Good Germans

Good Germans

✦

A Child's Fateful Journey Through Hitler's Third Reich

An Autobiographical Novel

Hal Marienthal

iUniverse, Inc.
New York Lincoln Shanghai

Good Germans
A Child's Fateful Journey Through Hitler's Third Reich

Copyright © 2005 by Hal Marienthal

iUniverse books may be ordered through booksellers or by contacting:

iUniverse
2021 Pine Lake Road, Suite 100
Lincoln, NE 68512
www.iuniverse.com
1-800-Authors (1-800-288-4677)

ISBN-13: 978-0-595-36859-4 (pbk)
ISBN-13: 978-0-595-81269-1 (ebk)
ISBN-10: 0-595-36859-X (pbk)
ISBN-10: 0-595-81269-4 (ebk)

Printed in the United States of America

To Sabine—
Without whom there is no journey

Contents

Acknowledgments

Gerd Richter-Kiewning of Studio Hamburg, Germany, for valuable research assistance; HAPAG GmbH for keeping superb records and making them available; Dipl.-Ing. Richard Weidle for his amazing energy and tireless help in authenticating the Stuttgart environment; Gisela Rossow for all of her research help; Michael Langner, General Manager, KHFM, Albuquerque, New Mexico, for indispensable technical information; Dr. Walter Wells for giving so graciously of his time, his expertise and his keen editorial eye; Uwe and Nancy Reimer, great nourishers of mind and body; Dr. Kenneth Lincoln of UCLA, Los Angeles, California for always being there when needed with friendship, insight, research and pistachios; Stewart Kane of the College of Santa Fe for invaluable technical assistance; Douglas C. Brown, Immigration & Naturalization Service, Albuquerque, New Mexico for finding needed documents; Dr. Lee Levin, Santa Fe, New Mexico, for significant medical background and information; Eve Warscher of Stuttgart's *Israelitische Glaubensgemeinschaft* for her help in finding long-ago names and places; Prof. Dr.Klaus-Jürgen Müller, Professor Emeritus, Hamburg University for validating the novel's historical accuracy; the archivists of Dortmund, Stuttgart and Hamburg for finding and reproducing invaluable iconographic materials and of course, my beloved friend, Stefan Weidle, who made it all happen in the first place and whose insights, trust and skills gave the entire undertaking a solid, professional foundation.

Foreword

Good Germans has been a work in process for more than fifty years. An urgency to tell this story has always been there, prodding, occasionally surfacing in other vaguely related shards of writing. Excuses for procrastination were easy to find: There were children to support, the ordinary demands of family life, career pressures; in sum, a subtle patina of emotional camouflage cunningly applied to keep the work from getting started. Nevertheless, the compulsion to do so never dissolved.

Stefan Weidle, my German publisher, entered my life unplanned, although as wisdom proclaims in our new age, one often gets what one anticipates. I told him my story and he was sufficiently intrigued to make a commitment to publish. Remarkable! To be sure, there was hesitancy on my part. To scrape around in my memories for months was a daunting prospect. Once I maintained a therapist in oriental splendor precisely to put the demons of my past to sleep peacefully and, if possible, permanently. That turned out to be an indifferent solution; the beasts became drowsy but remained on guard.

Stefan suggested that I write my story as a novel. That effectively ended a half-century of resistance. A novel made it possible to inject psychic distance and a layer of creative objectivity between one of mankind's most convulsive eras and me. My intent is not to distort reality, nor, as Socrates put it, to make the worse appear the better. At best, reality was bad enough. What the novel form made possible was a prudent recreation of events and feelings remote in time and thus subject to unruly synapses.

Even now, so many years later, the story of my early life touches me deeply. Painful as it sometimes was, I have done my best to recall incidents, names, places and dates with consistency and fidelity. However, as well as the autobiography of a young boy, this is also the novel of an era. I have changed some names, not necessarily to protect the innocent but because, after more than a half century, I don't always recall them with total accuracy. At other times such changes were felicitous in the context of the novel. For purposes of literary invention I have also created several characters, mostly drawn from personal experience, others culled from archival research. From its inception, the novel's guiding principle has been to tell the harrowing story of a boy's life in a credible, compelling way at a time, and in a place, when the shadow of evil shrouded mankind.

I am deeply grateful for what life has brought me as an adult: Loving and supportive wives, a quintet of astonishing children, good friends, the opportunity to serve my adopted country and a long, absorbing career as a writer and teacher. On rare occasions, mostly in pre-dawn hours, the demons of my past bare their fangs and growl, albeit somewhat aimlessly. They remind me of where I have been and what I have become. I have learned to accept their presence, but with all my heart I wish they would rest in peace.

Hal Marienthal
Asheville, North Carolina, 2005

1

Horst Schumann held up the flyer, brushed glue on each corner from the pot at his feet and quickly pasted the hammer-and-sickle design over Hitler's picture. The glaring notice obliterated a message announcing the Führer's upcoming radio address to the nation. Horst's arm ached from exertion. Almost done, he thought, only a dozen more. Suddenly a nearby tavern door flew open. For a brief moment, a shaft of light illuminated a noisy band of uniformed men. Their steel-plated boots clacked on the concrete as they marched toward Horst's hiding place. Desperate to avoid discovery, he crouched behind the kiosk, thankful for a dark night. Laughing and singing, the men passed within a few feet, too drunk to notice the boy pressed against the pillar. His body tense with fear, Horst sighed deeply as the Nazis turned a corner, then gathered his supplies and quietly moved on. A close one, he thought, but soon it will be done. He hoped the others had been as lucky. He knew Papa would be pleased.

◆   ◆   ◆

Dick Malkin hated March in Chicago. The wind shrieked off Lake Michigan, howled like a banshee through Lincoln Park's bare-leafed trees before shattering on gray high rises fronting the west side of Lake Shore Drive.

Dick was indifferent to the prestige of living on The Drive. Of course it was pleasant to live near the park and it was a good address. That meant a lot to Rae, but they could barely afford the rent and she kept the steam on all night. Their one-bedroom flat was always hot and stuffy. Waiting for spring made him impatient. What he could stand least about this time of year was waking up in the dark, always hearing the wind's icy lament rattling his windows.

"Nobody in Chicago should have to do this," Dick moaned as he reluctantly climbed out of bed, "not when it's that cold out there." Well, that was the produce business. South Water Market opened at three in the morning and he had to be present when trucks dumped their cargo on the loading docks. By five, restaurant buyers ordered potatoes and onions. Sure, his partner Max could handle routines but when it came to buying and selling everybody wanted to deal directly with Dick. A nice guy, an honest man.

"Breakfast is ready. Coffee's getting cold," Rae yelled at him through the bathroom door.

Funny, he thought, brushing a few remaining gray strands over his scalp, she says the same thing every morning. Still, he had to give her credit. For a plump Jewish princess she did okay, seldom complained about his early hours. Not that her life was that hard. The business was in good shape; even in a Depression people ate potatoes and onions. Only fun-and-games money was scarce. They took in a movie on Saturday nights, went for chop suey at Song Hee's on Thursdays and every Tuesday Rae and her sisters played mah jongg. They paid their Temple Sholom membership on the installment plan and that was about it. He often wondered how people with large families managed to survive. After they were married he and Rae tried to have children, but it wasn't *bescheert*. Too late to worry about it, now that they were in their fifties. Many couples didn't have children and lived a good life. Dick admitted that having a son would have been nice, maybe even a daughter. He empathized with Rae, knew how she envied her sisters with their *bar mitzvahs* and confirmations, the bragging about report cards, Judy going out with her young doctor and Harry, who was going to law school, dating the Rabbi's daughter. Apparently it went on all afternoon during their mah jongg game. Not having bragging rights just about drove her crazy. She was in a foul mood every Tuesday night.

Then there was this whole business with the German boy. It was all so confusing. Nearly a year ago, when cousin Clara first suggested that they adopt her nephew Horst, he thought it a ridiculous idea. In the first place they were too old.

"Not only our age, Clara, but why should we take on another burden right in the middle of a Depression?" he had said that evening when they went for ice cream after the movie. "What the heck do we know about raising a twelve year old?"

Rae, of course, immediately fell in love with the idea, had the boy dressed in three-piece suits from Field's before she learned to pronounce his name.

"Horse," she said, "what kind of a name is Horse?"

"Horst, with a *t* on the end. Common German name, but I'm sure he wouldn't mind if you changed it. Listen," Clara insisted, "what needs changing more than his name is his future. Do I have to tell you what's going on? You heard Binstock's sermon last Friday."

It was the start of her campaign. Not a day passed that Clara Weiss, mother of two strapping sons, didn't bombard Rae with phone calls about the bliss of motherhood, the joy of having a son to carry on the family name. "Think of the *mitzvah* offered to God by rescuing a human being from Germany. Such a hell hole!" Dinner conversations at the Malkins centered increasingly on countless advantages to be derived from bringing to the United States one Horst Schumann, the only son of Clara Weiss' brother, Oskar. Lately, the dialogue began at breakfast.

"Drink your coffee. It's getting cold. You want eggs?"

"Thanks, just toast." He ate in silence, stared bleakly at the curtained windows. Even the garage was icy. His mind numbed at the thought. He already felt raw winds scrape his skin. Rae hovered, fidgeted with a need to communicate. She pulled up a chair.

"You'll call him today?"

"Who?"

"Please, Dick. It's too early for games."

"Look Rae, Luckman's in Congress. That's in Washington, not Chicago." He peered at her over the edge of his cup. Maybe she'd drop it just this once. April would be a better time to talk, with the windows open, the steam off.

"He has a Chicago office, Dick. Some of our money went into that office. At least make an appointment. The man who runs things, I forget his name…"

"Farber. Bert Farber."

"Right, Farber. The one you've been bringing potatoes and onions to ever since the election."

"Come on Rae, be fair. He gets me into Wrigley free the whole season."

"I don't give a damn about Wrigley," she snapped. That startled him. When was the last time she'd used a swear word? "I care about you and me," she said, locking on his eyes. "I care a lot about what happens to that boy."

"Me too, Rae. I do too, but do we have to discuss it this early?"

"When else? In the evening, when you're tired? On weekends you listen to football games. I don't complain. You work hard. I know how you feel. Adopting a young boy scares me too; I don't have to tell you. But maybe we could make it work; maybe it's really possible. Shouldn't we find out if Luckman would help us bring the child here? Maybe he can, maybe he can't. At least we'd know that much." She pulled her housecoat tightly together, nervously crumpled a piece of toast. "Will you, Dick?"

Her depth of feelings moved him. She wanted this so bad.

"Okay, I'll call Farber for an appointment. He'll ask questions, Rae. We don't have answers. Invite Clara for dinner. I mean, it's her nephew. She should know things like birthdays and addresses, that kind of stuff. Okay?"

She helped him on with his coat, kissed him on the mouth. Another new wrinkle. He pushed the button for the elevator. What the heck, he thought, what's one more mouth to feed? Hey, maybe the boy would like baseball. A Sunday doubleheader at Wrigley in July with your own kid? Now wouldn't that be something! The Cubs in summer, the Bears in fall. He smiled. "Wouldn't that be terrific," he said to the elevator door as it opened. The wind blew icy whistles through the alley next to the building. The garage was dark and cold but for the first time this bleak Chicago winter Dick Malkin felt that spring was just around the corner.

◆   ◆   ◆

In 1935 Dortmund was on nobody's tour list of German cities. It featured no romantic, medieval castles, no museums demanding critical attention. The former Hansa city, founded in the Middle Ages, thrived on coal and iron and the shipping its river provided. Most of its inhabitants were complacently middle class.

It was by no means an ugly city. Tree-lined boulevards cut a graceful swath through clean and comfortable neighborhoods, spilled traffic into a small, attractive municipal center. Dortmund's breweries and coal helped fuel the Reich's economy. Party fiat had long ago squashed ancient trade union feuds over control of the mines. As usual, winter weather along the Ruhr was disagreeable, but it didn't stop Party organizers who worked feverishly to beautify the city, plan a rally and ready the Westfalenhalle for the Führer's upcoming visit, his first to the town. Flags festooned most homes and office buildings; enormous swastikas fluttered from public buildings and Hitler Youth marching bands energetically rehearsed their routines.

Horst Schumann had different concerns. After last night's near disaster, his day grew steadily worse. Before he was fully awake, he felt a familiar twist in his gut, sniffed the cloying reek of urine. He hated the way his skin crawled against the soppy cling of his pajama bottoms. Gretchen was in such a foul mood lately, this was sure to set her off. She'd stick his nose into the wet sheet, probably whack his ass again with that yellow stick of hers. As on all such mornings, the thought of escaping before she found out flitted through his mind. His father was in the kitchen eating a roll, drinking coffee, reading. Always reading.

"Bastard," Oskar muttered, slapping a rumpled copy of the viciously anti-Semitic *Der Stürmer* on the kitchen table, spilling coffee. "Goddamn lying bastard Streicher with those endless lousy lies he prints. Who the hell in his right mind would believe an old Jew would nail his housekeeper to a cross? Such nonsense. Goddammit, I'd like to dance on that bastard's grave." He saw his son standing in the doorway, looking lost and nervous. "What's the matter? Something go wrong last night?"

"No Papa. I had a close call, but I posted them all."

"Terrific. Then why so glum? You having a hard time too?" The boy just stood there. "Come on Horst, eat something before you go to school."

"Papa…" Silence. A fly droned near the ceiling.

"So, what is it?"

"I did it again."

Oskar sighed. Last night's meeting was a disaster. Westfalia's Communist Party was falling apart. They were supposed to distribute at least five hundred copies of his interpretation of Bolenkhov's attack on National Socialist economics, best thing he'd written lately, too. Isador Herz was there to print the flyers, but only Horst and three comrades showed up to distribute them. Maybe they thought Oskar Schumann would go around putting up posters all by himself. Who knows where the rest were hiding? Maybe in jail; maybe dead, for all Oskar knew. Maybe they joined the Nazi Party to get a free meal and warm boots, he mused, ruefully. Now here was a really big problem. His son, this nice looking boy with wavy brown hair and those large, sad eyes, pissed in his bed again. Oskar had the crap beaten out of him several times, was hounded by a murdering government and confronted by a nagging *schikse* wife. He'd lost a lot of weight and most of his faith, but not his humor. How would Karl Marx have handled a son who pissed in his bed? He smiled to himself.

"Go," he said. "Go, before she gets out of the bathroom. I'll cover for you. I'll tell her you went to school early to see if it's still open. Take a *brötchen*, get the hell out of here."

Horst stuck a roll in his pocket, picked up his rucksack and slid down the banister to the ground floor. Walter was already waiting for him, sitting on the curb in front of the professional laundry, the Victoria Wäscherei, drawing pictures, like he always did. Horst often thought his friend was born with a crayon in that skinny, bony hand. He sketched animals and flowers, beautiful, delicate images of birds sitting on branches so real you could see buds growing out of the wood. Funny, the birds looked just as scrawny as Walter, awkward creatures, a scared, pleading look in their eyes. Horst hated that look. Walter worked mostly with colored pencils, but when things were rough at the Parisers the pictures were black. Today he was using a piece of charcoal. A bad sign.

"Let's go," Horst said.

"Wait for Gitte?"

"Better not. Isador, Papa and I were at a meeting last night and things didn't go well. Almost nobody showed up to put up flyers. I had to paste up twice as many as usual. Maybe Pflug knows that Isador is running the mimeo."

"Oh no!"

"It's possible. Maybe Gitte and her father are staying with friends, just in case. Anyway, let's move, Walter. Maybe school's open today. If we run, we can avoid Eckert."

The Jewish Volksschule, a junior high school, was the only school they were allowed to attend. There was no money to pay the staff, books and supplies were scarce. Sometimes they had heat, but mostly it was colder inside than out. It had once been a crowded, vital school; now only a few students and some volunteer teachers huddled in two or three classrooms, the cold sweat of common fear saturating the peeling plaster.

To get there in the mornings was a daily struggle. Situated at the top of a palisade looking toward the railway station, the school was nearly three kilometers from their own neighborhood. A grammar school and the city's largest high school lay in the same direction. A steady stream of uniforms, young scouts giggling, playing games, imitating older Hitler Youth members, formed a gauntlet run each morning by a dwindling number of Jewish kids. "Dirty Jew" was one of the milder epithets hurled at them. Currently more popular was a line from Horst Wessel's song: *Wenn Judenblut Auf's Messer Spritzt*, "When Jews' Blood Spurts Upon the Knife," accompanied by appropriate gestures. All sorts of debris was thrown, clothes ripped, books torn. After school it was worse. Then they behaved like animals released from their cages. All day long teachers had lauded their racial superiority, inflamed disgust toward everything Jewish, "those Hebrew swine, those bloodsuckers that want to corrupt our Reich." After school Horst stayed out of their way.

In friendlier days Horst played soccer and stickball with Hans Eckert, a robust, fair-haired boy. They had grudgingly admired each other's skills. Eckert was two years older, bigger and more powerful, but Horst was quicker. They played well off each other. Eckert's father joined the S.A., the Storm Troopers, a year ago, his son the Hitler Youth soon after. Hans became a leader, Horst Schumann his enemy.

Schwanenstrasse crossed Weiherstrasse where the Opera House, spattered with pigeon droppings, hunched like an exhausted fortress. Across the street a neon sign read *Café Lüchtemeyer*. Eckert and his companions waited, restlessly milled around the café's revolving door.

"Look who's here," said Eckert, as if it were happening for the first time. "It's Pariser and Schumann, our local Jewish geniuses. Hey Schumann, how's your Commie father?" They all laughed, without humor. "Ask him if it's true, Klaus," Eckert commanded.

"Hey Schumann," said the boy, Klaus, "is it true they carve a secret sign into every Jew's prick after he's born?"

Horst stood mute. Enraged, he stared at Eckert who fiddled with his belt and stared back insolently. Both knew the game was unfair, six of them with knives and power, with the right to humiliate. Walter clutched his sketchpad like a shield and prayed he would not soil himself. People passed by, gawked for a moment, and hurried on. Why bother to stop, they'd seen worse. Eckert ripped the sketchpad from Walter's hand, tore off the cover.

"Birds," he snorted, "always birds. You're a bird lover, a goddamn poof, Pariser, a piece of filthy perverted Jewish shit." He crumpled the sketchpad, threw it in the gutter. "Let's go, guys. Why be late for two fucking Hebes." They stomped off, feeling good. Eckert turned, smiled.

"I'll look for you after school, Schumann. Somebody told me about a new game called Aryans and Jews. Like Cowboys and Indians. We could learn the game together, Schumann. You should be able to play a Jew. Wouldn't that be fun?" He smiled again, re-joined his comrades.

Walter, near tears, picked his pad out of the gutter, tried to straighten it. "He's getting meaner than ever."

"They all are, all over Dortmund, and it will probably get worse." They sat on the curb, angry and frightened, their future like stones under their hearts.

"What are we going to do?"

"I don't know. You can go to school if you want to, but I'm not. Eckert wasn't kidding. He'll be waiting for me."

Horst rose slowly, sniffed the air. "Come on, Pariser. Too cold on the sidewalk. Let's look at the mines."

"The mines? You want to see the coal mines again?"

"Yes, I want to see the coal mines again."

"What for?"

"I'm not sure. I just know I want to go."

Walter had often watched Horst do strange things, peek in odd corners, test holes in fences, disappear into spaces Walter didn't even know existed. Strange. Some day maybe he'd explain, but right now it was best just to tag along.

◆   ◆   ◆

Clara Weiss baked a potato kugel, her contribution to dinner at the Malkins. She and Hermann always felt uneasy visiting Lake Shore Drive. It had nothing to do with Dick and Rae, they were swell people. What made Clara nervous were apartment buildings along The Drive, where the rich Jews lived, the ones who owned liquor stores and movie houses. It smelled different here than on Clark Street, stuffier and less friendly. You never saw people on the sidewalks. What did they do, she sometimes wondered, go all their lives straight from the elevator to their cars? What if the elevator breaks down? She giggled as she pictured those women trip down ten flights of stairs in tight skirts and spiked heels. She wasn't kvetching, not about that. She and Hermann had made a good life in America. Cleaning and pressing hats all day was boring, but it paid the rent on the store and the apartment. The Depression hurt, but the family got enough to eat, especially potatoes. She had good boys. After school they helped in the shop and were paid two dollars every Friday. Aaron used one of his dollars for piano lessons, practiced faithfully on the second-hand upright Dick had given him for his *bar mitzvah*. Clara thought her boy was a born entertainer.

"Good kugel, Clara." Dick patted his stomach.

"Why not? You brought the potatoes, I'm just the cook."

Rae was impatient. "Come on people, there's no time to talk about potatoes. It's late and we have a lot of things to discuss. You'll be glad to know Dick called Luckman's office." The Weisses, delighted by the news, knew Rae was hooked. Could it be that Dick had finally come around too? About time!

Family concerns were in Clara's genes. She and Oskar were the oldest of ten children born to Jakob and Alma Schumann in Zeltingen, a tiny German wine village on the banks of the Mosel. Jakob supported his brood by running a shoe repair shop. He also served as rabbi to the town's Jewish community, nearly a fourth of it his own family. When Jakob wasn't fixing shoes, he mended souls in the leather-and-dye-smelling storeroom in the back of the shop. He wasn't universally loved. The vintners in the area resented him fiercely because Jakob was a left-wing activist who wrote and distributed pamphlets claiming that the region's wealth was built on the backs of laborers, especially the bent ones of grape pickers. He was a decent man who gave generously of himself, including finally his heart, which quit when Clara was eighteen. Being bright and energetic, the children learned to make ends meet. Oskar, the eldest and after his father's death the family's nominal head, assumed responsibility by losing himself in reading, a contentment to which Jakob, too, had devoted much of his life.

Clara became everybody's mother when Alma lay bed-ridden, following the youngest child's birth. The task consumed Clara, soured her attitude and eroded her sunny disposition. Desperate for relief, she trained her younger sisters to take over and wrote to her father's cousin Joseph in Chicago, asking if she could come for a visit. He was agreeable. Joseph's son introduced her to Hermann Weiss, a fellow student at the local *yeshiva*. Hermann wasn't overly bright, but he had nice curly hair, a courtly manner and a decent job in a hat cleaning shop. He liked Clara immediately, admired her robust figure and thick, wavy hair. On their first date Clara let him kiss her on the cheek, the next evening on her mouth. He proposed a week before her visa expired. It was a small wedding filled with dancing, laughter and good food. She wrote to her family, felt considerable guilt, but she never looked back. She was a loving wife to Hermann, a good mother to her sons, but sometimes, often at odd moments, she missed her brother Oskar, that gentle, dreaming companion of her childhood.

"So what did you tell Luckman?" she asked.

"I didn't talk to Luckman. I talked to Farber, the guy who runs his Chicago office. He said the House is setting up procedures."

"What does that mean? What procedures?"

Dick looked guardedly at the faces around him, knew they were anxious to prod him into action. "Procedures, Clara, procedures, ferchrissakes."

"Calm down, Dick. Clara's only asking," Rae cautioned.

Dick sighed. Maybe they were right and he was just being pigheaded. "Okay, procedures, an order to things. Farber says the number of Jews trying to leave Germany has doubled in the last few months."

"No wonder."

"No wonder is right, Hermann. Because of the volume, they're setting up priorities in Washington, like who gets a visa first and what kind of documents they need to leave Germany. Even Farber doesn't know all the details, but he said Luckman's on top of it. I'm supposed to make an appointment with Farber next week."

"Are you making the appointment?"

"I'm supposed to."

"Yes, but are you going to?" Rae and Clara exclaimed with one voice.

There it was. Shit or get off the pot, a recurring dilemma. Aware of Rae's anxiety, he avoided looking at her. Clara sat mute, supplicating, accusing, hoping. Hermann toyed nervously with his napkin.

A twelve-year-old kid in the house who can't speak English, Dick thought. Christ almighty! Start worrying about schools, getting a bigger place, problems nobody wanted. Problems, okay, but sure as hell nothing like the ones Jews were having in Germany. He could still hear Binstock's voice last week, lacerating the congregation.

"I don't know what rocks your hearts are made of, you people out there," he'd shouted, "with your comfortable lives, enjoying the safety of this wonderful country. But the Jews of Germany need your help. They need it now! Not next year, not next month, not next week. They need it now! Stop kidding yourselves. You, Milton Rosenberg, with your sister and her husband in Berlin. You, Lenny Cohen, with your penthouse at 3800. Sell one of your Cadillacs and bring your niece Rifka and her kids out of that hellhole. You, Dick Malkin, what's the matter with you? Clara Weiss wants you to adopt her nephew. She told me. So did Rae. Come on, give the kid a lease on life, not a death sentence. You people think I'm kidding? Hitler is a madman. Anybody who doesn't believe what he says in *Mein Kampf* about wiping out the Jews has his head in the sand. Wouldn't hurt you to read it! I've asked you for money, all the money you can spare. And what do I get? It's a Depression, Rabbi. Business is bad, Rabbi. We have to take care of our own, Rabbi. Damn it, these *are* your own and if you don't help, nobody will. They will all perish. So help me God." He had burst off the pulpit, whispered something to the Cantor and sat down. The Cantor finished the service. Nobody in the congregation had seen Binstock this angry before and they were moved. Sure, the Rabbi seemed a little hysterical but still, there was a lot of truth to what he said. They'd read the papers, seen the newsreels.

Dick knew in his heart what was right. No, at his age adopting a boy of twelve wouldn't be easy, but it felt like the right thing to do. Strange, he thought, how much harder doing the right thing often seemed to be. In the end it usually turns out better; not all the time, but usually. Besides, just imagine taking your son to Wrigley for a Fourth of July double-header.

"Relax, guys," he smiled. "I'll see Farber Monday morning. Never too late to become a father, right Rae?"

Rae started bawling. Dick gave her his handkerchief. "Now Clara, we need your help. Here are things we have to put together."

They talked until three in the morning, when Dick usually got up for work. But today was Saturday, the Sabbath, a time to rest, to pray, a time to give thanks.

2

In his sparse, orderly office, a dozen files scattered before him, Roland Pflug, Rollo to his intimates, was keenly aware of the occasion and the gravity of his responsibilities as Dortmund's *Gruppenleiter*, the head of the city's expanding SA Division. A newcomer to Party discipline, a card-carrying member only since 1933, Pflug knew that senior Party officials would closely watch his performance in matters connected with the Führer's upcoming visit. Ambitious *Gauleiter* Paul Terhoven, North-Westfalia's area commander and an early Hitler supporter, made this amply clear on a personal visit, reinforced by detailed memos. Mistakes would not be tolerated, not on this, the Führer's first visit to Dortmund from where his speech would be broadcast throughout Europe.

"No mistakes of any kind," the sallow-faced, balding Terhoven had said at the *Kneipe*, the tavern across from Party headquarters. For emphasis he'd banged his empty glass on the table. "I don't have to tell you what this visit means to me. To us," he added dryly.

Pflug knew perfectly well. Although a newcomer to National Socialist politics, he rose in rank faster than others because of his energy and administrative skills. Being Gustav Pflug's son helped, of course. Nor did it hurt that he resembled his late father, like him tall, rawboned, his black hair cut short, green eyes intense above a nose slightly too large for his slender face. People were drawn to him. Even so, to become *Ortsgruppenleiter*, the region's nominal Party boss at twenty-eight was unusual. Older party members still eyed him suspiciously. Like Rollo's father, most of them had come out of the army, struggled with Hitler in the rough days when one had to fight for the right to belong to the Party and wear the swastika armband. The Party was everything to them, their religion, their dream and also their bread and butter. Rollo, on the other hand, represented a new kind of Nazi, a wise guy out of the university. Acceptance came slowly.

Pflug's immediate concern was to confirm specific procedures, although Terhoven's directives were precise. The scope of logistics was a major consideration: the Führer's route from the airport was to be densely lined with cheering citizens, including a generous number of flower-carrying women and children. All buildings along the route were to display Nazi banners, the larger the better.

"Dortmund should look like you could eat off its sidewalks," Terhoven had said, "and check the loudspeaker system, Rollo, carefully, not like those assholes in Hanover last month. If Hess has to wait again to start the rally I'll have you shot," he'd grinned. Pflug didn't doubt he might be tempted. "Ah, one more thing while I think of it." Terhoven ordered a beer, ruminated as if the thought were new. "I hear that Communists float around your district. I hear they still print their filthy shit, contaminate good Germans with Bolshevist Jew lies. Hard to believe, Rollo. Not true, is it?"

Pflug, about to drink, replaced his glass on the table. "It's being taken care of," he said, sounding determined.

"Good. I don't have to tell you what would happen if the Führer saw signs of Communists on his visit, do I?"

Terhoven's warning was unmistakable. Pflug heaped the files together. "Frau Schuster," he called to his secretary, "Tell Böhm I want to see him."

Heiko Böhm, his adjutant, four years older than Pflug, was a coal miner out of work when he joined the Nazis in 1931. He saw Party membership as a way out of poverty, out of the claws of unemployment ripping his pride and manhood. Böhm, who hated school, went into the mines when he was sixteen. It was rough there, a bloody battleground between Communist organizers and traditional trade unionists. In one of those pitched battles he acquired the scar that ran livid across his left cheek. He was proud of the scar, wore it like a medal. It suited his appearance, the too-large ears, icy blue eyes, the constant, restless shrugging of his thick shoulders. Böhm deeply distrusted Communists with their books and pamphlets, all that bullshit about thesis and antithesis, their constant harangues against free enterprise. He was good with his fists, never dodged a fight and slept like a babe on days when he'd enlightened some Commies or Jews into submission. The SA and Böhm were made for each other.

He had mixed feelings when they assigned him to headquarters, to help organize Dortmund's section of the German Labor Front. It took him off the street. At first he liked working for Pflug who was smart, organized, and a hard worker. Böhm was proud when Rollo picked him as his adjutant. In the last six months, however, Böhm felt strong misgivings. What was bothering his boss? Rollo seemed withdrawn, less friendly. Only a week ago they found Communist flyers pasted on shop windows and fences, but Pflug didn't appear concerned. Strange. He felt uneasy walking into Pflug's office.

"Sit, Heiko, this won't take long." Pflug shoved the files to the edge of the desk. "You know what these are."

Böhm glanced down. "Of course. The trouble makers."

"Right. I want them gone."

"Permanently?" Böhm smiled. This was more like it.

"What do you mean, permanently?"

"Come on, Rollo. A week or so as our honored guests. That should give us the names of everybody we're still looking for. We find them and ship them all to Dachau for a long vacation." He chuckled.

"Maybe later, Heiko, there are no orders, at least not yet. Right now I'm concerned about Hitler's visit. I want everybody in these files off the street until the Führer leaves."

"Off the street? You want me to put them in a hotel?"

They glared at each other. It's happening again, thought Böhm, a softness, an uncertainty about dealing with the city's riff-raff. He'd make a note, pass it up the line if necessary. "Plenty of space in the basement," he said. "I'll do what's necessary."

"I'm sure you will."

They made a priority list: Schumann and his kid, Horst; leave the Jew-loving wife alone for now since policies about that were not clear. Certainly Herz, the furniture finisher. Leave his daughter Brigitte alone for now, even though rumor has it that the little bitch plays with boys' cocks to get them to hand out Bolshevik flyers. Lifshitz the lawyer, Grünberg, the doctor, Koerner, Pfarrer Thalmann, who needs to learn he can't corrupt people just because he's a priest. The list drawn, Böhm gathered up the files.

"Take care of it Heiko and don't overdo it."

"Heil Hitler, Rollo."

"Heil Hitler."

Rollo was lost in thought, his boots scraping the top of his desk. Why did he always give Böhm the dirty work? Wasn't he, Pflug, capable of it? Wasn't that his duty, his commitment to the Party? He struggled to wipe such questions from his mind, but as always they persisted, gnawed at his brain, sent bolts of pain through a space behind his right eyeball. Duty to the Party. Böhm found that easy; as ordered, eat your monthly one-dish dinner, collect money for Winter Relief, hate Jews and Communists and worship the Führer. Simple. As he reflected on the drawn-up list, the leather merchant, Oskar Schumann, came to mind.

Schumann. Why was that pinch-nosed, shambling, near-sighted Jew so goddamn irritating? Pflug remembered him from a previous arrest as if it were yesterday. As an act of routine harassment, Böhm had personally conducted the question-and-answer sessions, prodding these Semitic cretins with an array of gadgets designed to elicit answers. Pflug, his stomach roiling at the prospect, had forced himself to go into the basement. He found Schumann tied to a chair, his smashed glasses dangling ludicrously from one ear. Some blood had seeped from his nose and crusted his stubbled cheeks, but he was quite conscious, wary. Böhm ordered the beating continued. Schumann's body flinched, but his eyes locked on Rollo's face, never wavered. Pflug saw pain in those tired, watery eyes, humiliation and fear, but also something else that perplexed him, a look of softness and a curious hint of humor. Schumann's eyes caught Pflug's, read vulnerability there and mocked him.

Pflug had sent the whole filthy bunch packing, had watched from his office window as they stumbled out. Schumann's son, a skinny kid with dark wavy hair, his ragged shirt torn, had gently taken his father's arm; then he had turned and scoured the building with a hatred so savage it had twisted his face. Rollo couldn't forget the boy's unmasked fury. Hostility that intense didn't belong on a child's face. Tonight, after they put their son and daughter to bed, he would discuss his jumbled state of mind with Rika. She would help him straighten out his head and, as so often before, stop him from doing something stupid. He put on his overcoat and turned out the office lights.

"Heil Hitler, Herr Pflug."

"Heil Hitler, Frau Schuster."

3

Horst and Walter headed south, toward Dorstfeld, in the direction of the mines. Walking warmed them, sharpened their hunger. They nibbled on Horst's roll, shook shriveled apples out of a tree, but found them inedible. Horst was more watchful than usual, borrowed a pencil and tore pages from Walter's notebook to make sketches of landmarks, street corners and churches, then painstakingly labeled them with crabbed block letters as if he'd just learned to write.

Horst had dragged Walter here once before. The place was forbidding, a dispirited landscape dotted with unpainted tool sheds, broken down colliers, tram tracks seemingly leading nowhere. Mountainous slag humps emitted an acrid smell. The entire west end was fenced, "*Verboten!*" signs posted prominently. A few workers in sooty clothes, wearing helmets, crossed the open fields, disappeared into unseen entrances. A black limousine, flying a swastika, was parked at a two-story brick building.

"Administration," Horst muttered.

"How can you tell?"

Horst only shrugged. "Let's go over to the other side where we saw the old tram cars."

The whole place reeked of decay. The tramcars had rusted; some tracks were missing where they led into mine openings, now carelessly boarded up. Horst pried off a rotten plank, peered into one shaft, a wooden ladder leading into the unlit tunnel. He firmly gripped its vertical posts, tested the rungs and noted with satisfaction that they supported his weight and nailed back the cover, using a stone as a hammer. He inspected several shafts, made additional sketches, wrote a few comments under each. Walter shuddered as he began to understand.

"Hiding places. You're looking for hiding places. You think something is coming, don't you?"

Horst nodded. They were crouched against an abandoned shed; the winter sun barely warmed their bodies. Walter stared at Horst with deep wonder.

"Yes, Walter, I think it's coming. I think it's coming pretty soon. It gets scarier and scarier. I'm not surprised. The last few years have been terrible." Even to his friend, Horst found it painful to relate the story of his years away from Dortmund, tried hard to forget them, although at times he couldn't help but remember.

In nineteen twenty-nine he was only six years old when his mother, Toni, died in childbirth, but there was to be no new brother or sister. She was twenty-eight, a dark beauty, a gentle, smiling woman who had dressed him in velvet pants when he and Oskar went to Café Corso on Sunday mornings to drink hot chocolate and listen to string ensembles. His sister, Liselotte, two years older, stayed home to help her mother. When Toni died, Oskar's world fell apart. He could not imagine raising two children by himself. His brothers and sisters had emigrated, Clara and two others to America, several more to South Africa. Only he and his brother Walter remained in Germany. Oskar tried, haphazardly, to be an adequate parent, but the task overwhelmed him. He had meetings to attend, pamphlets to write, books to read. The KPD, Germany's Communist Party, was at war with right wing elements, especially those brown-shirted monsters making political waves. He, Oskar, was a soldier in the trenches, his weapons a gifted pen and a nimble mind. In his heart he believed the KPD needed him more than his children. He made necessary provisions, drove his six-year-old son and eight-year-old daughter to the Jewish orphanage in Paderborn, said tearful good-byes, promised to visit them often and went home feeling misgivings, but also considerable relief. He had a meeting to attend that weekend in Cologne. What would he have done with the children? Besides, the arrangement was temporary. The country would come to its senses, his side would win, his children would come home and they would all live together in a better world. Oskar saw the future clearly.

At the orphanage in Paderborn, Horst was assigned to a dormitory with twenty other boys. He felt acutely sorry for himself, lay awake for hours watching shadows, listening to restless cries. On many mornings he woke exhausted, only to discover that he had wet his bed. He was scolded, warned not to let it happen again. The place was not set up for bed wetters, he was told. He stayed awake as long as he could, tried desperately to control himself, but it was the same story nearly every night. They made him dry his sheet on a clothesline, let him sleep on the same one for several weeks. Why waste a clean sheet, they said. The other boys, finding someone even more miserable than themselves, made constant fun of him, called him nicknames like "Horst Pee Pee" and "The River Boy." The staff hated the extra work and did nothing to discourage the name-calling. Liselotte, on the other hand, made peace with the place. For the first time in her life she could play with friends her own age. She was a quiet, obedient child who hated to see her brother humiliated, but there was nothing she could do about it.

Seven months at Paderborn turned Horst into an alert, cautious, wily animal, far too old for his age. Oskar visited rarely, listened half-heartedly to staff complaints and his son's pleas and then departed, trailing empty promises. At Succoth, the harvest festival, the children were marched to the edge of nearby woods to gather branches and vines needed to build the holiday's traditional arbor. Horst asked Liselotte to accompany him, led her a short distance into the forest.

"I'm sorry, Lise, but I'm leaving. I'm leaving for good." She looked at him, saw that he meant it, started to cry. "Don't cry, Lise," he pleaded, "please don't cry."

"You're my brother, Horst! You're just a little boy. Where will you go? What will you do?"

"I don't know, but I can't stay here anymore. I hate it. I hate it!"

"What am I going to tell Papa?"

"I don't know, Lise. Tell him how much I hate it here. Tell him I will call. I'll call him on the telephone. Maybe I can write to him or something. I will write to you too, real soon."

"You don't know how to write," she sobbed.

"I can learn to write," he said, "I'll find a way. I have to leave. I think I would die if I had to stay here any longer."

She hugged him fiercely, so scared she thought she would lose her breath. He was her brother and she loved him. Horst and Papa were all she had left in the world and Papa didn't care about her anymore. Her heart broke as she watched him move deeper into the woods. He turned, smiled at her and waved. He was so small, she thought, what would happen to him? He turned once more and gave a final wave before he disappeared among the trees. It was the last time they would see each other.

"Why?" asked Walter, "what happened to you? What happened to her?"

"She died."

"How? When?"

"I don't know. She died in that place a year later. Oskar said it was appendicitis, but I'm not sure; he doesn't want to talk about it."

"What about you? Where did you go? What did you do?" Walter was astounded by what he heard. "Didn't they look for you?"

"Maybe, but who knows? No, I don't think they ever did. They probably thought I'd come creeping back. So did Papa, I guess, but I didn't."

He stared into the distance, visiting old ghosts, remembering things, then shrugged and came back to the present. The sky had clouded over, a hint of snow in the air. Horst took an old, worn sweater from his rucksack, pulled it on.

"It's getting late, Pariser. Let's go home."

"Horst? Tell me, where did you go?"

"To the country, to a lot of places. I'll tell you about it some other time." Horst walked to the colliery entrance, made a quick sketch there, looked around as if to print details on his mind, like a map. "We'd better split up," he said. "If there's trouble, at least it'll only be one of us. You know the way?"

"Sure."

"You go first. I want to poke around. See you in the morning. Maybe tomorrow we can avoid those bastards." He smiled, watched Walter walk toward the horizon, wandered around, and tested a water tap at the side of the dilapidated building. His eyes measured the distance between the edges of the abandoned shafts to a nearby grove of trees. Two hundred meters, he noted, closed his rucksack and left.

With practiced caution he picked his route home through sparsely populated neighborhoods. Even at a distance he felt the pounding boots, the deafening fifes and drums, the trumpet blasts and measured cadence of Horst Wessel's song, the whole strident cacophony that saturated Dortmund's atmosphere this icy March in preparation for the coming of its God, the Führer. Careful, he warned himself, best to be very careful.

He rarely came into his apartment through the Weiherstrasse entrance. With the help of Toni's money, Oskar had bought this three-story apartment house and an adjacent one on Neue Strasse. Early on, Horst discovered that drain pipes between the buildings left a space large enough to wedge through, terminating just above the balcony of his apartment. A wooden rod to beat carpets extended into an alley below as did the rear door of Herz's furniture shop and, at the far end, storage lockers that belonged to Ruhmann's Delikatessen. Hardly anyone used the alley; still, better to be cautious. He edged through the crawl space, pushed his rucksack ahead, peered over the edge, saw nobody and made the short leap to the balcony. Far safer than the street entrance, he often left this way. These days one never knew. He walked quietly into the L-shaped apartment, its bedrooms and bathroom to the rear, the kitchen, food closet, sitting room and living rooms near the front door. In plusher days it had been a luxury apartment. He still remembered his mother at the piano in the sitting room, singing Lieder in her tiny voice.

No one was home, Oskar most likely at a meeting. Gretchen was probably visiting her family, as she did more and more often. He dropped his rucksack in the hall. For some reason a light had been left on in the kitchen. He was hungry, but the food closet was empty except for some bread, a few cooked potatoes and a withered piece of sausage. He poured himself a glass of water and took his meal into the living room, with its broken crystal chandelier, stuffed furniture and dusty oak cases, overflowing with Oskar's precious books. Through the room's narrow bay windows Horst sensed the throb of marching bands, heard the exultant shouts of men and women transfigured by spectacle. He sat in his chair, empty of mind, waiting for something, but he knew not what. Not for the first time, he felt utterly alone.

4

"Please go in Mr. Malkin," the receptionist said, "Mr. Farber can see you now. First door on the right."

Dick met Bert Farber in 1932, during Warren "Luck" Luckman's successful run for the House. Luckman credited much of his success to Farber, his campaign manager, a former Chicago Tribune staff reporter and shrewd political analyst who had wisely hitched Luckman's wagon to Franklin Roosevelt's rising star. As the 1936 elections approached, Luckman lusted after a Senate seat and with FDR's support his chances were excellent. Farber now ran Luckman's Chicago office, a complex assignment. He labored prodigiously to keep Chicago's Democratic machine functioning smoothly, pledged judicious congressional support whenever appropriate. His toughest job, however, was to line up contributors with deep pockets to fill his party's war chest.

Farber targeted his markets carefully. Downstate Illinois would likely go Republican, but Chicago was a Democratic stronghold. Luckman, a Jew, could count on the city's sizeable West Side Jewish vote, including throngs of recent eastern European immigrants who owned small retail shops and services. Long-established Jews with financial clout lived mainly south, in Hyde Park, or north, along Lake Shore Drive. Farber's persistent problem was how to reach them. They vigilantly guarded their privacy.

When Dick Malkin first approached him about bringing a relative out of Germany, Farber listened carefully. Dick didn't look that impressive, a short, balding, paunchy man, but he was likeable, a warm person, a faithful Democrat, an efficient worker in Luckman's campaign. Moreover, he lived on Lake Shore Drive amidst the fat cats, although he didn't act like them. Farber knew Malkin to be a respected member of Temple Sholom, an officer of its Men's Club which Farber had addressed several times. Rabbi Leonard Binstock, a national religious leader, fulminated against indifference to the plight of German Jews in the press, on radio, in meeting halls, wherever he found an audience. Now here was Dick Malkin, a temple member, a responsible citizen, a committed Democrat, and personally involved in Binstock's cause. Farber recognized a juicy public relations prospect, a compelling icebreaker, when he saw one.

"Nice to see you, Dick. Have a seat." Farber settled on one of the facing couches, fished a cigarillo from a mother-of-pearl humidor, flicked a lighter and waved at the smoke cloud. "How's Rae?"

"Fine, Bert, just fine. A little anxious, but she's fine."

"What's she anxious about?" Farber knew perfectly well, he'd checked the file, but better to let people make their own case. He offered the humidor. Dick accepted, lit up and relaxed.

"We've decided to go ahead with it, Bert. We want to adopt the German boy. His name is Horst. That's with a *t*. Horst Schumann. With two *ens*."

Great news, Dick. Congratulations."

"Yeah, well, the boy doesn't know about it yet. Maybe he won't want to come."

"Out of Germany? You have to be kidding. He's not a *meschuggene*, is he?"

"Hope not. They say it's growing worse over there. A zillion Jews trying to leave, most of them to America, at least that's what we hear."

"Best country in the world."

"You bet. What I want to talk to you about…"

"Don't bother, Dick. You want Luckman's help to get your boy out. You've come to the right man. I'm sure you know he's on Foreign Relations. Next session he's chairing Ways and Means. You're one of the people who put him there. He owes you. Count on us."

"Bert, that's great, really great! Any idea what we have to do to start this?"

"I don't know much about adoption. You'll probably need a lawyer. Tannenbaum at Sholom should be able to help you. Immigration is something else again. There are two ways to bring the boy to America. One is through normal channels, regular Immigration and Naturalization procedure, but that could take forever. INS is swamped these days. Never enough help, especially abroad."

"The other way?" Dick tried not to sound anxious.

"I'm asking Luck to go to the floor with a piece of legislation, to let the boy enter by Act of Congress. Our staff legal eagle, Alan Horwitz…you ever meet Horwitz?"

"Last year, at the Jewish American Congress dinner. He was on the panel."

Bert nodded. "Of course. Horwitz knows his stuff. He's coming over this afternoon. I'll ask him to draw up the document. I'm going to Washington on Thursday. I'll take it with me. Luck has a lot on his mind, but believe me, Dick, he'll give this matter high priority. It's important to him."

"I'm really grateful, Bert. You know I won't forget. In the meantime is there anything Rae and I can do? Anything we should be putting together?"

"As a matter of fact there is." He asked his secretary to bring in the Malkin file, the forms they had received from INS.

"I sent for this when we first talked," said Farber. "It's a regular INS application requesting admission to the U.S. Asks all kinds of basic questions, some data I'm sure we'll need sooner or later even if we go through Congress. Mail it to Germany, have them fill it out and get it back to me as soon as possible, the sooner the better, okay?" He plumped down in back of his desk. Dick knew the meeting was over and shook Farber's hand.

"Thanks, Bert. Please thank Luck for us. We're really grateful." He opened the door, started to walk out.

"Oh Dick, one more thing."

"Yes, Bert?"

"I still have friends at the Trib. They would like this story."

"They would?"

"Sure. How many Congressmen can you name, personally trying to save a Jewish boy from Hitler's clutches?"

"Will that help Horst?"

"Couldn't hurt, Dick. Couldn't hurt."

"Then do it, Bert." He closed the office door softly, folded the INS form, tucked it into his suit pocket and left. When he exited into downtown traffic, several pedestrians returned his smile.

◆   ◆   ◆

Gretchen Schumann, nee Krause, boarded the No. 44 tram at the Levering-strasse end station. Depending on traffic crossing Dortmund's center, the ride home might take an hour, even this late. Ordinarily she enjoyed the time alone, the fact that nobody knew where she was and the comforting thought that she need do nothing but watch the scenery or other passengers. She liked to float through the city, snug in her window seat, idle thoughts drifting through her mind. Her daydreams were sometimes erotic. She would glance slyly at fellow passengers, younger men if any were on board and create delicious fantasies around them. One of her favorites was to have a man look into her eyes, be instantly attracted and move to her side. At first he would be shy, but also charming in a boyish way. He would tell her how appealing she was, how captivated he was by her long, blonde hair and her slim figure. She would act coolly, then warm a little. His name would always be exotic, perhaps French, like Pierre, at other times Spanish, maybe Don Pasquale or Jose. She also liked Italian names like

Luigi or Paolo. Dreaming about handsome young men sitting close, softly pressing against her, made her feel so enchanted that she often found it difficult to return to reality.

No Latin lovers tonight however, no quandary about reality. Ever since this morning, reality had descended like puffs of poison gas on the head of thirty-six year old Gretchen Schumann. Dinner at her parents was a catastrophe. Until recently such get-togethers centered mainly on pot roast and pastry; the food, like the conversation, tended to be banal, but safe and *gemütlich*. Hedwig, at sixty-one and Reinhardt, at sixty-three, were past the point of interfering in the lives of their daughters. Ilse, the eldest, had married Rupert Koch, a decent fellow, a carpenter who drank beer as hard as he worked, but who was also a good father to Katje, the Krause's pleasant little granddaughter.

Gretchen's marriage to Oskar Schumann required greater adjustment. The Krauses did not consider themselves anti-Semitic. In fact, Schumann was the first Jew they knew personally. Oh sure, they gave business to Dobritsky the tailor, but their discourse extended only to repair directions and customary amenities. Also when Marmelstein and his pushcart came around with fresh fruit and vegetables, they bought when they had money. Schumann was a different sort, so pushy, always talking, reading, and arguing politics. Reinhardt made it clear from the beginning that he disliked Communist talk in his house, especially when Ilse and Rupert were there. Listening to Schumann's left-wing propaganda for a whole evening totally infuriated Reinhardt. It wasn't that he was a Nazi sympathizer. Well, he wasn't exactly antagonistic, either. In the privacy of his mind Reinhardt admitted that he thoroughly disliked his Jewish son-in-law, a rabblerouser who thought he knew everything. "The Nazis are right about some things," Reinhardt would confess to Hedwig. "A lot of yelling and marching and loud band music and everybody going around Heil Hitlering, but that will quiet down one of these days." The good thing was that more people had jobs; also food prices had come down so ordinary folks could afford to eat well again. True, a few heads got bashed and some Jewish shops messed up. "Too bad," Reinhardt would mutter when the subject arose, "it's the price that has to be paid." Reinhardt wasn't quite certain what he meant by that, what the price was or what it had to be paid for, but he was sure Jews were different from ordinary, decent, god-fearing Germans like himself. Well, thank heaven Oskar wasn't visiting anymore. Grete said her husband didn't feel welcome at the Krauses, which was fine with Reinhardt. Maybe Grete could find herself a new husband, a good Christian man. Sooner or later having a Jewish son-in-law was sure to mean trouble for the whole family.

Gretchen had been in a foul mood all day. It began, as it did so often, with Horst's stinking bed. She always took the sheet to the laundry downstairs, but the mattress was heavy and had to be dragged to the balcony to dry. Sometimes she lost all self-control and whipped his bottom. That never improved her disposition and certainly didn't reduce the episodes. She knew the boy needed help, some kind of doctor. He was a good kid, not nasty or anything, just so withdrawn and private. She didn't know how to reach him and that made her nervous. Lately, merely getting out of bed upset her. Everything around her was changing, the way people looked and treated her, the cleaning lady who came on Thursdays, Ruhmann at the delikatessen, Frau Lempert at the butcher shop. They hardly spoke to her, never even said "Good morning." She felt so angry. Wasn't she the same person? Didn't she pay cash like everyone else? Why should they behave so coldly just because she was married to a Jewish man? Her feelings had come to a head a few weeks ago. She and her best friend, Ulrike Raabe, had met at a downtown café.

"Gretchen, I'd better just come out and say it."

"What? What is it?" she asked, but she knew.

"Gretchen, Karl Heinrich has been promoted. He's the new director of Westfalen's National Youth Corps. He's an important man in the Party. You know that I like you, we've been friends for twenty years, but I can't see you anymore as long as you're married to...to..." She chewed on her lower lip, twisted a ring on her finger.

"To a Jew, Ulrike. Might as well say the word. Nobody can hear you."

"That's right Grete, a Jew. I'm sorry it worked out like this. I hope you'll be all right. Maybe when things are different we'll see each other again." She put money on the table, gathered up her purse and walked out without another word. Gretchen had felt a deep emptiness in her chest.

Today was worse than usual. When she came out of the bathroom, Oskar lingered in the kitchen, drinking coffee. "Horst left already, Gretchen. He did it again. You know what I mean. Couldn't face you this morning. He's having a bad time." He peered at her balefully. "We're all having a bad time. I'm sorry. I'm really sorry. Maybe we can go out this week to a concert or the theater. I'll try and collect money today, see some old customers, those still willing to talk to me. Gretchen, I'm so sorry. My god, what has happened to us?"

He had dressed quickly and left the apartment.

"What's happened to us?" echoed in her mind as she sat at the table, chilly in her bathrobe. She stared at the crumpled weekly, *Der Stürmer:* "Jew Drinks Christian Virgin's Blood," threw it in the trashcan. She knew from the beginning it wasn't an ideal marriage, but life with Oskar had started out pleasantly, even with hope. Now look at it, only four years later. She poured a fresh cup of coffee, lit a cigarette and keenly remembered the day they met.

She had gone to the Opera House, a Saturday matinee of "The Merry Widow," had enjoyed the music, the singing and clever sets. Afterward she went across the street to Café Lüchtemeyer for coffee, cake and a smoke. When the gentleman at the next table offered his lighter, she accepted. They made small talk.

"You come here often?" she asked.

"I live on Weiherstrasse, a few minutes away. I own the building."

She knew he said that to impress her, but maybe it was true. He wasn't handsome and his hair was thinning, but his eyes twinkled behind his thick glasses. He certainly looked well dressed, had clean fingernails and shined shoes. Gretchen noticed things like that about men.

"I live with my parents near Scharnhorst," she said.

"You're a long way from home."

"I don't mind the ride. I sing all the music I hear in the theater."

"Out loud?"

"No, in my head," she laughed.

That was the beginning. He didn't rush things, but she managed to meet him most Saturday afternoons. On their third date they went to the theater at the Hiltropwall, then visited the nearby synagogue. That's when she discovered he was a Jew. It made no difference to her. For several years she had worked at the Günter-Meyer department store, owned by Jews. Many fellow workers were Jewish, mostly nice people, no different from anyone else. She was distressed by the ugly graffiti written on walls, on houses and fences, mean things about "dirty Jews," "Jews, the Enemy of the People," "Red Jews" and what not. Schumann was not serious about his Jewishness. He had been a corporal in the German army and considered himself a good German. He was also a devoted Communist. She found that out after a picnic in Westfalenpark while putting the food basket in the trunk of the Opel. Bundles of literature were stacked under a blanket, pamphlets about the rights of the proletariat, the evils of right wing aggression, a lot of other stuff. She questioned him and he didn't protest. He was proud to have written some of it. Well, she had no interest in politics so it didn't bother her, not then.

It was her good time of the month and she decided to sleep with him. When she offered to cook dinner that evening he knew what was on her mind, enjoyed the meal and led her gently to bed. He was a considerate lover, passionate and patient, but afterward he talked when all she cared about was sleep. She certainly didn't want to make love and then listen to a lecture about Karl Marx. She shrugged it off, told her family about him, moved her clothes into his apartment and two months later a judge in the Rathaus married them. Frau Gretchen Schumann. She liked the sound of it.

The erosion in their marriage came imperceptibly. He was always writing at his desk, going to meetings, whispering in the sitting room with disheveled, unshaven, rough-looking men who left KPD pamphlets and other Communist literature lying around. She hated that. He often came home with blood on his face, torn clothes, bruised bones. "Nazi bastards," he whimpered as she cleaned him up. She couldn't understand why he kept doing it. It all seemed so futile, like attacking an angry beast by calling it names. The Nazis were clearly in power. To write and hand out Communist leaflets brought Oskar nothing but beatings, so what was the use?

After Horst returned to Dortmund her relationship to Oskar further deteriorated. She didn't know all the details and probably never would. She knew the boy ran away from an orphanage in Paderborn where Oskar placed him after the mother died. Temporarily, Oskar said when he told her the story, unable to look her straight in the eye. She thought it very strange, all of it. Nobody heard from the child until 1932. That autumn, Oskar's brother, Walter, called from his village in the Hunsrück. Horst had appeared on his doorstep out of nowhere, tired and hungry. The brother had put him on a train and dispatched him to Dortmund.

She had tried her best, but her relationship to Horst was strained from the outset. He was sullen, secretive and fiercely independent, like a restless animal in captivity. He also wet his bed, not every night, but often enough to be a nuisance. As the bond between father and son tightened, her rapport with her husband weakened. They seldom made love anymore, rarely spent special moments together. Politics consumed Oskar, inundated everyone connected to him. Their married life collapsed further after Hitler came to power. Oskar felt betrayed by Germans and the rest of the civilized world. He threw himself even more into Communist causes and took frightful beatings as a result. They were now with few friends and less money, most likely without a future as well.

A nasty blow fell today. Her family made it clear that Oskar was too dangerous to have around and no longer welcome at their home. Rupert thought a divorce appropriate and they all agreed. She had stomped out of the house, furious. What were families for? Weren't families supposed to help each other in times of trouble? What was she to do? Of course she knew decisions had to be made, but right now she was too confused and scared to think clearly.

She arrived at her Schwanenstrasse exit, clenched her jaws and got off. A light was burning in the hallway, but Oskar was not home. Horst was asleep in his room. She thought he might be faking to avoid confrontation, but she couldn't be sure. She took a warm bath, fell into a fitful sleep and woke briefly when Oskar joined her in bed much later. They mumbled greetings and curled up on their own sides.

A hard, insistent rap on the door instantly woke them. For some reason Gretchen checked the clock on her night table. It was four in the morning and totally black outside. She climbed out of bed, turned on the overhead light and slipped on her robe, her heart pounding in her throat. Oskar yanked his pants on, suspenders dangled at his sides.

"What's the use," he said, "let them in," and disappeared into the bathroom.

Horst also woke at the first rap, knew exactly what was happening. Without hesitation he grabbed his shirt and pants, his sweater and shoes, and climbed over the balcony wall and into the drainage opening. He scurried around the block to the far corner of Weiherstrasse. From there he could see parked sedans, their lights dimmed. Five or six Storm Troopers shoved Oskar out the doorway and into the back of a car. Isador Herz from next door, still in nightclothes, was hauled into another one. Two guards posted themselves in front of the building. Horst saw apartment lights go on, heard some yelling and Gretchen cursing the guards. He knew there would be no returning to his place tonight, perhaps never again. He was homeless once more.

5

From his corner office in the north wing of Stuttgart's majestic old castle, converted in 1934 to the services of the Third Reich, Dr. Klaus Becker, SS stalwart, Senior Civil Servant and trusted guardian of *Büro Ribbentrop's* burgeoning Division of Visas, had a clear view of the city's ornate railway station, tucked picturesquely between Heilbronner Strasse and Cannstatter Strasse. Dr. Becker was exceedingly busy, but never so burdened that he could not enjoy, if only for a moment, the glorious view of the castle's surrounding gardens and, to the west, the University's somber, but impressive structures. Becker, debonair and mannerly, appreciated beauty in all its forms, from blossoming flowers to blooming young women, both copiously available to the Führer's more compelling and faithful disciples. At first he had chafed at relocating his department from Berlin's Foreign Office nerve center to this lovely, but decidedly bucolic outpost. Only recently had he begun to appreciate, then to admire, the move's utility.

He cast a last glance at the gardens, stubbed out his cigarette with a sigh and turned to a sheaf of directives received only this morning from *Oberregierungsrat* Heinz Naumann, his Senior Administrator. He buzzed for his secretary.

"Yes, Doctor Becker?"

"Please sit down, Fräulein Grimm. We have organizing to do." As always, her presence agitated him. As always, he warned himself not to be stupid. A man simply did not dip his pen in the office inkwell. "I want Schweiger, Hartung, Deppmüller, Schirardi and Hofmeister in my office at three."

"Schirardi is in Frankfurt."

"Find his assistant, the fat one who looks like Göring."

"Kullmeier, sir." She suppressed a giggle.

"He'll have to do. I've marked the new directives from Berlin. All departments are affected. Please have copies ready, also files for sub-sections. Identify copies to match cover sheets. Make separate files for visa applications from Europeans, Americans and other parts of the world, identical to the way Berlin organized it."

"Major changes, sir?"

"Decidedly. From now on we will need to deal with four distinct regulations. The most complicated ones are for Jews running off to America, Hartung's section." He heaved another sigh. "Get his material to him as soon as possible, he functions best in the mornings. Advise the others that I want the information chewed and digested by this afternoon. And Fräulein Grimm, make careful notes please in case we have questions for Berlin. Oh yes, advise Minister Neumann that we received his directives and will implement them at once. You know what to say."

"Of course, Dr. Becker."

"Fräulein Grimm?" Her skirt cupped her buttocks like a goalkeeper's hands clutching a ball. He couldn't resist the gambit. "I meant to ask you. Are you happy here?" She stared at him. "I mean, do you like your job?"

"Shit," Andrea Grimm thought, "six weeks in a pleasant office, good pay, close to home and here it comes again. New politics, same old stupid game." She managed a smile.

"Very much, Dr. Becker. Best job I've ever had I told my boyfriend last night, right after our Party meeting." She turned to the doorway. "Will there be anything else?"

He shook his head.

"Then I'll get on this immediately, Dr. Becker." She strode out.

Becker sighed with regret. She was so tempting. Still, he rued his advance, appreciated how she handled the situation. Perhaps it was better this way. On the other hand, women were known to change their minds. They are so clever, thought Becker, and returned to administrative worries. Except for Hartung, who presented a different problem, he trusted his staff.

At eleven that morning, shortly after Andrea Grimm delivered the information to his office, barely moments after his first drink, Dietrich Hartung called in Paula Zeidler, his assistant. She knew, of course, that he drank. She had been with him almost sixteen years, long before he joined the SS. He was already drinking then, but not nearly as much. These days he hit the bottle hard, was less diligent than in earlier days. Still, he was good to her. They were comfortable with each other and she covered for him whenever possible. Max Zeidler, her father, lost an arm for the Kaiser during the war. The Zeidlers had always been loyal. She was proud of that.

"Work, Frau Zeidler. New orders from Berlin. Becker wants a meeting this afternoon."

"Andrea told me."

"Berlin is putting on pressure. How many Jews are now on our list who want to join that great American leader, President Rosenfeld?"

"Roughly two thousand. Berlin is sending more, another five or six hundred."

"Damn. Do they think we're machines?" He heaved his pear-shaped body out of his chair, paced the floor, and rubbed the flask in his pocket as if expecting a genie to appear with the answer. "Jews," he muttered, "all day long Jews and more Jews." He plopped down. "Wouldn't it be beautiful if we could just pack 'em up and ship 'em out? Maybe to Africa with the rest of the niggers?"

"The meeting is at three, Herr Hartung. Time to get organized."

"You're right. Call the department in here after lunch. We'll see what we can work out."

"No lunch. Not today." She gathered her papers together. "Too much to do before three."

He glared at her, ran a finger over his veined nose, feeling the alcohol, already wanting more. "You're right again. Damn. You're always right."

Hartung met his staff at the civil servants' conference table, larger than the one in his office. He sometimes wondered when the Party would make this collection of smug clerks toe the line, but right now he needed them. They went to work.

Later, in Becker's office, Hartung clearly and precisely explicated Berlin's directives. Jews applying for American exit visas were to be divided into distinct groups: the bulk from working class and shopkeeper backgrounds, a sizeable number from professional ranks, and finally a select cluster with extensive financial reputations and with foreign, political, and industrial connections. The Party's interest in all three groups was exclusively one of money: its structure, its volume and, most importantly, a need to develop precise methods for its extraction from Jews who possessed it.

"Actually," preened Hartung, "it's quite simple. In the future, visa applications from Jews will be considered only if they include a financial statement verified at local levels. Berlin assumes all Jews lie about their money and will always try to sneak out with it. They'll find it much harder to hide assets while still in their own communities. That should also take a load off us here in Stuttgart."

"Excellent," said Becker.

"Jews without money fall into a different category," Hartung continued.

"Which is?" former policeman Rolf Schweiger, now Border Security, wanted to know.

"Not yet totally clear, Rolf. They may have to stay in Germany, unless you want to buy them a ticket to America and maybe a new suit and a piece of luggage to go with it, eh?" That got a laugh.

"What else, Dietrich?" Becker was growing impatient.

"A tricky one. Many Jews have connections in the United States, with rich relatives, with Jew organizations that have plenty of dough, even with politicians who expect something out of it and are willing to pay for the privilege. Berlin wants to keep an especially close watch on those. Before they are permitted to leave they have to come here, to Stuttgart, for a personal interview, to explain their connection."

"Very good." Becker was pleased. "Make them pay before they run off to Palestine and New York. They're a sly bunch, Dietrich, watch your ass."

The meeting lasted three productive hours. Fräulein Grimm served refreshments and Becker complimented the group on the efficiency with which they had attacked this complex assignment.

"Heil Hitler, Dr. Becker."

"Heil Hitler. Oh Dietrich, a moment please."

Fräulein Grimm made a discreet exit, left the two men behind. Becker rubbed his eyes with his knuckles.

"Dietrich, we're all under tension. A lot of responsibility. Berlin, the Führer, our superiors, everybody expects things from us."

"I understand, sir."

"Ah. And exactly what is it you understand?"

"That…well…that they expect things from us." Hartung rubbed his nose, felt sweat gather in the crease under his collar. "Something wrong? Are there complaints about my work?"

Becker lit an English oval, wondered for a brief moment how long his supply would last, leaned against the edge of his desk and exhaled smoke in Hartung's general direction. "Your work? No, there's nothing wrong with your work. There's something wrong with you."

"With me?"

"Dietrich! We're not fools here, you know. We all need to relax from time to time, have a beer, a schnapps or a glass of wine. But we do so on our own time, not on department time, not on SS time, not on the Führer's time. Understand what I'm saying?"

"Yes, I do. Of course I do." The sweat ran down Hartung's spine and his left eye twitched. "But everything seems to be piling up."

"Even more reason to keep a clear head. We have a half million Jews in this country. Any idea how many of them want to desert the Fatherland? Half of them? Maybe all of them, for all we know. Actually, who gives a damn? In this office it's the rich ones we're after, the ones who want to rob us blind, those who want to run off with money stolen from good Germans. Are you following me?"

"Perfectly, Dr. Becker."

"Good." He snuffed out his cigarette, eased into a leather chair. "Get smart, Hartung. Where Jews are concerned, Berlin expects us to be the nation's watchdog. In this office we're not dealing with broken-down Polish yids hauling candlesticks around on pushcarts. We're handling clever ones, sharp operators who want to move their money to New York and London, to start banks, to finance newspapers so they can print their filthy Hebrew propaganda. I warn you, Hartung, mistakes could be costly, extremely costly. Frankly, I don't want to pay for your mistakes."

"Mistakes? What mistakes have I?..."

"Not yet, Dietrich, not yet, but from now on no more drinking during the work day. Oh for god's sake, don't act so surprised. Everybody knows you drink on the job. I smell booze on your breath right now!"

"Please forgive me, Dr. Becker. It won't happen again. I'm sorry. I'm really sorry. I assure you I will stop."

Becker picked up a file, scanned it and smiled without parting his lips. "Yes, you will, Dietrich. I'm sure you will." He raised a limp hand. "Heil Hitler."

"Heil Hitler," snapped Hartung and fled. He wiped the sweat from his neck, crossed the long corridor, descended to his office and ignored Frau Zeidler's questioning look. He slammed his door and collapsed in his swivel chair. The job was too much for him; it weighed a ton.

Not so long ago he was an insurance adjuster, a well-paid accountant and a highly esteemed officer of *Vereinigte Deutsche Versicherung GmbH*, the prosperous United German Insurance Company, owned and operated by the Jewish brothers Grumbauer, Leon and Markus. The Grumbauers took *Mein Kampf* seriously, closed the business, sold their homes and late in 1933 joined their uncle's insurance company in Buenos Aires. The Grumbauers had been kind to him and taught him plenty. The SS, too, came to value his skills, his contacts with the Jewish financial world, his extensive information about Jewish business practices. They considered him precisely the right man for the job. At first he had reveled in the recognition, relished the feeling of power, but nothing prepared him for the magnitude of this assignment, the mounting pressure of decisions that increasingly involved matters of life and death. He slipped the silver-plated whiskey flask out of his pants pocket and took a deep swig. As on most days, he would empty its contents and bring it home in his briefcase.

◆   ◆   ◆

The raid on his home and the arrest of his father came as a shock. Once again, Horst Schumann embarked on the depressing ritual of finding a place to hide, hopefully a warm one this time, preferably one accessible to food and water. The sun had not yet risen. It was bitterly cold, but thank heaven he had the foresight to grab his sweater. Morosely hugging his knees, he hunched against the wind on a bench in the Hoeschpark. He wondered if he would see his father again and would he be recognizable? Horst fought against tears of anger, frustration, and misery, but they welled in his eyes. No use to cry; better to find a place out of the cold. He considered the Krauses. Would they take him in and hide him for a few days until he could find a new spot? Best to forget that idea. Reinhardt liked him, but was scared about anything that involved Oskar, also probably why Oma Krause wasn't too friendly these days. Maybe sneak into his school? It was heated sometimes. Forget it, too dangerous. Twice last month a security detachment searched the building, probably looking for the mimeograph machine. The last time they came he had fled out a side door, crossed the Burgwall and lost himself in the service yard of the Ritter brewery, a possible hideout. He had seen steam rise from grates that adjoined several square buildings. Steam meant heat. He had also spied small wooden structures, probably tool sheds. Long ago he learned to notice such things.

Even this early in the morning Horst took nothing for granted. He circled Heiligegartenstrasse and crossed over Leopoldstrasse, thereby avoided the railroad station's bright lights. The dark, deserted-looking brewery complex smelled of malt and hops. He looked around carefully. The tool sheds were off to the side and fenced, but he climbed over easily. Two of the sheds were unlocked, one heaped with boxes of beer glass coasters, many spilled on the floor. The other, stuffed with empty grain sacks, appeared more inviting. Dawn was approaching and he had to act fast. At one end of the wooden structure he discovered a small window and unlocked it. That would serve as an emergency exit. He burrowed into the bales of sacks, arranged them to provide a peephole. He still had a piece of bread and a half-eaten apple, started to bite into the bread, but changed his mind. Better to save it. Besides, he was too tired to eat. He dozed fitfully. Old memories jabbed his consciousness, poignant reminders of the first of many lonely nights after he ran away from Paderborn.

How well he remembered that night! He had walked north for no particular reason, with no idea where to go or what to do. He was only six years old, always had someone to look after him and give him direction. He had thought vaguely about telephoning his father, but did not know where to find a telephone or how to operate one. He also had no money. He was sure you needed money to use a telephone. He had no food either, but that didn't worry him. He saw lots of apples on trees and this was the season for berries. Surely somebody was searching for him right now. Maybe they had called the police. He kept looking over his shoulder in the direction from which he had come. What if the police suddenly appeared? What would he do? He knew only that he could not stay in that terrible place. Not anymore. If they caught him he would run away again. He would run away even if they tied him up and locked him in the cellar. Could they keep him tied up forever? He didn't think so. They would have to let him out sometime. Then he would escape once more, this time to the end of the world. They couldn't find him there. He knew if Papa realized how unhappy he was he would bring him home, and Liselotte too.

He walked until early evening. Lots of ripe blueberries and gooseberries grew along the road. He picked some. They were juicy and sweet. Just before dark he came to a small village with a few farmhouses and some shops like a bakery and a butcher, but not much more.

After all the walking his feet hurt. On the other side of the village he could see the banks of a river. He took off his shoes and stockings and put his feet into the cold water. It felt wonderful. He cupped his hands and drank from the stream. Great trees surrounded him, their leaves already thick on the ground. He couldn't walk any farther. He looked in the direction of the village but didn't see anyone. Maybe they weren't looking for him after all. He was cold and crawled under the leaves to keep warm.

His eyes felt so heavy he had to close them. Maybe tomorrow he would go back. Maybe he could learn not to wet his bed and the children wouldn't laugh at him all the time. He missed Liselotte. Maybe Papa would truly take them both home. He could almost hear the way the violins sang when he and Papa went to Café Corso on Sunday mornings. Mutti liked to dress him in the black velvet suit with the white collar. She said it made him look handsome with his baby-soft skin and his nice smile. Papa always let him have a hot chocolate with spoonfuls of whipped cream on top. Papa had only a small glass of something green that tasted like licorice. Afterward they went to the zoo or just walked around and looked into store windows. In the winter they wore their overcoats and rubber boots because it was cold.

He dug deeper into the leaves of trees that grew on the banks of the Lippe, curled up into a ball for warmth and safety. He dreamed of his Papa and Mutti, of lions and bears in the zoo, of violins that sang in the Café Corso where waiters in white coats and black ties served mountains of whipped cream floating on lakes of hot chocolate.

Now, six years later, loneliness remained his steadfast companion. Now, in the wooden shed of a Dortmund brewery, lying under sacks smelling of grain, his knees pulled against his body for warmth and protection, his mind nearly numbed by despair, Horst Schumann wept a child's tears, but quickly decided that was a waste of time. Silently he mouthed the alphabet and then practiced multiplication tables, all the way to one hundred times one hundred. Finally, he tapped inaudible messages on his knees to the outside world in the Morse code a boy at school had taught him. Dots and dashes spelled out longings, hope, and want and went into the atmosphere until that, too, became a useless exercise. Then he lay still, stared into the darkness, and waited for morning.

6

The *Steinwache*, Dortmund's main police station, squatted like a run-down warehouse at the foot of a palisade called Hoher Wall. Located in an industrial section, human enterprise had transformed its surrounding landscape into barren vistas of cement.

In 1935, the city's regional Party boss, *Ortsgruppenleiter* Roland Pflug, conducted his primary duties in this building. From his fourth floor window Pflug looked at an enormous swastika banner attached to the roof of the building and fluttering just below eye level. Despite the structure's plain looks and deteriorated condition, Pflug detested the prospect of moving to the imposing new headquarters, now approaching completion in the nearby Hansaplatz. He was comfortable with his plain, but familiar environment although he understood the move's rationale. Relations between the Party's SA and SS divisions had deteriorated; Berlin wanted to centralize activities and exercise stronger control. Nord-Westfalen's expanding political sectors clamored for places to meet, to plan, to ritualize. Each branch wanted more elbowroom, a larger arena in which to exert power. Even his adjutant, Böhm, had lodged a complaint, had cited gross inadequacy of current interrogation facilities and thoughtfully appended an equipment list designed to accomplish his tasks more thoroughly.

Heiko Böhm. Pflug heaved a sigh. At this very moment his right-hand man undoubtedly performed those very tasks in the basement, in one of those dingy, smelly, concrete cubicles with rusty ceiling pipes that ran to the building's corroding boiler. The mere thought of descending into that basement made Pflug's skin crawl, yet one more function of being a loyal Party member that became harder to sustain. Last night's exchange with his wife, Rika, although it went past midnight, had not relieved his troubled mind.

"I know you hate the work, but what are your alternatives?" She dimmed the lights.

"I could ask for a transfer."

"To what?"

"I don't know. Maybe run The Union of Young German Women or the local branch of the National Teachers Union."

She looked at him with raised eyebrows.

"That's right, I'm being facetious. No, dearest Rika, there are no alternatives. They picked me for this job and dealing with enemies of the state is part of it. Either I perform or Terhoven kicks me out. Period."

Rika found Rollo's hand and held it tight. "Maybe in time it gets easier."

"Maybe. Maybe like Böhm I could also become an expert on locating peoples' vital organs. Who knows when that might be useful."

"What a terrible thought." She flinched, pulled the cover to her shoulders. "It really scares me, Rollo. We used to talk about the future."

"I seem to remember."

"About raising Heinz and Trudi in a better world."

"Rika, please!"

"Now we worry how to live through tomorrow."

"I don't want to think about tomorrow."

"I wouldn't either, not if my job depended on torturing people."

"It's not why I'm there, for heaven's sake!"

"If it were, I wouldn't be married to you. When you joined, the Party made promises, Rollo. But have they kept them? Have you achieved what you hoped for?"

"I don't know, Rika." He took a deep breath. "No, that's not true. I do know. It's not what I hoped for, not by far."

They lay side-by-side, alone with their thoughts. Rika, aware of the truth, was reluctant to open old wounds. When they met at Freiburg University, Rollo wanted to be a teacher, to lose himself in research and joyously embrace the pristine world of higher mathematics. Only loyalty to Gustav, his father, could have diverted Rollo from that path and transform him into a Party official. Rika's feelings about her father-in-law, the late Gustav Pflug, were sharply tangled.

Gustav Pflug was a corporal in the Kaiser's artillery when the Great War collapsed. At that time his young wife, Johanna, and his son, Roland, lived in Essen with Gustav's parents. Gustav's father, Heinrich, worked for Krupps where he helped to forge steel into cannons, to earn money so that Gustav might go to school when the shooting stopped, become somebody and buy a home of his own. When Gustav returned from the war, Heinrich's dreams for him vanished when the money he had saved became worthless paper.

"Stop thinking about your father," Rika said, reading her husband's mind. "It's not all his fault. We had choices, Rollo. Just because Gustav joined the Party…"

"He had choices too."

"After what was done to him?"

True, that was a bad time, a turning point. Heinrich and Gustav were disappointed again and again, seeking work and finding only rejection. One day, weary and frustrated, they pooled their resources and stopped for a beer. A band of *Red Falcons*, a militant Communist detachment, invaded the tavern, flung handbills on tables, shouted Bolshevist slogans and KPD propaganda. Gustav kept his temper, turned his back. They grabbed him to make him listen, but Heinrich interfered and was knocked to the floor as others joined the short, brutal fight. Bottles were smashed, jagged shards used as weapons. A stocky, bearded youth slashed Gustav's wrist, opened a large vein in his forearm and severed the main tendon. Heinrich bound the wrist and rushed Gustav to a hospital. In time the wound healed, but Gustav's spirit, like his arm, was permanently crippled. He joined the Nazi movement in 1923, stayed with it when Hitler went to prison, earned a meager living as an organizer. Two healthy arms weren't needed to make street corner speeches; leaflets could be handed out with the left hand, so could the Nazi salute. In young Rollo's house revenge and hatred were served nightly along with dinner. When Hitler came to power, Gustav persuaded his son to join him. Rollo did so reluctantly.

He propped himself up with a pillow, with a need to explore further. "Yes, Rika, even after they hurt him he had choices, even then. I'm convinced he hated Communists more than he loved Hitler. He loathed Marx and Lenin. He despised left wing notions, especially the concept of giving power to the people, especially to people like those bastards in the tavern who thought they had power. Of course Gustav was shortsighted. He connected everything about Communism only with his crippled arm. He believed in Hitler, but mostly, I think, he lived for revenge."

"And you were there to help him get it."

"Maybe. It's possible. He was a bitter man. He had a limited view of the world, but the Party gave him stature, a sense of belonging."

"He was also thrilled when you joined."

"What are you saying?"

"I'm saying that he wanted a partner. He wanted you to share his fate."

"But Rika, Gustav knew I worked like a dog to become a teacher. I can't imagine he'd be happy to know my job depends on tormenting people, even if they're Bolsheviks and Jews."

"You're Gustav Pflug's son, my love. They'll never let you forget that. They want you to think like him. They admire how you organize things, how everybody respects you. They think you're great with people and it's true, you are. The trouble is, SS big shots don't regard human beings the way you do. For them, a little torture comes with the territory. Gustav would have supported that."

Hard as it was for Rollo to admit it, Rika was right. "Yes, he probably would have. The question is, how long can I stand it?"

Rika was deeply afraid for him. Lately, such demons of conscience made nightly visits. "Whatever you do, my darling, they must never suspect how you truly feel. If you let them think that you don't respect their ways, they'll make you pay. I don't have to remind you about Röhm and Strasser. Fake it if you have to, Rollo, but stay in control until the time is right. Better options are bound to turn up. Maybe not right away, but sooner or later they will, I promise you." She turned out the light, kissed his cheek and nestled closer, wanting so much to give him some of her strength.

His mind in turmoil, Rollo went into the living room, browsed through unread professional publications, but couldn't concentrate. Rika's remarks hit a deep nerve. He loved his wife. He kept things from her. He kept them from her precisely because he loved her. She didn't need to remind him about Röhm. Since his Party chief's assassination, attitudes toward the SA's remaining leaders had changed. Lutze, who took Röhm's place, was a loyal Nazi. Why then did Interior send someone from the SS to supervise the Hansaplatz move? Nobody could to it more efficiently than he, Pflug. He had lived in Dortmund most of his life, knew the people, had faithfully performed his duties. Communist literature had almost disappeared. Even now the troublemakers were locked in the basement, all except Schumann's kid. He got away. What was his name again? Horst? Clever boy. If he were my son, Pflug thought, I'd be proud of him. They had raided at four in the morning and still didn't catch the youngster. Well, so what? Where could he go?

Reflecting on Schumann's son reminded him of his own children. He checked on Heinz and Trudi, watched their sleeping faces until a wave of nausea told him a migraine was tightening its grip. Hitler's radio speech two days ago still echoed in his brain. "You must be ready to lay down your life for the Reich," the Führer had screamed. "You must root out evil in our nation. You must make whatever sacrifices are necessary." It was an hour of frenzy, of hatred and malice. Rika promised that something would come up sooner or later. Pflug thought of himself as an intelligent man with a well-ordered mind. He had been involved in his Party's power structure for more than two years now. "I know what's coming up, my dear wife," Roland Pflug murmured sourly into the night, "and it's coming up sooner, not later. War is what's coming up and I will be in it." He was a loyal

German, a National Socialist by choice. He had made compromises, some he deplored. He had many flaws, but he was not a Heiko Böhm!

The mere thought of Böhm wrenched Rollo back to the present. He stared out the window, envious of people below pursuing the ordinary. Envy would change nothing; Böhm was still in the basement, an awareness that made Rollo fretful. No way to stall any longer; he had to go down there, if only to show interest. After all, the raid had been successful, more than a dozen potential troublemakers off the street, at least until the Führer left. He had given orders for the prisoners to be questioned, not physically abused, but knew perfectly well that where Herz, Koerner, Schumann and other Communists were concerned, Böhm would decide what constituted physical abuse. Schumann, for one, was thoroughly acquainted with Böhm's methods. Pflug wanted to see that perplexing man again, hoped he was still in one piece and conscious. In odd moments Pflug recalled their last confrontation, the amused scorn with which Schumann's eyes had stared at him out of a bloodied face. Well, there was no choice; might as well go down there and see if the Jew still had his sense of humor. Pflug straightened his tie, pulled on his cap, assumed an authoritarian posture and exited.

"I'll be downstairs, Frau Schuster. With Böhm."

She stared at him. "With Böhm?" she asked. "In the basement? Will you be all right?" She blushed deeply at such boldness.

"Yes, I'm sure I will," he said, but without conviction.

◆   ◆   ◆

"Read it again," Rae pleaded, "maybe we missed something. Maybe we don't sound concerned enough. Shouldn't we send pictures of ourselves, Clara? They'll have to translate that stupid INS form or pay somebody to do it. Should we send money? Can they exchange dollars in Germany?"

"Sweetheart, slow down," Dick laughed. "One step at a time."

For hours they'd hunched over pads of paper in the kitchen behind *H & C Weiss & Sons, Hat Cleaners*, composing a letter to Oskar and Horst Schumann, oblivious to the fact that neither the father or the son was in shape to receive it. The letter was written in English; Clara would make a translation.

"Read it again, Clara. Let's hear how it sounds."

"No, Rae, enough is enough. You want to memorize it?"

"So, how many times in my life am I going to ask a boy to be my son, tell me?"

"Do it," Dick smiled at his cousin, "it's not that long."

Clara made a face, took the coffee pot off the stove, filled their cups once more and pushed a plate of mandelbrot in their direction. "Eat," she said.

"Read," said Rae.

My Dear Brother Oskar,

Some other time we will talk about how we have been and what we are doing. Right now there is something more important. I wrote you a long time ago that we have relatives here in Chicago. I am very close to Richard and Regina Malkin. Richard is our second cousin. His father Benjamin was the brother of our cousin Sigmund Loeb from Simmern unter Daun. They are wonderful people, very kind and thoughtful. They have a swell apartment on one of the best streets in Chicago and Richard has a fine business in potatoes and onions.

Here is the big news! The Malkins would like to bring Horst to Chicago and adopt him. How's that? We hear all kinds of stories about what those terrible Nazis are doing to the Jews. So we hope nothing terrible has happened to you or Horst. Here in America the boy would have a great chance. He would have a fine home, two people who would love him. He would get a good education and become a real Mensch. If you agree to let him come, and of course it also has to be agreeable to Horst, the Malkins would begin to put all the papers together like the visas and the passport and the ticket on the ship. It's not as easy as it used to be when I came over because the Nazis are making all kinds of trouble but Dick and Rae (that's what they call themselves) are sure it can be done, especially Dick, who knows some important people who will help him. So what do you say? If you and Horst are willing you will let us know right away. Write to my address: Clara Weiss, 1522 North Clark Street, Chicago, Illinois, U.S.A. You must fill out the paper from the American government. It's in the envelope. The Malkins thought maybe it would cost something to translate the questions. So they wanted to send some money just in case things aren't so good in the leather business right now. We've put twenty dollars into the letter. You can change it into Marks at any bank, Oskar. If you need more we will send more.

Please write as soon as you can. I know this is not an easy decision to make, I mean letting your son go away. I only wish Liselotte were still alive and could come too but that's life. So Horst will have his chance and then later I'm sure you will want to leave that awful country too. Please hurry and answer.

Your sister

Rae, Dick and Clara were silent for a while. In the background Hermann's press thumped a steady rhythm, hissed short bursts of steam, clanged as it opened. It was a solemn moment in which, they felt, something important ought to be said, something quotable at future family gatherings.

"Sounds good to me," Dick finally conceded. "How about you, Rae?"

"We didn't describe ourselves, how old we are, what we look like."

"Next letter, Rae. This one will do fine for now."

Dick turned to his cousin. "Terrific work, Clara. Here's twenty and money for a new ribbon. Time to go. I have to be at the market soon." He filched a few cookies from the plate, said good night to Hermann. The women stood in the kitchen, eyes glowing, then burst into tears.

"Oh Clara," Rae sobbed, "it has to come true. It just has to. I want it so much."

"Go home," Clara said, wiping her eyes. "God willing, he'll get here. And he will, I feel it in my bones. When it comes to my bones, God never lies."

The Malkins drove home without talking. The wind howled down Lake Shore Drive but on this April night they hardly noticed.

7

Horst was alerted by sounds of the morning shift arriving at the brewery. His throat was parched. Still tired and frightened, he only wanted to stay in his nice warm sacks, doing nothing at all. He wasn't sure what he needed more, to drink or to piss.

He looked cautiously out the window. A few yards away workers unlocked a section of fence and rolled it aside for a truck to enter. Horst knew he had to leave; with so much activity in the vicinity someone was bound to spot him. He relieved himself against the shed, waited patiently until shielded by the truck and walked out behind it. Near the street entrance workers glanced in his direction but didn't bother him. He took a familiar route toward Romberg Park, in the direction of the zoo, a place where he always felt safe. Walter loved it there too, was always surrounded by children fascinated with the way he drew pictures of monkeys, lions and birds.

It was early, the zoo still closed. Horst used the drinking fountain at the entrance, ate the last of his food, sat on a stone bench and considered his options. He was anxious to go home and clean himself, but Weiherstrasse was a bad idea. By the end of the day, after dark, he would contact Walter. He would use the cuckoo signal his friend had taught him. Walter would give him something to eat.

Horst was keenly aware why the Nazis wanted to catch him. Although he was only twelve years old, they knew he put Communist flyers on kiosks, on walls and car windows, that he sometimes painted hammers and sickles on fences. Also, he was Oskar Schumann's son, child of a Communist and the son of a Jew, in Nazi eyes more than enough reason to hunt him. He shuddered, wondered if his father was alive. Lately he always wondered if his father was still alive. Walter might be able to find out. Maybe Grete knew something. Better forget Grete; she was plenty scared herself. The Krauses didn't want to see any of them. Right now it was only important to find a new hiding place.

One day he and Walter had roamed the city and watched workers go in and out of a hole in the street. The hole was so big two men could use it at the same time. Despite Walter's impatience, Horst insisted on watching. He moved as close as possible, but couldn't see much because a striped barrier with blinking lights surrounded the opening. An iron ladder went down one side, but apparently not deep because workers easily passed tools to the bottom. When the crew finished loading equipment, the last man out had closed the two covers, which had handles, but no locks. Signs were painted on the covers, red and white ones, also bolts of lightning and warnings about electricity. The hole was near Born Strasse; Horst was sure he could find it. It might be safe there, at least for a short while. After he met Walter tonight he would go there

The zoo finally opened. A bus drove up, loaded with small children. Many more would arrive during the day. He would hang around as long as it looked safe. The zoo was safer than the streets. When he and Walter visited the zoo together, Walter stayed with the birds and small animals, his sketchpad always ready. Horst preferred the tigers and leopards, but mostly a beautiful black panther named Ali. He could stand for hours watching Ali. When the panther moved close to the bars, Horst would concentrate on its green eyes which never blinked, only stared, as if trying to figure something out. Horst loved the panther, daydreamed about opening its cage. How wonderful it would be to see that shiny black cat run like the wind, leap over the wall and disappear. He tried to imagine what Ali might do once he was free, but that got too complicated because there was no jungle on the other side, just streets and houses and people. Horst always stopped his daydream when Ali soared through the air. Today, the graceful beast lay in its cave. Its tail hung out and it never stirred. Horst moved on to the deers and antelopes, then sat on a bench and waited. The deer didn't do much except pull on grass and munch. As he sat there, he reflected that it was exactly like this, watching deer nibble grass, when he first met Norma and Hubert, Ludi and Pauline.

He had been on his own then for a year, Paderborn already a dim memory. He often wondered about Liselotte, whether she was all right, but in time even that concern faded. He had decided long ago that nobody was looking for him, not the police, not his father. If they had really tried they could have found him. He didn't go to some strange land or sailed to Africa, right? He had only wandered twenty-five miles, as far as Bielefeld.

Bielefeld was crowded and he didn't stay. He learned to forage for food, became adept at finding places to sleep. Near small towns like Rheda and Wiedenbrück and even near bigger ones like Gütersloh, safe dark forests provided shelter at night. When it rained he took chances, crept into barns with warm, good-smelling hay, but often dogs discovered him and barked and howled. He hated dogs. In small villages he would usually go to a bakery and ask if he could help in exchange for bread. Most bakers chased him away, but once in a while he met a kind baker with a kind wife and when they saw that he was hungry, that he meant no harm, they let him sweep floors, wash windows, or whatever was needed. They often asked, "Where do you live? Why aren't you in school? Where are your parents?" He would stammer, try to say something that made sense, but they knew he was lying and told him to go away because they didn't want trouble.

In the winter of 1931 Horst walked south. He thought it would be warmer. He only reached Lippstadt, which wasn't very far south and not warmer at all. In Lippstadt, however, his luck changed. At the end of town he found The Village Bakery, a sign proclaiming a Pavel Czerny to be its proprietor.

Horst looked through the window. A tall, thin man worked alone, mixing, heating ovens and tending the kneading machines. It was early, long before sunrise.

"What you want boy? I'm busy. Come back when I open." The baker had a slight accent.

"I'm hungry."

"Lots of people hungry. You got money?"

Horst shook his head.

"No? No money? So what the hell you want from me? Go to the city bakery. They're rich, they feed you." He had laughed at his own joke, moved away, doing things, and ignored Horst who just stood there sniffing, smelling, hungering. Czerny walked by and handed him a *schnecke*, still warm. Horst bit into the sweet dough with such relish it made Czerny laugh.

"You can say *danke*, little bastard?"

"Thank you, oh yes, thank you very much. I want to pay you. I don't have money but I know how to work."

"Ah. What can you do?"

"I can sweep and measure flour. I can put things in cases where they belong. I can do lots of little things."

Czerny was a good-hearted man although he hollered a lot, usually at his old ovens which didn't maintain temperature, other times at customers after they left, accusing them of not paying their accounts on time, of not paying at all and of giving their bigger orders to the Stadtbäckerei. He was born in the Sudentenland, learned to bake in the German army during the Great War. He claimed to have known a Josef Schumann in the army, a good cook, an interesting Jew. Any relation? Clearly he knew Horst was a Jew, but didn't seem to care. He had never married, although he wanted children of his own. He liked Horst and saw how much he longed to help. The boy needed a place to rest, so Czerny fixed a bed in a storage room, near the toilet. Horst was always awake by the time preparations began. Each morning he swept the bakery spotless, washed display cases, scrubbed pans and utensils until they shone. After a while Czerny let him handle bread, stood him on milk crates to reach the oven.

Horst stayed in Lippstadt until spring, 1932. He soon knew the customers, memorized what to put in their baskets. In addition to Horst, a girl from the village, Elsa, worked part-time in the store. At first she was mistrustful of Horst, but eventually welcomed his help.

It was a bright, sunny Saturday in the middle of May. The bakery had closed at noon. Elsa was removing trays of unsold merchandise, bringing it to the storage locker, while Horst and Czerny set up for Monday's baking. A car drove into the lot and parked next to the baker's delivery truck. Two men in SA uniform, one red-nosed, large and beefy, the other slim and mean looking, stepped out and stomped in.

"Are you Czerny?" the slim one asked.

"Yes, I'm Czerny. What you want?"

They looked straight at Horst. "You've got this piece of Jewish shit working for you. We've had complaints from customers. They don't want their food touched by a filthy Jew. You understand, Czerny?"

"Why they don't go to Stadtbäckerei instead? Maybe there they don't get poisoned."

"You're a loud mouth, Czerny," the fat one said, "a Jew-loving loud mouth. You need a lesson." They pulled leather truncheons from their belts, smashed trays and buckets filled with flour, salt and sugar, dumped sacks of grain on the floor, brushed themselves off and moved to the door.

"That was just a warning, Czerny," the thin one said, "next time not only the equipment gets hurt. Throw the Jew out before you open Monday if you know what's good for you." They marched out.

It took hours to clean the place. Elsa went home, scared, crying. "Sons of bitches," fumed Czerny, "dirty, cowardly bastards; real brave men with clubs and knives. Thank god they don't run the country, not yet."

"What happens if they do?" Horst asked in a small voice.

"God help us." Czerny stared into the distance as if seeing monsters. "Stay in this weekend," he said, "we figure out something. Maybe they exaggerate."

Horst knew they didn't exaggerate. Slowly at first, he had seen the violence increase steadily. Now brown shirts were everywhere, sang the Horst Wessel song, marched in the streets, gave speeches and handed out leaflets on corners. More and more people performed the Nazi salute, young people at first, but later the older ones, too. Hitler's picture was plastered on kiosks, on fences, on walls of public buildings. In Gütersloh he saw two shops smeared with paint. The words said, "Don't buy from Jews."

He knew they'd be back. Even with his limited view he began to understand that he was an outcast, hated by many people for no reason other than that he was a Jew. He was thankful to Czerny for many things; for letting him stay and be useful, for bringing him simple books to read and for paper on which to practice writing. He had become better at both. Czerny had even talked about sending him to school after the summer. He stacked the books on the mixing table and printed a note, careful to spell everything correctly:

THANK YOU HERR CZERNY. THANK YOU FOR THE GOOD FOOD AND A NICE PLACE TO SLEEP. THANK YOU FOR BEING MY FRIEND. YOU MADE ME FEEL HAPPY. IT IS MUCH BETTER I GO AWAY. THEY WILL COME BACK. THEN THEY WILL HURT US MUCH MORE. MAYBE WE SEE EACH OTHER AGAIN. I HOPE SO.
YOUR FRIEND HORST

He left after midnight when the streets were empty. He thought Czerny wouldn't mind if he took the books, which he loved. The Czech had no use for them. He was better off than when he arrived. Czerny had bought him a leather rucksack, a new pair of shoes, wool socks, sturdy corduroy shorts and two baker's shirts, too large, but fine when tucked into pants. Horst was usually rewarded with a little cash bonus when they worked long hours on holidays, or for birthday parties. He saved every penny and finally bought a pocketknife at Scheelmann's Hardware Store. It had two blades and a screwdriver. On one of the blades it said "Solingen." When he touched his knife in the pocket of his new corduroy shorts, Horst felt safe. He didn't know which he loved more, his knife or his books. He packed a bottle of water, a bag of rolls, some *schnecken* and a Danish.

Although his rucksack was heavy he walked fast, away from Lippstadt, away from Czerny. His baker friend would be safe, but Horst missed him already. By sunset he crossed the Möhne river at Belecke, saw signs pointing to the Arnsberger Woods, a good place to spend the night, among his old friends, the trees.

The next day, a warm and sunny one, brought many families to the forest's nature park. The children fed deer and ducks or played in the grass. With envy in his heart, Horst wished he could join them. Not far from him a family spread out a blanket, and while the mother arranged food, the children and their dog amused themselves with a ball. Once the ball rolled over to Horst. He picked it up and threw it back.

"Thank you," the boy said, "would you like to play with us?"

"Oh yes." Horst didn't hesitate a second. "I would like that very much."

They played for more than an hour. The boy's name was Ludwig, but his mother called him Ludi. Ludi Klingen. The girl was Pauline and the dog was Wally.

"I am Horst. Horst Schumann."

"Are you from this area, Horst?" the mother inquired in a friendly manner. Horst felt comfortable in her presence. She was a short, sturdy woman, with cropped brown hair cut in bangs, and gentle, green eyes. "Are you here with your parents?" she asked, but he didn't answer and she didn't insist.

They all settled on the blanket and the mother, Norma, invited Horst to join in the picnic. He wasn't hungry, but longed to stay. It felt so good to laugh and play that he never wanted it to stop. Also the sausages smelled great; he just couldn't say no.

The Klingens told him about themselves, of their house in Arnsberg, that Norma taught German and History in the Volksschule and that Hubert owned an auto repair shop. After the meal Hubert started a game with Ludi and Pauline and Norma called Horst to her side.

"Would you help me clean up?"

"Yes, gladly."

Together they put things back in the basket. That finished, Norma pulled a small book from her bag and held it toward him.

"Do you like poetry?"

He wasn't sure what poetry was.

"I don't know, Frau Klingen."

"Call me Norma. You can call my husband Hubert. He doesn't mind, honestly. Sit here for a minute and let me read you a short poem. It's from a book called "Germany—A Winter's Tale:"

> The fish is excellent, Mother dear,
> but it needs to be eaten in quiet.
> It's so easy to get a bone in one's throat:
> a highly dangerous diet.

They laughed. She put the book in her lap, looked straight into his eyes. "It's by a man named Heine, Heinrich Heine. He was a fine poet, very funny sometimes. I often read his work to my pupils."

"I've never heard of him, Norma."

"Some people don't want me to read his poems anymore."

"Why not?"

"Because he was Jewish." She saw him wince. "You guessed that, didn't you?"

"Yes."

"You're Jewish, aren't you, Horst?"

"Yes."

"You seem so scared when you say that, like somebody is going to hurt you. Are you scared because you're a Jew?"

"Yes, I am."

Hubert and the children played noisily, Wally yipping his dachshund bark with abandon. Norma returned the Heine book to her bag, fished out some rock candy, offered him a piece.

"You do have parents, don't you?"

"No, I don't. Yes, I do. I have a father."

"Where is he?"

He couldn't help it. Tears came to his eyes. He turned his head but she saw. He wasn't used to kindness. Czerny had been kind, but this was different. He wasn't used to kindness from a woman; he didn't know how to respond.

"I don't know. I don't know where he is. Somewhere. I don't know."

"Did you run away from home?"

"Yes."

"Your father is surely searching for you. He must be terribly worried. When did you run away?"

He hesitated. She obviously wanted an answer. "Two years ago. He's not looking for me anymore."

Norma was so shocked she nearly stopped breathing. She stared at the strange boy in front of her. His hair was a little too long, but he looked healthy, wore good shoes, new pants and a decent shirt. It was his eyes. Those eyes made him different. They were the saddest eyes she had ever seen in a child. She knew she had to do something. All her life Norma had fixed what was broken; birds with torn wings, plants that were old and dying. When they went fishing she threw back what she caught, could not stand to see a fish gasp for air. She was aware of every scratch on her children's bodies, wouldn't allow a flea near Wally if she could help it. The sadness in this child's eyes was unbearable. She would change that. She would make him whole.

"Come to Arnsberg for a few days," Norma said with an encouraging smile, quietly prayed Hubert would go along. "We have an extra room. You can see the whole town from there. Then in a few days you may go wherever you want. You can take a bath and wash your clothes."

"I don't have any more clothes."

She tousled his hair. "Ludi has shirts and pants he doesn't wear. I'm sure some will fit."

Horst swallowed hard to stop new tears. He liked Norma. She was a miracle to him and for a moment he experienced complete happiness. "Oh, I think that would be great. Thank you, Norma!" He ran off to play ball with Ludi and Pauline. They had to be careful because Wally kept getting in the way trying to bite the ball. In the distance he watched Norma talk to Hubert who was hunched over, nervously tugging at the grass. Horst's heart sank. He could actually feel what Hubert was thinking. "Take a stranger into the house? Not only a stranger, but also a Jew?" No way.

They packed the Chevrolet. Horst put on his backpack, but Hubert stopped him.

"Not comfortable in a car with a rucksack on," he said. "Sit in front. Let me tell you about Arnsberg while we drive."

Hubert learned long ago not to interfere with Norma's wounded birds, not until they healed and could fly again. Still, this was an awkward time. If she had to rescue someone, why did it have to be a Jew? Talk about Jews on the radio and in the newspapers was increasing, most of it hateful, narrow-minded, and thoroughly irritating. Even so, plenty of Christian kids around who needed help; why couldn't Jews take care of their own?

Despite Hubert's misgivings, it was a happy summer. June and July flew by. Ludi generously shared his young friends, often invited Horst to come along. Norma, always the teacher, furthered his education during many an evening. She taught him how to write better, introduced him to German grammar, and helped him discover world history and famous people like the Italian explorer, Columbus, and the French Kaiser, Napoleon. Horst, in turn, assisted Hubert in the garage, did simple jobs like changing oil and water in cars, checking air in tires. He learned how to use tools, gauges and machinery. Norma continued to ask about his family but Horst avoided answers. He didn't want to spoil things. Dortmund was too close. If he told the Klingens he came from Dortmund they might try to find his father, a father he still loved, but a father he also hated. He could not forgive Oskar for putting him in the orphanage; it was Oskar who had failed to find him, so he didn't say much. Other than her questions, Norma was wonderful.

In August of 1932 everything changed. Arnsberg's National Socialists held their first rally. Hundreds of brown shirts from other cities joined in. Suddenly swastikas were everywhere. Ludi was fascinated with the Nazis, with their flags and their marching, with their uniforms, their belts and boots and their sharp, flashing knives. He hung around boys his age whose fathers belonged to the Party. Alarmed, Norma and Hubert tried unsuccessfully to control their son. Horst saw Ludi less and less; instead spent increasingly more time in the library or in Hubert's shop.

Late in August, as Horst was cleaning tools with gasoline, a customer called for his car. Hubert wiped his hands.

"Car's ready, Herr Kallenburg. Had to overhaul the carburetor, a clogged valve. Runs fine now. I'll get your bill."

"A moment, Herr Klingen. You have a moment?"

"Of course."

"Nice boy, your Ludi."

"Thank you."

"Yes, a very nice boy. He and my Egon often play together. They were talking the other day. Something about a boy, the one who lives at your house? There is another boy living at your house, isn't there, Herr Klingen?"

Hubert sucked in his breath, sharply.

"This boy, he's Jewish, isn't he? That's what Ludi said, but you know how boys are."

"He's Jewish."

"Well, I just wanted to know, to hear it from the horse's mouth, so to speak."

Hubert took the money, remained silent.

Kallenburg started the motor, turned down his window. "Oh Klingen, one more thing."

"What?" Hubert snapped, barely controlling his temper.

"As you know, I'm a director on Arnsberg's school board. We had a meeting a few nights ago about new contracts for teachers, who does a good job, who should be hired, you know, that sort of thing. An odd coincidence; your wife's name came up."

Hubert clenched his fists, breathed hard through his nose.

"It's probably nothing," Kallenburg smirked, "but some directors wondered why Frau Klingen is interested in having a Jewish child in her house. Perhaps you can tell me."

"Why don't you ask her?"

Kallenburg put his car in gear. "Yes, I may do that. I'm sure somebody will. Good day, Herr Klingen."

Hubert seethed with anger. He was ready to explode. Horst made himself as small as he could, stored the tools, changed pants and left, roamed aimlessly along the river before he dared to go home. He saw Hubert's car parked in the driveway, heard him furiously arguing with Norma, stood frozen and listened.

"None of his business! Why didn't you tell him it was none of his business? How could you let him humiliate the boy? How could you?"

"The boy, the boy! Damn it, with you it's always the boy. I hate Kallenburg as much as you do, you know that, but how about my shop? How about your job? I like Horst but he's a Jew, Norma. No matter how you want to look at it, he's a Jew. That's a simple fact. You want Ludi and Pauline to go around school being called Jew-lovers?"

"And when did you join the Nazi Party?"

That did it. They smashed dishes and glasses, hurled angry, hurtful words at each other, followed by sobbing and after a while by an eerie silence. Horst tried to sneak into his room, but Norma saw him. Although they knew Horst had heard the fight, they said nothing. Supper was like a funeral. During the night, for the first time since leaving Paderborn, he wet his bed.

The next day the atmosphere was poisoned. Ludi hardly spoke to him. Even Pauline, only six, behaved differently, as if she didn't want to catch a disease. Hubert mumbled that business had slowed, that he didn't need help in the garage. The pressure on Norma grew stronger. Horst wet his bed nearly every night. Norma washed the sheets without comment, but one day she simply blew up.

"I can't," she screamed. "I can't smell your bed anymore. It makes me sick. You make me sick."

In August the weather was warm so it wouldn't be too bad. After another silent supper, Hubert went out and Norma mended socks. Horst fetched the Heine book she had given him weeks before. He didn't understand most of it, but he loved the sound. He asked if he could recite her a poem.

> That is a magic kettle wherein
> Strange powers are bubbling and humming.
> Stick your head in the circle and you shall see
> The shape of the future that's coming.

He closed the book when he saw tears in Norma's eyes. So, she had understood. He hugged her, fiercely.

"Thank you, Norma, thank you for everything."

"Horst. It won't stay like this, I promise you. It will change for the better. It must get better."

"Yes, Norma, I'm sure it will."

He packed what he came with, careful not to take anything that wasn't his. At midnight he tiptoed down the stairs. He was sure that Norma and Hubert heard him, but they didn't move. What else could they do?

That night he rested under a bridge crossing the river, leaned for support into a curve of stones. He had tried so hard to belong, to become one of them, but he was a Jew. He saw ever more clearly how hard it was to be a Jew in this time and in this place.

8

Pflug found Oskar roped to a pipe, alone in a basement cubicle. Someone had slapped his face hard, a handprint still visible across one cheek. His glasses lay smashed on the concrete. He was shirtless. His pants, pulled over long underwear, hung from one suspender strap, the other was ripped off. A trickle of dried blood protruded from one nostril. Pflug pulled up a metal chair, straddled it.

"You're stupid, Schumann," he said. "If you had any brains you'd be long gone, anywhere but in Dortmund."

Oskar sniffed through his clogged nose. "Where's better?" he mumbled.

"How about Moscow, Schumann? Wouldn't you be happier there? You could do your bit for the Red Revolution, write forever about power to the people."

"Untie me, Pflug and I'll go right now." Oskar tried to smile. His pain had subsided. He wasn't sure what he read in Pflug's eyes, but it wasn't death. Something else, something he couldn't put his finger on any more than the last time; melancholy, sadness, perhaps a touch of sympathy. Sympathy? Sympathy from Pflug? Was he going crazy? Possibly, but he was sure he wouldn't die today.

"Where's your kid?" asked Pflug, "the one you keep sending around pasting up Communist literature?"

Oskar relaxed. So they haven't caught him, he thought.

"No, Schumann, we haven't caught him, but we will. We'll also find your mimeograph machine and your literature and destroy it. Be smart, Schumann, save yourself more pain. Tell me where all your comrades are hiding."

Oskar tried to see things clearly, difficult without his glasses. He stared at Pflug. From somewhere in the basement came sounds like twigs snapping, dull thumps such as women make when beating carpets, then muffled cries. Fear rose in his throat, bilious and irritating. Suddenly he understood the look in Pflug's eyes. Pflug was afraid! Oskar didn't know of what and didn't much care. He only cared that he wouldn't die. Not today.

Pflug heaved a sigh, stood up and replaced the chair against the wall. "Okay, Schumann, have it your own way. Maybe Böhm is more persuasive. I should tell you that we're building rest camps for people like you, with nice wooden bunks and a copy of the Manifesto under each pillow. All paid for by the State." He picked up the shattered, twisted glasses, carefully hung them on Oskar's ears. "I'll make a reservation for you when a place opens." He turned and walked out briskly.

◆   ◆   ◆

Walter heard the whistle, immediately ran downstairs and found Horst crouched in a dark corner of the hallway. "Are you all right?" he whispered.

"I'm hungry."

"Mama will fix you something."

"Good. They're looking for me. I can't stay."

"I know. Where are you going?"

"Remember those men who repaired something in a hole, the one with the fence around it? It was on Born Strasse."

"I remember. I hated the place."

"But it's safe. It has to do for tonight. If I have food and water I'll be okay. Maybe you have a sweater for me?"

"What else do you want?"

"Nothing right now. I'll come back after Hitler leaves Dortmund. Maybe then they'll let Papa go. Please take a look and see if they're watching our house."

Walter filled a laundry bag of stuff for his friend. It was heavy, but that was okay with Horst. The walk to Born Strasse was short. He avoided bright lights, crossed Borsigstrasse, found the iron gates in a commercial area, without traffic at night. He liked that, put down his bundle, tugged at one lid and found it lighter than expected. By pulling hard he could lift it enough to wedge a leg under. He made sure his bag was knotted and inched his body through the opening. His foot touched the iron ladder. He grabbed the top rung with one hand and released the lid. It made a sharp sound. "Shit!"

Light bulbs in small cages illuminated a labyrinth of tunnels and pipes, gauges with wheels that turned valves on and off. Smaller pipes, fastened to concrete walls, bore identity tags in different colors, terminating at junction boxes equipped with meters and switches. Horst peered into several tunnels looking for a hiding place in case someone came down unexpectedly. The whole place smelled of waste and garbage. He held his nose, but that didn't help. Even in dim light he saw that the largest tunnel ended at a sluice gate controlling sewage, brackish effluence flowing over a retainer, like water over a dam. He heard it plunge to somewhere lower, probably toward a treatment plant. He felt sick, nausea rose in his throat. Never mind, if he had to throw up this would be the perfect place to do it. It was also perfect for hiding; he was sure that nobody, absolutely nobody, would follow him into a hole that smelled like a lake of shit.

As his eyes grew accustomed to the semi-darkness he emptied his rucksack, found an apple, cheese and bread neatly wrapped in Walter's wool sweater and a piece of licorice in a paper bag at the bottom. The licorice made him smile. With nothing left to do, no other precautions required, tired, too weary to be frightened, he smoothed the ground as best he could, propped the rucksack in a corner and fit his body to the wall. Water gurgled at the sluice gate. I will never have to come here again, he told himself, said it over and over like a prayer. He tried to be more cheerful, a difficult task in a place like this. He imagined happier times; hoped Czerny had kept out of trouble. Even in this smelly pit he could taste Czerny's *schnecken*. He pictured Norma and Hubert when he first met them, recalled his own salty tears when Norma noticed his loneliness and understood his need. And Liselotte, how sad she looked when he left her. He thought of his father, so bitter, but still able to laugh at times. His eyes grew heavy. He searched fiercely for pleasant pictures, like his Mutti in an apron, cooking in their kitchen, in the sitting room as she put his fingers on the piano keys. Then he couldn't think anymore. In the month of August, 1935, in a foul-smelling cave underneath the Born Strasse, he drew Walter's sweater around him, curled up on the hard concrete and slept.

9

In a tiny alcove adjoining her bedroom, Hildegard Kube fingered a few remaining beads and intoned a final "Hail Mary" before she hid her well-worn rosary and precious Madonna-and-Child statuette under a tea cozy. She mourned the necessity to conceal her communion with the Holy Family. Lifetime habits were not easily broken, but Frau Kube also recognized a need for prudence in her changing world.

She regretted that her husband, Otto, did not share her commitment to Jesus. However, after twenty-four years of a reasonably tranquil marriage she was resigned to solitary worship. Even Otto's early enlistment in the Party had not greatly disturbed her. He insisted that his job in Hamburg's small, but esteemed Ministry of Transportation was coveted by friends and relatives of influential Party members, that his civil service status was threatened if he did not join. Perhaps true, but she personally knew several government employees who had not entered the Party and none seemed overly anxious about their jobs. In her heart, Hildegard Kube was aware of the truth. Otto was delighted with the order and discipline imposed by Nazi dictum. He loved the uniform, the polished boots, the shiny belt and the hearty camaraderie of middle-aged men with a common cause, strutting about and swapping harmless lies over schnapps and beer after their weekly meetings. Most of all he cherished companions with whom to celebrate bigotry, an opportunity to vent life and career frustrations by blaming personal failures on others, mostly on Jews. Hildegard was uncomfortable with such prejudice, as it contradicted her concepts of Christian love. On the other hand, she was reluctant to let religious convictions affect her domestic life. She enjoyed her job in Hapag's ticket office and her cozy home in the suburbs.

Unfortunately, her son had adopted most of his father's poisonous attitudes. Sixteen year-old Gottfried became a Hitler Youth shortly after Otto joined the SA. In 1934, returning home from a Nuremberg rally, the boy regaled his admiring father with a ditty he had learned there. Hildegard was appalled. The words, as best she could recall, said 'No evil priest can prevent us from feeling that we are the children of Hitler. We follow not Christ, but Horst Wessel. Away with incense and holy water. The Church can go hang for all we care. The Swastika brings salvation on earth. I want to follow it step by step. Baldur von Schirach, take me along!'

From that day on, Hildegard Kube celebrated her devotion to Christ in the sanctuary of her heart and, as opportunity permitted, in her bedroom alcove. This morning both Otto and Gottfried left a bit early. She tidied the apartment, enjoyed a moment with her Lord, buttered a roll, washed it down with a cup of tea, wheeled her bicycle out of the garage and commenced her ride along the Alster, appreciating as always the river's tranquility and the way the early morning sun reflected on old mansions, pavilions and well-maintained parks that graced both banks of this beloved waterway. It stimulated her to begin her workday by inhaling the fragrance of late-summer blooms and the resinous smell of trees along the bicycle path. She used the streetcar in winter, but now was a wonderful time to be out in the Hamburg air. In the old days she had often thanked Jesus for such earthly delights by performing a novena at St. Michaelis Kirche before pedaling to her Alsterdamm office, but Otto and Gottfried's attitudes made her reluctant to continue the ritual. She wasn't certain if the Party knew she was Catholic, or if they even cared. No official threats had been made against Catholics, at least not yet. Nevertheless, Otto didn't announce her religious affiliation publicly. Even in fiercely independent Hamburg it paid to protect oneself.

A few weeks ago something so disturbing had occurred that it made her edgy to this day. Shortly after she had opened the office, two men in black leather coats, eyes cold as ice, presented credentials from the Geheime Staats Polizei, the dreaded Gestapo.

"Hildegard Kube?" the taller, blond one, demanded to know.

"Yes, I'm Hildegard Kube."

"We won't take much of your time, Frau Kube." He opened a billfold that featured his photograph, attached to an official identification card, and then pointed to the telephone. "Herr Eberhardt will confirm our business and the legality of this visit."

"You mean call him now?"

"Yes. Now."

She dialed Eberhardt's number, urgently tried to disguise her inner turmoil. Who had snitched on her? She knew that children were encouraged to inform authorities about anti-social behavior, even that of their parents. Had Gottfried secretly observed her prayers, discovered her rosary and statue in the alcove? Had praying to Jesus become a crime?

"Herr Eberhardt? Hildegard Kube here. Two men from the Gestapo are in my office. I was told to call you."

There was only a moment's hesitation at the other end. "Listen carefully, Frau Kube. Cooperate with them. Give them any information and documents they request. I assume full responsibility."

"Of course, Herr Eberhardt."

"And Frau Kube, be discreet. Company affairs should remain…well, company affairs. You do understand, don't you?"

"Of course, Herr Eberhardt."

"Good. I know I can rely on you." He hung up.

They had no interest in her religious beliefs. They wanted to see passenger manifests, specifics on how they were compiled. They asked about ticket distribution, procedures used to check reservations against passenger lists. What happened to unused tickets? What controls assured identifications to be legitimate? She had answers for most questions, but some details disturbed them.

"If you should be ill a day or two before a voyage, is someone trained to take your place, Frau Kube?" asked the short, heavy-set policeman, "someone familiar with forms and procedures?"

"Not at this time, but I'm certain Herr Eberhardt would find a capable substitute to fill in."

"I see. And as to identifications, who verifies your judgment?"

"I don't quite understand."

"Is it possible," the taller man interjected, "for tickets to fall into the wrong hands? Are you trained to detect false documents?"

"It's possible, but I've been in this office for eleven years and I'm careful."

"Yes, Frau Kube, undoubtedly." Both men made copious notes, thanked her stiffly, and left.

On her way home she considered telling Otto what happened. As a government employee he might know the meaning of the incident, but Otto would relish telling his companions that his wife was visited by the Gestapo and how important her job was. Eberhardt's closing admonition had been explicit. Don't be stupid, Hildegard, she murmured to herself, best to keep your faith in Jesus and your mouth shut.

10

Truck tires rattled the metal gates and woke Horst out of an uneasy sleep. He edged toward the sewage tunnel, but heard nothing more; the brief moment of panic passed as another car approached. Soon these sounds reassured him. They were ordinary noises, welcomed intrusions into the discomforting silence of his self-imposed dungeon. He stretched his stiff and cold body, relieved himself in the sewage tunnel and decided he couldn't make it smell any worse. He moistened his hands with drops from his meager water supply and wiped them on his shirt, conscious of performing ordinary acts. Old habits. He slaked his thirst with small gulps from the water bottle, wondered what time it was and how long before he could safely leave. Perhaps later, when there was less morning traffic, he might risk a quick look outside. Now it was important only to think of other possibilities. He had all day to do so, a long, endless day. He shuffled idly around the bunker, examined dials and tags barely illuminated by the dim lights. No point fooling around with those, they meant nothing to him. He left them untouched, retreated to his alcove, made a pillow of Walter's sweater and tried to find a comfortable position. Boredom stared him in the face, soon joined by old, familiar demons of despair that he could not totally suppress.

Three tough years roaming Westfalia's countryside and two more dodging a hostile bureaucracy convinced Horst Schumann that his contract with life extended no further than food, shelter and, if possible, a little affection. After that came pleasure, to be taken as found. In this dreary bunker, flattened like a giant insect against a concrete wall beneath a dangerous, adversary world, he bit off a piece of licorice, felt its sweet juice flow down his throat as it obliterated, if only for a moment, the sewage tunnel's foul odor.

A transformer started with a hum, so loud that it made Horst jump. His right arm throbbed, the one that hurt when he slept on it. The left one didn't trouble him anymore. For a brief moment he recalled that terrible afternoon, two years ago, when Günter broke his arms. Was that two years ago already? The memory made him dizzy. Panic rose in his throat, crept down his spine with icy fingers. He rubbed his limb to erase the sensation of pain. "Don't think about it," he muttered, "not now, not in this place."

Another, then another rattle of the iron. He groped for what was left of his licorice. He debated saving it, ate it anyway, relished its familiar taste, comforted by the feel of bits stuck in his teeth, the reassuring chore of extracting tiny pieces with his finger nail, chewing them until they dissolved. He felt stronger, but increasingly restless. He paced from dial to dial, read tags, anything to occupy his mind and shut out his growing loneliness and fear. He hated those feelings, knew that unless he guarded against them they would invade and sneak foul into his body, like worms wriggling into unreachable spaces.

Thank god for trucks that banged on the iron gates above his head, sounds that connected him with the outside world. Could he possibly dare to simply climb out and run, never mind the consequences? But what if people on the sidewalk noticed him, caught him, and delivered him to the police? What if the police beat him up just like they beat up Oskar? He was miserable in this hole, but he would be much more miserable in the hands of the police. "I know I can't stand it any longer," Horst whispered, desperate and yet ashamed of his own weakness. He couldn't stay, but he couldn't leave. He was too dispirited to think clearly, his outlook too bleak to be optimistic. "Papa," he sobbed, and wretchedly beat fists on a concrete wall. "Papa, make it get better. Oh god, please make it get better. Please." He wiped his nose and eyes, fiercely hugged Walter's sweater, forced himself to think of better times, of sun prickling his skin, of meat filling his mouth, of flannel covers trapping his body heat and protecting him against the cold. With eyes wide open he stared into the gloom, into the dim yellow bulbs that lit his cavern. He felt totally trapped, ready to give up.

Give up? No! Never!! He was not going to give up. Not now. Not tomorrow. Not *ever*. Then and there, at that very moment, he decided his life had to change. It had to change completely. Not sometime in the future, but now, immediately. He had survived many things, but survival was no longer enough. He would have been unable to explain it, but he knew he would somehow escape from this mess. His friend Walter was scared even when there was nothing to be scared about. Horst didn't want forever to look over his shoulder, always afraid that an enemy was chasing him. He had seen the same behavior in Oskar. Was Oskar okay? He would think about his father later. Now he had to be brave, to keep up his courage. He knew he could. He learned long ago not to be afraid of the dark. When night came he would leave this sewer, leave this stupid panic and this dumb loneliness behind.

Several trucks jangled the iron, transformers continued to hum. At this stage of his life, Horst Schumann was unfamiliar with words like "soul" and "spirit." To consider himself a survivor would have implied that he clearly understood the concept of an untimely death and how to avoid it. He had, in fact, succeeded in doing so in the past, was surely even now in the process of surviving. But his inner self had so far refused to see life implicitly and perpetually at risk. When he experienced fear and despair to the marrow of his bones, he resisted with all his strength. When he was hungry he was convinced he would find food. When he was homeless, he trusted himself to find shelter. In moments of loneliness, he opened up to people. He never chose such behavior willfully; he was hopeful by instinct, a survivor by practice.

A burst of water rushed its muted roar through the sluice gate. Vaguely aware of sounds mingling in antiphonal harmony, Horst returned again to images of another time, to August, 1932, his season of belongings and endings, to an Eden gained and lost. His heart felt heavy. He pictured the Klingens, mainly Norma. He had so wanted her to love and hug him, to make her proud of the way he improved his spelling, his writing, especially his reading. He could now finish a book in a week if it wasn't too long or difficult. Only in those last days of August did he begin to understand Norma and Hubert's dilemma. They were kind and generous people who loved children, not just their own. Their many decent friends, teachers, store clerks, people from church, had liked and accepted Horst. Then the Nazis paraded through town and within days everything changed. The troublemakers came from elsewhere, not only from Arnsberg. The rally was noisy, emotional, and skillfully planned. Afterward, troopers remained, strutted through the city in gangs of six or eight, a rowdy bunch who blew their own horns, harangued people on sidewalks, pasted up sheets of hatred against Jews and Communists. They made speeches on street corners, in beer halls, wherever they found an audience. Their fanaticism, their promises of jobs for the unemployed, their pledges to recover national pride, to restore laws and order, even their love of brute power, seeped into Arnsberg's consciousness. Suddenly, Horst's presence made life confusing and difficult for the Klingens. Even now, two years later, Horst still felt the pain of that parting.

As he sat in this gloomy cave, Horst clearly recalled the day he had left. Drifting south, he came to the outskirts of Limburg-an-der-Lahn. After walking all day he was hungry, thirsty, and very tired. He saw the Limburg sign and instead of the paved highway that led into the city's center he took the country lane along the Lahn River. Next to a grove of birches, a small community of repair shops and service businesses formed a rustic suburb. That's where he first met Bjorn Milfs, the largest man he had ever seen. Milfs, a blacksmith, shoed horses, built metal gates, repaired wagons and helped to maintain Limburg's iron bridges.

Milfs worked hard. When he wasn't working he drank beer in his small stone house, adjacent to his smithy.

Leaning on an iron post against which was propped a wagon, its rear wheels removed, Milfs was drinking water from a tin cup. Horst didn't mean to stare, but couldn't help it. Nearly seven feet tall, the man loomed like a human tower, with bulging arms and a massive neck supporting a great round head from which cascaded wildly disorganized strands of sooty, yellow hair. His black leather apron covered a bare chest; his shoulders gleamed with sweat. He looked like Thor, that god whose picture Horst had seen in one of Ludi's books. Thor eyed him with amusement, gulped water, returned Horst's stare.

"Want something, kid?"

"Yes. Please. I'd like some water."

The giant swallowed what was left and tossed his cup at Horst, who dropped it.

"Pump's down that way. Bring it back when you're finished." He rumbled off to the smithy.

Horst pumped, drank his fill, hurried back to the shop. The man never looked up. "Set it on the box."

Horst put the cup down and watched the blacksmith's every move, hypnotized by his strength. He had never seen such muscles, couldn't tear himself away. Now the man heated an iron rod in the glowing hearth.

"Want something else? I'm busy."

"I'm hungry."

Thor plopped the rod into a tub of water, which sizzled and steamed, used tongs to lift an ember from the hearth and lit a cigarette.

"Hungry? What do you think this is? It's a blacksmith shop, not a restaurant."

"I'm sorry. I'm starved. I don't want to bother you. I'm sorry. I'll go." He walked out, unhappy to leave the warmth and strength of the place. At the road he turned, saw Milfs in the doorway. They looked at each other.

"Okay, kid, come back. For heaven's sake, don't stand there. I'll give you something to eat. You can work for your supper."

Horst ran the short distance back to the smithy. The giant banked the fire and closed the flue.

"You got a name?"

"Horst."

"I'm Milfs. That's Norwegian, if you're wondering. There's a broom and a dustpan and a bucket in that corner. Start sweeping."

Horst swept the earth, which was hard as concrete, picked up spilled coal, dropped it into the bin, caught Milfs' approving look. Milfs choked the hearth with a fire hood, cleaned off the shoeing anvil and large vise, carefully hung hammers on a rack, checked the dying fire and removed the iron spike from the water bucket.

"Take those two pails and fill them at the pump."

Horst did as told. They went into the house, washed their hands and faces in the tiny bathroom. The towel they used wasn't very clean. Horst thought of Norma who did laundry almost every day and ironed everything. Milfs fried a panful of bratwurst, boiled Brussels sprouts and served the meal with a huge chunk of dark bread on homemade tin plates. He handed Horst a glass of water, poured a metal pot full of beer from a large bottle.

"What's your story, kid?"

Over the years Horst had learned that his lies mostly turned out bad. He liked this man. He was big but gentle and, like Czerny, gruff on the outside, soft on the inside, glad to have company. He had never lied to Czerny, which had worked out fine. He would tell the truth now.

"I ran away from an orphanage three years ago because I hated it."

"What do you mean, three years ago?"

"Well, I was six then. Now I'm nine."

"So where have you been?"

"Different places. Different people."

"Like me, right? Different people like me."

"Yes, a little. Sometimes they let me stay for a day, sometimes much longer. In the last place I was with a really nice family for almost four months. That's the longest I've ever been with anybody."

"Then why did you run away again?"

"I had to."

"You had to? Did you steal something?"

Horst shook his head emphatically. "No! Oh no! Nothing like that."

"It's okay. Don't tell me if you don't want to."

"I don't mind. What's the difference? I had to leave because I'm a Jew."

Milfs sat for a long minute, then picked up the empty plates, dumped them in the sink, fetched a fresh bottle of beer from a bucket of cold water, filled two metal pots and shoved one toward Horst.

"Have some. You've earned it. Do Jews drink beer?"

"I don't know, Milfs. I think so. I think they drink what everybody else drinks."

Milfs looked at him, grinned. "Naturally. Of course they do. Tell you what. Finish your beer. You look ready to pass out. I don't know what kids do before they go to bed, but whatever it is, do it. There's a storage room in the back of the house; has an old mattress on the floor. Let's find you a blanket and pillow. We'll talk more tomorrow." Out of a trunk in the corner Milfs fished an enormous, slightly worn garment. "Here's an old night shirt you can sleep in. A little big, but so what. Do Jews sleep in night shirts?"

"Only at night, Milfs."

The big man's laugh thundered from that massive chest. He wiped his eyes on the dirty dishtowel, showed Horst the spare room.

"Good night, boy. Get some sleep."

"Milfs?"

"What?"

"Thanks, thanks very, very much."

"It's okay, go to sleep." He turned out the lights and shut the door. Two minutes later Horst was gone to the world.

He stayed with Bjorn Milfs for several weeks, did odd jobs, cleaned the house and learned the work of a blacksmith. He liked Milfs more every day. They talked in the evenings, but Horst was often so exhausted he fell asleep right after supper. One morning, in the middle of September, Milfs hitched his homemade trailer to his Citroen. "We need supplies. Nails, beer, sausage, stuff. Let's eat breakfast in town."

They drove to Limburg. Even at a distance the cathedral's towers loomed majestically from the top of a rock. Once across the Lahn, Milfs followed the city's narrow, winding streets until they came to their first stop, a hardware store.

"I get horseshoe nails here. Could make them myself, but that takes too much time."

In the store's windows flyers announced a Nazi rally, its featured speaker to be Robert Ley, chief of the Labor Front. Milfs saw Horst flinch and put a reassuring hand on his shoulder.

"Don't worry. Behmer won't eat you." Inside, a short, stocky man with a gray mustache was busy, putting things on shelves.

"Milfs? Where have you been? Thought you took your business to Engelhof."

"That thief? No thanks. Business is slow, Heinrich; fewer wagons to fix, not so many horses. People are buying cars."

The shopkeeper came to the counter, looked closely at Horst. "Got yourself an assistant?"

"Sure, why not? He's young; don't have to pay him much."

"What's your name, young man?" Behmer asked.

"Horst."

"Just Horst?"

"Schumann. Horst Schumann."

The two men's eyes met, slowly, silently.

"You know where the nails are, Bjorn. Take what you need."

Behmer resumed his fussing at the shelves, cast sidelong glances at Horst. Milfs selected a carton, inspected tools, picked a small wrench and paid cash.

"Coming to the rally, Bjorn?"

"What rally?"

"Don't play dumb. Sunday afternoon, in the square. Ley is speaking."

"Who's Ley?"

"I'll tell you who's Ley. Ley's the future, Milfs! The future, like Hitler. He's going to talk about Germans going back to work, making their own money and keeping it instead of giving it to the Jews." He stared at Horst whose face had frozen. "Join us Sunday, Bjorn. We can use big men like you in the Party."

Milfs opened the door. "Sure, Heinrich. Sunday. I'll think about it."

"The future, Bjorn. A new Reich. Heil Hitler."

Behmer's eyes glittered with passion, his right arm held rigid in the Nazi salute.

Horst and Milfs hardly talked as they made their rounds. Swastikas hung from nearly every window, kiosks were plastered with messages against Communists and Jews. Flyers about the rally covered houses, walls and fences. Many men wore Nazi uniforms, even some shop clerks. On the city square they ate bratwurst at a sausage stand. Several people, probably customers, nodded toward Milfs, who barely nodded back. A waitress tried to flirt, but the blacksmith's thoughts were elsewhere. Some uniformed SA members heatedly argued with a group of people at a nearby table. Horst desperately wanted to leave.

Slowly they made their way home. After a supper of pork chops and potatoes, Milfs poured a small glass of beer for Horst and lit a cigarette.

"Schumann, huh? Listen to me, Horst Schumann. Listen real carefully." He drank then, furiously puffed smoke into the air. "You're a nice boy. Not very big, not very strong, but for a Jew you're all right. They say Jews are supposed to be smart, but you're not so smart. For a Jew who's supposed to be smart you're pretty damn dumb."

It was the longest speech Horst heard him make in three weeks. He knew there was more to come.

"Schumann, give it to me straight. No bullshit, no playing dumb just because you're a kid. Do you have relatives?"

"Yes Milfs, I have a sister in an orphanage, in Paderborn. I have a father, maybe in Dortmund."

"A father? Maybe in Dortmund? A goddamn father, Schumann? Then what the hell are you doing here?"

While Horst spoke, Milfs drank more beer, smoked, grew angrier and angrier and finally erupted.

"That's a lousy story, Schumann. That's a really bad story. Your father is a Communist and he put you away in an orphanage and you're mighty pissed off with him? You know, I don't blame you. Now think hard. Besides him, is there any place else you could go, anybody who knows you?"

"Yes Milfs."

"Who?"

"My father has a brother."

"Where?"

"Somewhere in the mountains. It's called the Hunsick, I think."

"Hunsrück, Schumann, Hunsrück. What town in the Hunsrück?"

"Something like Kasselbaum. I don't remember exactly."

From his bedroom Milfs fetched an old map of Germany, torn at the folds, laid it on the table, ran a finger over the area labeled Hunsrück.

"Ah, here it is! Kastellaun, not Kasselbaum."

Horst recognized the name. Milfs continued the questions.

"So, that's your uncle. You know your uncle's name?"

"Yes, it's Walter. Walter Schumann."

"How come you never went to see your Uncle Walter?"

Horst hesitated. His old, stupid fear made him shiver, but Milfs pretended not to notice. "Because he would have sent me to my father. Then I would have had to go back to the orphanage. I'm not going to the orphanage again, Milfs. I'm not."

Milfs held out his hands. "Okay, okay, I understand, but you can't keep running around the country. You can't do that."

"Why not?"

"Come on, Schumann! You know why not. You saw why not in Arnsberg. You saw why not again today." He shoved his chair aside, stalked around the room. "The Nazis are in. Hitler is in. Those bastards hate Jews. Believe me, Schumann, they won't take it easy on you because you're small. You're a Jew and they'll beat you up. I saw it in Behmer's face. That son of a bitch!"

"What do you think I should do?"

"I think you should go to Kastellaun and check in with your Uncle Walter. You can't wander around forever hoping somebody's going to feed you. The country's not safe for you anymore, Horst, and it'll get worse."

Horst knew that Milfs was right. He was tired of moving on and on, always on the lookout for somebody to take him in. He wanted to go to school, to have friends, to play with children his age. "I'll try and see my uncle, Milfs, but I don't know how to get there. Will you help me?"

Early the next morning the blacksmith unhitched his trailer from the Citroen. He made Horst pack his belongings in the rucksack, added a chocolate bar, a piece of cheese and some bread and drove him to Limburg's railroad station. At the information booth Milfs had the clerk print the exact information of how to get to Kastellaun, made sure Horst clearly understood it, and then purchased a one-way ticket. They ate sausage and fried potatoes as they sat next to each other on a wooden bench, saying little.

"Milfs."

"What?"

"Why are you doing this?"

"Doing what?"

"Why are you helping me? What difference does it make to you?"

Horst's giant friend frowned slightly. "I don't know, I really don't. Maybe it's because I'd like to have a kid like you."

Horst's heart jumped. He so badly wanted to stay with Milfs although he knew that was impossible. "Like me, Milfs? Like me?"

"Well, maybe not exactly like you. Maybe a Norwegian kid with blond hair and blue eyes, but you're okay. You work hard, you don't complain. You're okay, Schumann, especially for a dumb Jew." His huge hand ruffled Horst's hair, shyly, quickly.

Milfs waited until the train pulled in, went into the compartment, put Horst's rucksack into the net above the seat, tousled his hair one more time and walked out. He stood on the platform and waved good-bye as the train pulled out. Horst leaned out the window and waved back until he couldn't see his friend anymore. Then tears came; not for long, but he felt them on his cheeks and lips, hot and salty. He so badly would have liked to stay. Milfs had never looked down on him because he was young, had treated him fairly and with patience and had even taught him small things about the blacksmith trade, like how to straighten horse-shoe nails and bend glowing iron. He was so big and powerful. Horst knew he would very much miss the man and the safety he had felt in his company.

Early that evening he arrived in Kastellaun, a small, dusty town that smelled of cow manure. Next to the station he approached the owner of a tobacco shop, asked whether he knew a Walter Schumann. The man pointed across the plaza.

"Go to the end of the square and make a right turn; that's Besengasse, where most of our Jews live. Second house on the left is Schumann's place. Has an iron rooster on the roof. Can't miss it." Horst said thank you, followed the directions and found the house.

Walter Schumann and his wife, Bertha, were not particularly happy to see their nephew. They had three children of their own, money was tight, the prospect of another mouth to feed no blessing. Few of Jakob Schumann's offspring had remained close. Walter had not seen his brother in years. He shared nothing with Oskar; their political and social perspectives were far apart. Walter planned to emigrate to California, to join one of his brothers in the jewelry business. He wanted no complications in his life, especially if they concerned his Communist sibling. He and Bertha asked a few more routine questions, how long ago Horst had left Paderborn, where had he been, but saw quickly that their nephew was in no mood to answer. After dinner Horst was given a place to sleep in the attic. Early the next morning Walter took him to the post office where telephones were available. He called Oskar, hoped fervently to reach him at home. He was lucky. Oskar received the news of Horst's arrival in Kastellaun with astonishment, exchanged a few words with his son and assured him that everything would be taken care of with Walter's help. The following day Horst boarded a train to Koblenz, changed connections in Cologne and finally arrived in Dortmund in the evening. Oskar waited at the station with a strange woman standing next to him. He introduced her as Gretchen, his wife.

"Your new step-mother," was the way he put it. He looked at his nine-year old son as if seeing him for the first time, which, in a sense, he was.

"I'm glad to meet you," Gretchen ventured, aware that her life just became considerably more entangled.

Horst didn't know what to say. He certainly couldn't imagine what to call the blond lady. He felt awkward and uncomfortable toward both of them. They walked out of the station in a daze, desperately searching for ways to communicate, some means to break through a shared uneasiness.

"Papa." The word sounded peculiar and alien to Horst. "Do you...I mean, do we still live on Weiherstrasse? Is Liselotte coming to live with us now?"

The expression on his father's face, the troubled look that passed between husband and wife, made Horst's heart sink.

"I'm sorry, son. I really wish I didn't have to tell you. Your sister...she couldn't... "Liselotte became very ill, Horst, and she died in Paderborn. More than two years ago." Grete looked pale but determined. "I'm sorry. I'm very sorry. I never got to meet your sister."

A sharp, terrible pain exploded in Horst, as if a knife were plunged into his chest. He stared at them. He did not understand. He could not believe their words. He felt sick. Numb and cold and mute he climbed into the car.

They drove home to Weiherstrasse in the old Opel. Nothing had changed; the Viktoria Wäscherei still occupied space on the street level. Oskar carried Horst's rucksack, showed him into his old room next to the balcony and suggested he best go to sleep since it had been a long day. Horst walked around the four walls in which he had spent half his life and felt like a stranger. He also felt completely alone. Liselotte? It isn't true, is it? It can't be! They didn't let you die, not in that awful place. They couldn't. They could never, ever do that! That night, for the first time since Arnsberg, he wet his bed.

11

Street noises interrupted his musings, drifted dimly through the iron gates, sounds of traffic and people. Horst tried to shake off the memory of his return to Dortmund. That feeling of being apart and estranged never quite left him. Even now, two years later, he hated that feeling. He had expected to be glad to see his father, to be where he belonged, where he wouldn't be thrown out because he was a Jew.

Not yet quite awake, fleeting fragments came to him from earlier in his life, when he and Liselotte were wrapped in the protective arms of Papa and Mutti, when he and Oskar, holding hands, walked up Café Corso's marble steps on Sunday mornings, when he sat on his father's lap in the big brown leather chair that swallowed them as they looked at pictures in one of Papa's wonderful books. Horst realized once again that a part of him loved his father, he was sure of that. He didn't know exactly why; it was just something he knew inside. But another part hated his father, he was sure of that, too. Horst understood hate very well. He hated Oskar for putting him into the orphanage. He hated him for the thousand times he had shivered in hay lofts, under bundles of leaves, after hunting for food in alleys, behind restaurants, never-endingly aching and longing for love and protection, always hoping, always wishing that Papa was looking for him, that Papa was just around the corner. He hated him for the awful moments when blisters hurt so much from walking the road all day, when he prayed Papa would pull up behind him in the Opel, fling the doors open and yell "Here you are Horst! Been looking for you everywhere. Climb in, we're going home!" It never happened.

A stifling silence cut into his reverie, made him fully alert, acutely aware that no car had rattled the iron gates for some time. His stomach growled. Dizzy from hunger, he ate a piece of bread and cheese, stretched his cramped legs, walked around the bunker and felt better. He knew he had dozed intermittently, thought it might be early evening, but time functioned differently in a place where dirty, yellow light bulbs never changed color and made no distinction between day and night. He heard traffic noises; probably people on their way home from work. With great caution he climbed up the rungs and pushed against one of the gates. It moved, but he couldn't hold it open. He climbed back, put his sweater between his teeth, climbed up again and wedged the sweater under the gate to make a narrow opening. It was almost dark outside. To be on the safe side he waited another half hour, then gathered his things and pushed his way out. No signs of people or traffic. He let the gate drop softly, moved quickly into a recessed doorway, certain no one had seen him. It felt good to be in the open air, away from foul smells and dark thoughts. With renewed vitality he hurried to Walter's house, cautiously hugged buildings along the way.

Walter was waiting for the whistle and relieved to see Horst. From a dark corner in the alley they watched Oskar's apartment. A light glowed in the kitchen, probably Gretchen.

"How did it go?"

"Spooky, Walter, but a good hiding place. What's going on?"

"They've arrested a lot of Jews, most of your father's friends, anybody they thought was a Communist."

"And Oskar? What happened to him?"

Walter looked down at his feet, hesitated. "David Lifschitz tried to go to school yesterday. He saw people at the police station being hauled out of cars. David's father was one of them. I think that's where Oskar is, too."

The last time his father was hauled in by the Nazis, he had come out in bad shape. Horst cringed. Helpless rage made him clench his fists. Walter kept on talking. "David said other kids are trying to find places to hide."

"Who?"

"Soli Rabinowitz, the sons of Dr. Grünberg, the one who fixed your arms."

"Albert and Karl."

"Lisa Koerner. Gitte, too."

"Where are they now?"

"David said they would meet tonight at school and use the door with the broken lock to get in the basement."

Horst liked the idea. "Good, I will go there."

"Can I come?" Rather than stay in his parents' apartment, Walter wanted to hide with his friends. Horst discouraged him.

"The Nazis aren't after you. It's more important that you keep watch here and find out what you can. Tomorrow night I'll whistle. And Walter, I'm starved. You think your parents mind if…"

Within minutes Walter brought sliced salami, a piece of bread and two carrots. Horst took the food gratefully.

"We'll all be fine, Walter. Don't worry. Keep your eyes open. Everything's going to be okay." He waved, went through the alley door and was gone.

"From your mouth to God's ear," Walter implored into the gloomy night. It was his father's favorite saying when divine intercession was urgently needed. Walter determined that right now God's help was urgently needed.

◆   ◆   ◆

On September 2nd, 1935, Dick and Rae Malkin signed for a registered letter from the offices of the Honorable Warren Luckman, The House of Representatives, Washington, D.C. The letter's signature was not rubber-stamped like the bulk of his correspondence, but endorsed personally by the Congressman.

August 28, 1935

Mr. And Mrs. Richard Malkin
3520 Lake Shore Drive
Chicago, Illinois

Dear Dick and Rae:

It is with considerable pleasure that I inform you of the introduction and passage of House Bill #A-03685083 under whose provision entry into the United States of America is granted to one Horst Schumann of Weiherstrasse 4 in the city of Dortmund, Germany, for the purpose of his adoption by you, the Malkins.

Notification of this Act of Congress will be forwarded to all requisite agencies, domestic and foreign, and arrangement for appropriate documents, including a United States entry visa, will be issued through the State Department's Embassy in Berlin.

I must point out that while the U.S. Congress may grant entry into this country, final approval for emigration resides with the German government. While I foresee no major difficulties, Germany's current political and social atmosphere should be kept in mind. I have instructed my staff to keep me posted on all developments. If necessary, I will commit further governmental resources to bring this matter to a successful conclusion.

Should additional documentation be necessary, or if you have any questions, don't hesitate to call Bert Farber in my Chicago office.

With best regards,

Warren Luckman

A handwritten post-script followed the signature:

Dear Dick and Rae,

Everything will work out fine. We'll have the boy here in no time. We have to. He'll be voting some day soon.

Best wishes,

"Luck"

12

No matter how hard he tried, Martin Lutz could not sleep. His duties in connection with the Führer's upcoming speech swam in the troubled waters of his psyche like voracious sharks, eager to eat him alive. Even his girlfriend Ursula's soft hand, protectively cradling his now flaccid penis, did nothing to alleviate his anxiety. They had made love before midnight and, as usual, their coupling had concluded in mutual satisfaction. While her entrancing fingertips spun carnal fantasies, his mind remained fixed on tomorrow's events.

He had suffered a frightening dream several days before, a vision so horrible it had made him scream. He had awakened, bathed in sweat. In this nightmare the Führer walked to the rostrum, patiently waited for cascades of "Sieg Heils" to abate, nodded the multitude into an ecstatic hush and spoke into a cluster of microphones. Nothing came out. Not a word could be heard, not in the Westfalenhalle, not in Dortmund, not in Germany, not in Europe, not anywhere at all. The Führer had continued to speak into the deafening silence for a sentence or two, had stopped, then stared with suppurating malevolence at the man in charge of broadcast technology, twenty-two year old Martin Lutz, at that moment crouched in the radio booth, praying for the earth to open and swallow him whole. His anguished moan had awakened Ursula. She had comforted him and lulled him into an uneasy sleep. In the morning the nightmare remained vividly before his eyes.

Today was the big event and he was well prepared. He slipped out of bed in the predawn dark, dressed quietly in the bathroom and drove the specially equipped, half-panel Mercedes to the Westfalenhalle, skirting downtown by using the Beurhaus entrance to Westfalen Park. He parked at the service elevator entrance and presented identification papers to an SS guard who meticulously checked his credentials. The license from his broadcast service company, *Westfalischer Rundfunk Dienst GmbH*, featured his photograph, seal-imprinted and initialed by a Party photographer. He ascended the elevator to the broadcast booth located under the roof of Dortmund's impressive convention hall. Even at this early hour there was already a considerable bustle in surrounding parking lots and in the building. From its dais, the Führer was to speak to the nation at eleven o'clock. Most activities throughout the Reich, including factory and office pur-

suits, eating and drinking in restaurants and bars, in fact all non-essential under-
takings, were discouraged for the duration of the address in order that all citizens
might share this intoxicating ritual without interference.

Lutz was aware of the assignment's magnitude. Although nervous, he relished
this opportunity to do something special, to put his technical training on the cutting edge. He believed there would be financial rewards from his company if he
performed well. He expected adulation from his social circle and counted on
unimaginable favors from his adoring Ursula. He scanned his checklist, hanging
on a clipboard in the control room, scanned it once more and began a complex,
but clearly defined procedure. On a heavy-duty dolly he brought up several loads
of equipment, installed the remote and power supply amplifiers in specific racks.
Not for the first time that week he plugged them together, checked tube plate
currents to verify that their combined output measured well above one hundred
percent. While loudspeakers were not his responsibility, he checked them anyway
since he needed to monitor their volume for crowd reactions. To do so, he
mounted the rostrum where, in a few hours, the Führer would address the world.
As he gazed over the empty hall, Lutz experienced for a very brief moment the
awesome sensation of being in the world's cynosure, the thrill of inspiring millions with the power of one's personal beliefs. The moment passed; he returned
to tasks more within his compass.

After sunrise, traffic grew intense. Several canteens opened, erected for the
comfort of a gathering army of service personnel. Lutz washed down a roll with a
fresh cup of coffee, then contacted the building's chief engineer to check on the
emergency generator to make certain its connections leading to his booth were
secure.

The broadcast's producer, dressed in full SS uniform and carrying a fine
leather briefcase, arrived at seven and introduced himself as Bernhard Oldenburg.
Assigned by the Greater German Broadcasting Corporation, one of Propaganda
Minister Goebbels' divisions, he had arrived from Berlin the night before and
immediately made arrangements with Martin Lutz's boss at Westfalischer Rundfunk. Oldenburg was polite, but brisk. His first telephone call went to Westfalia's
Telephone Central to certify connections between the broadcast booth and the
central transmitter, thereby assuring reception of the Führer's speech throughout
Germany and beyond. Telephone Central asked Lutz to vary volume control
through a full spectrum and assured Oldenburg that the system was ready. Next
on the list was Lothar Zimmermann of Broadcast Central's electrical transcription studio.

"It is now seven twenty-seven, Zimmermann. I am going to the rostrum, which will take me"...he glanced out the booth window..."approximately ten minutes. My associate will switch on the broadcast system precisely at seven forty-five. At that time he will confirm power input and you will begin electrical transcription. I will speak for exactly thirty seconds. You will record my voice and play it back when I return to the booth. Unless you have questions, I will now proceed."

He took a typed page from his briefcase, stepped to the rostrum, signaled Lutz and spoke slowly into the microphone, distinctly enunciating each word:

"This is Bernard Oldenburg speaking from the Westfalenhalle in Dortmund on the occasion of an address to be given on this day, September the second, nineteen hundred thirty-five, by our Führer, Adolf Hitler. The purpose of this announcement is to check the electrical transcription system being operated at this moment by Herr Lothar Zimmermann at Broadcast Central. Unless there are unforeseen circumstances, this will be the final check of that system."

He signaled to the booth. Lutz relayed the message to Zimmerman who moved the large platter to a phonograph. On Oldenburg's return, Zimmerman played back the speech. It sounded perfectly clear, even over the wire.

"Good work, Zimmermann. As per my memo, we begin recording at ten sharp. Please remain ready." He turned to Lutz. "Is there anything you need? Anything at all?"

"No sir. Nothing. Everything has been checked out."

"Good." Oldenburg placed a printed sheet on yet another clipboard. "Your copy of today's itinerary, Lutz. As you see, the Führer arrives at Dortmunder Flughafen at nine, in a little over an hour. His motorcade arrives here at nine forty-five. He will assemble with his comrades in the reception area and prepare for his entrance into the hall. You will activate the system at that time. *The Badenweiler March* will be played by the HJ Marching Band and at precisely ten the Party's standard bearers, preceded by a three-man drum corps, will enter the hall, followed by the Führer, flanked by comrades Hess and Göring. You will make every effort to record their walk to the rostrum. Don't stare at me, Lutz, I understand the difficulty; just do your best. The Führer will join his comrades at the rostrum, succeeded by a thirty second drum roll and the Horst Wessel song, played by the band and sung by the entire assembly. Next, a two minute greeting from Deputy Führer Hess, who introduces Bormann. Bormann speaks for two minutes. Next, two minute speeches by Göring, Ley, Von Schirach, and Streicher. At ten forty-five, Hess begins his introduction of the Führer, lasting until ten fifty-two. The audience will be encouraged to express its love and joy for five minutes. At ten fifty-seven the Führer moves to the microphones, allowing broadcast facilities that have made previous arrangements three minutes to sign on. At precisely eleven, the Führer begins his speech. Your responsibility is to operate this equipment with maximum efficiency, to capture each and every moment of the occasion with absolute fidelity and to ensure its transmission to Central Broadcasting. The proceedings of this occasion must be brought to the world's attention without distortion or the loss of one syllable. If that is not accomplished, Lutz, somebody will be held responsible. As that somebody is likely to be me, I wish to guard as far as possible against unfortunate calamities. Do I make myself perfectly clear?" He didn't wait for an answer, picked up his briefcase and walked to the door. "I'll be back at nine sharp and stay with you until our task is completed. Together we will record history." He closed the door softly behind him.

Amid the rising clamor of the great hall, the rattling sounds of drum and bugle corps tuning up in the parking lot, buffeted by waves of delirium wafting out of the city and seeping through the auditorium's open doors, Martin Lutz was aware only of his pounding heart, the lump in his throat. Automatically, he checked tube plate currents once again, made certain, beyond the least shadow of a doubt, that they registered above one hundred percent.

◆   ◆   ◆

A dangerous world mobilized around them, but none of the youngsters who gathered in the musty basement of a nearly abandoned school had come there to pray, although all were descendants of Abraham, that implacable forefather of generations of nomadic Semites. Only the Grünberg boys had some religious training and even they might have found it difficult to explain why Jews prayed to a deity whose image they were forbidden to illustrate and whose name could not be spoken. In exchange for such strictures, the Faceless, Nameless One, Blessed be He, ought at least to have granted them the right to live peacefully. No such luck. Instead, He had seemingly convinced them that they were Chosen for an exclusive covenant with Him. Exactly for *what* they were Chosen remained an enigma. How, where and why this contract was made in the first place, was also not clear. Moreover, their claim to uniqueness subjected them to endless attacks by other believers, all those who resented what they deemed as supreme arrogance on the part of a minor desert tribe.

These young Jews, now plotting survival in a cold school basement, would have gladly renounced all claims to theological distinction had they thought it would help them out of their current predicament. They might even have prayed, especially since not all of them were equally well equipped, physically, to withstand their present ordeal. Solomon Rabinowitz, the son of tall, intense street fighter Schmuel, was short, pudgy and lacked courage utterly, cast in his mother's likeness by genetic mishap and tolerated mainly for his uncanny ability to produce food out of thin air, a skill ascribed less to his keen nose than unbridled terror about missing a meal. David Lifschitz, son of lawyer Dov, was a stocky, curly-headed athlete, a brawler with fistic skills. Albert and Karl Grünberg, sons of respected physician Dr. Lev Grünberg, were handsome, slim, quiet intellectuals. Albert, at thirteen the older, hoped to be a surgeon while Karl dreamed of the concert stage, having given his first piano recital at the age of eight. Of the five, Horst Schumann was the one most experienced in the contrary art of survival, although all of them had had to cope, more frequently of late, with hardships brought on by their fathers' precarious politics. A parent imprisoned, their homes under surveillance, none looked on this crisis as an adventure.

David Lifschitz, raised by his lawyer father to face facts, asked for quiet so they could discuss their options. "We can't stay here," he said, "too close to headquarters. After Hitler talks they'll be on a rampage."

"We need food," murmured Solomon, already anxious about missing lunch.

"Sure, we need food, Soli." Horst poked him playfully in his soft belly, glad to be with friends after the last forty-eight hours. "We also need water and a safe hiding place, at least until we find out more about our fathers."

"What do you think they'll do with them?" asked Karl, a delicate boy, uneasy with physical discomfort.

Horst pretended not to hear, refused to have the unthinkable overwhelm them. Instead, he talked about his latest hiding place.

"In the goddamn sewer?" said David.

"It's not like being home, but it's not that bad, David. It doesn't smell good, but it's clean."

"What about rats?"

"Didn't see any."

"What if they find us? How do we get out?"

"Feet first."

Nobody laughed and as hard as they tried, nobody could think of alternatives. It would have to be the sewer. Horst described its exact location. They would split up now and meet at the bunker at dusk. A simple code was arranged, three knocks, a pause, three more knocks. Before then they needed to get word to their mothers to reassure them and to gather supplies for a few days, just in case. Horst counted on Walter to act as their lookout.

Chubby Solomon had his own concerns. "Can I make it down the ladder, Horst?"

"I'll put a chocolate bar at the bottom, Soli." For the first time that grim morning the boys shared a smile.

"Did you guys know," asked Albert, "that Papa took care of Pflug's son a few years ago? Swallowed a safety pin, or something. Maybe Pflug remembers and lets our fathers go after Hitler is gone."

"Yeah," grunted David, "and pigs can fly."

They decided to wait until the beginning of Hitler's speech. They had heard his radio talks before, were familiar with the routine. The voice would boom from loudspeakers mounted at every corner of the Bahnhof and at all public buildings. Everybody would be listening, whether they wanted to or not. The streets would be empty, a perfect time for them to be on their way. Only Albert owned a watch; it was eleven o'clock.

The voice of Rudolf Hess slammed through the walls.

"Es spricht der Führer!"

"Sieg Heils" roared into the air. In quick succession the boys left the school, took several directions toward their homes, toward food, toward whatever they thought they might need to sustain them. Horst headed for Neue Strasse and Walter, while Hitler's shrill voice saturated the atmosphere.

> "National Socialists! My German People!
>
> Fifteen years ago in our program we promised a revolution: and over Germany there has come a revolution, deep and mighty. Not externally have we conquered the old system, but in the hearts of men. All the ferments, which were destroying the people, have been banished—Marxism and just to the same extent our rootless and equally...

Rika Pflug knew she had to listen to Hitler's speech; Rollo would question her about it and value her opinion. Reluctantly, she banged down the lid of her spinet, folded the sheet music of the Chopin nocturne she was rehearsing, part of the recital she was scheduled to give at the *Städtische Musik Schule*. Hitler's speech had to be listened to; The Pflug home on Gutenbergstrasse faced the Südwall where large loudspeakers, mounted on ten-foot pillars, transmitted across most of the city's center. She never heard the Führer without wishing someone would give him voice lessons and teach him to modulate. In fact, several aspects about

National Socialism bothered Rika Pflug, not least the Party's dogmatic attitude toward music. For weeks she had prepared a Mozart concert, notating her own piano transpositions of overtures to *The Marriage of Figaro*, *Don Giovanni* and *Cosi Fan Tutti*. Two days ago a memo was placed in her school mailbox, signed by the secretary of the National Teachers Union, requesting that she change her program because Lorenzo da Ponte, a Jew, a baptized Jew to be sure, but a Jew nevertheless, wrote the opera libretti. Ridiculous, thought Rika, but complied.

As she turned on the radio she mused about Rollo, her kind, conflicted husband, presently enveloped by the Party faithful in a cocoon of pomp and circumstance. She knew he must have been thinking, even at this exhilarating moment, about the underside of the dark beast, the one that maimed bodies and muffled screams in concrete cubicles. Hesitantly she turned her attention to Hitler's words.

> …International bourgeois party system. In its place there has come a community of the German people in the economic sphere the Front of our workers. We have been in power only for two years. People must not imagine…

Heiko Böhm looked forward with great excitement to seeing his Führer in person. Before joining the procession leading into Westfalenhalle, Heiko made certain that the broadcast reached every nook and cranny in the headquarter's basement. He had arranged for extra loudspeakers to be connected to the radio, ordered an office worker to turn them to full volume at the start of the broadcast. He didn't want these Commie Jews to miss a single word, fervently hoped Hitler might announce a plan to ship them all to Kingdom Come, or at least to Dachau.

Oskar Schumann slumped against a wall, all too familiar with the rhetoric. He loathed Hitler's incessant ranting against so-called international bourgeois systems, his simplistic attacks on Bolshevism. Sledgehammer reasoning. Who among the people, or in the government for that matter, had ever read Marx or possessed even a rudimentary understanding of his Manifesto?

"That's right, Schumann, you big *macher*," he murmured into the malodorous air, "go ahead, invoke your irrefutable maxims and enlighten your beloved common man. While that fascist killer is bludgeoning millions into supporting his evil ways, you, you big shot Communist pamphlet writer, are flat on your ass in a concrete coffin begging some brown-shirted cretin to slip you a bowl of soup so you won't starve to death. Oh Jakob, my father, for what reason did you teach me to love underdogs?" He tried, unsuccessfully, to shut out the despot's relentless assaults seeping through the walls. For a brief moment he contemplated suicide, to cheat the bastards now and forever. He stared at the rusty pipes; too high to reach. He'd failed as provider, husband, father and brother, and certainly as a political mover and shaker. Sure as hell he'd screw up his suicide too, break an arm instead of his neck. He slumped in dejection while the devil droned on.

> …that our energy is exhausted. On the contrary, we stand only at the beginning of the new development. What we have created in two years is but the proclamation of that which will one day be.
> To all those who roam through Germany still cherishing their silent hopes…

In nearby Arnsberg, a scant hour's drive from Dortmund, Hubert Klingen listened to Hitler from under the hood of an American-made Buick sedan. Disconnecting the car's carburetor aroused in him more emotional response than Hitler's invectives. The Führer, National Socialism, Jews, Bolshevism, and Norma's leaving him all crackled in the background of his confused soul like static from a defective radio.

Four months ago Norma resigned her teaching post, informed him that she and the children were moving to Bingen to live with her parents until she could make other arrangements. She wasn't sure about a divorce, perhaps later. Apparently, Hubert thought, she wasn't sure about a lot of things, like whether she disliked living with him more than she disliked living in Arnsberg, or whether it was a lethal fusion of the two.

Inevitably, Hubert's feelings returned to the boy, the little Jew. He tried, unsuccessfully as always, to shoulder Horst with blame. He slammed down the Buick's hood; the car could wait. He wiped his hands, leaned heavily against his greasy desk, listened without truly hearing and sorrowed without tears.

> …So often in my life I have been a prophet and you have not believed me but have laughed at me and mocked me. But I wish to be a prophet still and I would say to you: you will never come back! That which today is will never fade away, and that which was will never return…

Ah! Was Hitler speaking directly to him? *That which was will never return.* Was that truly prophetic? Hubert missed his family, came slowly to understand the rupture's real causes. On many an evening they had talked about the boy, the emotions roused by his leaving. Norma had loved the boy, not more than her own children, but differently. He soothed her need to protect the hunted and to defy the hunters, while Hubert's concern was wholly for family. As a result both their careers had been threatened and Ludi teased mercilessly for having a Jew in his house. What the hell did Norma expect? Why wouldn't she understand? He owed this ragged little boy nothing. Hadn't he given him bed and board for a whole summer? Was his home a permanent hospice for run-away Jews?

Deep down inside Hubert Klingen knew the truth. The Nazis had gotten to him. It wasn't their parades, their music or uniforms that had wrenched him to the right. A decent and generous man, he was unmoved by trappings of political power. No! What attracted him was the Nazi promise of knowing where one belonged in society, a return to order. For Hubert, order had a clear-cut focus: fine German cars built in splendid German factories, maintained with superb German tools, barreling down awe-inspiring German highways. Also, order was Ludi, so straight, so full of spirit, so proud of acceptance by his peers. Hubert shared a personal ethos with millions of other Germans: he loved conformity, found idiosyncrasy inimical to his sense of well-being.

Hubert was only vaguely aware of the precise moment when he surrendered to the pressure and became a card-carrying Party member. Perhaps it happened at that rally in the spring of 1933 when Arnsberg's district commander demanded a one-day boycott of all Jewish businesses and nobody, absolutely nobody protested, including himself. When he joined the SA in 1934 Norma began to withdraw, slowly at first from the community, then more rapidly from him. Their lovemaking became mechanical, their conversations empty. She refused to join the women in the teachers union and finally resigned her job.

Perhaps they could patch it up. He hated living alone, badly missed the weekend cacophony of his children and the warmth of family meals. He suddenly felt old, slumped into a chair as the Führer's voice punctuated his misery.

> ...The German nation has no feeling of hatred towards England, America, or France; all it wants is peace and quiet. But these other nations are continually being stirred up to hatred of Germany and the German people by Jewish and non-Jewish agitators. And so, should the warmongers achieve what they are aiming at...

In southern Stuttgart, Minister Becker, chief of that lovely city's booming Visa Division, arranged for his overworked staff to listen to the Führer in the plush comfort of what was once, in the castle's patrician days, a lady's sitting room. Folding chairs, fully occupied, faced a satin-covered wall, now somewhat frayed and faded. For this and future occasions Becker had bought a fine new radio which sat on an antique end table next to porcelain trays loaded with cakes and an urn of coffee, to be served at the conclusion of the address. Attendance was mandatory, of course; a reminding memo had been distributed.

Fräulein Grimm at his side, Becker entered the salon shortly before the start of the speech, paused at the entrance, lightly brushed a sleeve against his secretary's silky blouse and ostentatiously guided her to their reserved seats. He knew that all eyes were on them and relished their envy. From time to time, as the speech progressed, he pressed his thigh against hers, longing for a twitch of response. Patience, he thought, sooner or later.

> …Our own people would be psychologically quite unprepared and which they would thus fail to grasp. The German nation must know who the men are who want to bring about a war by hook or by crook. It is my conviction that these people are mistaken in their calculations, for when once National Socialist propaganda is devoted to the answer of the attacks, we shall succeed just as we succeeded inside Germany herself in overcoming, through the convincing power of our propaganda, the Jewish world enemy…

Unobtrusively seated with Frau Zeidler near the rear, Dietrich Hartung received the Führer's message in a brain fogged by alcohol. He had nothing to drink this morning, his hangover resulting from yesterday's binge, an all-night skat game with old friends liberally lubricated by shots of schnapps, washed down with bottomless steins of good lager. Frau Zeidler poked him. Hartung sat up and made a brave effort to narrow the hazy expanse between his throbbing temples and the seemingly far-distant radio. Hitler's words, "the Jewish world enemy," nearly sobered him. Was his chancellor about to say something useful about eliminating mountains of enemies, those endless stacks of dossiers waiting to be processed? He needed a drink, furtively glanced at Becker, begrudged him his cold superiority and loathed his proximity to Andrea Grimm.

> …but there is one thing that everyone should realize: these attempts cannot influence Germany in the slightest as to the way in which she settles her Jewish problem. ON the contrary, in connection with the Jewish question I have this to say: it is a shameful spectacle to see how the whole democratic world is oozing sympathy for the poor tormented Jewish people, but remains hardhearted and obdurate when it comes to helping them—which is surely, in view of its attitude, an obvious duty…

Hartung agreed with the Führer. Let's take what the yids own then get them the hell out of here. He sternly determined not to drink the rest of the week and to clear up his backlog of work. With long-practiced instinct he reached into his pants pocket and caressed the comforting shape of the silver flask. Well, maybe just a nip or two before lunch to clear the head. "Not before you make the rounds after the speech," protested his inner voice, "not before you socialize to show everyone how sober you are. I mean everyone, including Becker. Especially Becker."

> ...If the rest of the world cries out with a hypocritical mien against this barbaric expulsion from Germany of such an irreplaceable and culturally eminently valuable element, we can only be astonished at the conclusions they draw from this situation. For how thankful they must be that we are releasing these precious apostles of culture, and placing them at the disposal of the rest of the world...

In the flatlands of Westfalia, the streets of rustic Lippstadt were as empty as Pavel Czerny's bakery, its citizens glued to their radios, mostly to one of the new mini-receivers selling at Willi's for only thirty-five Marks. Czerny didn't want to listen to Hitler's ranting, but there was no way to avoid it.

Less than a year ago, Willi Abenrode had opened a new shop, "Willi's Electrical Appliances, New and Used," directly across from Czerny's bakery. Abenrode worked in his store only in the mornings, when he sold vacuum cleaners, steam irons, radios, phonographs, and the like. In the afternoons his wife, the grossly overweight Bettina, watched the store while Willi pursued a greater passion at NSDAP headquarters as Lippstadt's radio warden. Abenrode had learned radio mechanics from his father, a licensed electrician, who had also taught his son to hate Jews, gypsies, bankers, niggers, Frenchmen, Polacks, Orientals, lawyers, priests, intellectuals and anybody who spoke with a foreign accent. Czerny's slavic inflections put him near the top of Willi's list of Undesirables. That Bettina spent many afternoons masticating her way through Czerny's irresistible *schneckens* further stoked Abenrode's nationalist fires. That Czech bastard was probably poisoning a special batch just for her. He had heard tales about a Jew kid working for Czerny a couple of years ago. Didn't surprise him a bit. After he opened the store in the summer of 1933, his first mission was to make certain that Berlin's policy—radio must reach all or it will reach none—was strictly enforced. He believed in leading by example. On the brick lintel above his store's entrance Willi mounted the largest speakers in his inventory and connected them to the best tuner/amplifier he could afford. He had turned on the system with intense satisfaction. The strains of the *Badenweiler March* signaled his Führer's approach, soared through Lippstadt's skies and invaded every near-by habitat, especially the bakery of Pavel Czerny, that Jew-loving, food-poisoning alien. Willi pictured Czerny listening to each of the fifty speeches Hitler broadcast that year, but if the

Czech hated it, he never let on; just kept selling *schnecken* to Bettina, who thrived on them.

> ...of other nations. The Jewish race will have to adapt itself to sound constructive activity as other nations do, or sooner or later it will succumb to a crisis of an inconceivable magnitude...

Czerny shuddered at the implications. Last year, after he married his assistant, Elsa, he thought he could settle down in this small community and raise a family. His homeland was on his mind. The Saar was annexed a few months ago. In the boiling cauldron of European politics maybe his Czech countrymen were next on the list of those who, like the Jews, needed to adapt to sound constructive activities. He thought seriously about emigrating, maybe to America. He and Elsa talked about it. Sometimes, on quiet winter evenings, when falling snow misted their vision, they also recalled the little Jewish boy, Horst, hoped he had found a peaceful place. Czerny kept the note the boy had left him, used it to mark Exodus in his Old Testament Bible.

> ...been ridiculed for it. During the time of my struggle for power it was in the first instance the Jewish race which only received my prophecies with laughter when I said I would one day take over the leadership of the State, and with it that of the whole nation, and that I would then among many other things settle the Jewish problem. Their laughter was uproarious...

In the frigid northern city of Hamburg, Hildegard and Otto Kube listened to the Führer together. Her office had no radio, but Hildegard got permission to hear Hitler's speech over loudspeakers on Hamburg's picturesque Rathausplatz. She had offered Otto to make lunch for both of them, to be eaten as they sat on folding chairs in the square.

Frau Kube was only mildly interested in what Hitler had to say. She knew she would miss nothing since Gottfried and his father re-hashed all the Führer's speeches far into the night, inundating her with gusts of enthusiasm until, in self-defense, she would slip off to bed. Not that they noticed. Actually, she hoped to pinch a little time after the speech for a bit of discreet shopping on Moenckeberg-strasse, maybe even indulge—the very thought gave her shivers of pleasure—in a *kaffe und kuchen* at that new little konditorei across the square.

> ...but I think that for some time now they have been laughing on the other side of their face...

Otto nudged her arm. "You hear, Hilde?" he whispered. "Boy, is he giving it to them. This will make those bloodsuckers stop and think."

Frau Kube nodded, her mind fixed on a wool coat she saw at a department store two weeks before. Just right for weather like this, she thought, and wondered if it would still be there. She also considered how long it was safe to stay away from the office, contemplated the possibility of eating her lunch while listening, but discarded that notion as too conspicuous. Otto would accuse her of being inattentive. She avoided anything that provoked him.

> ...Today I will once more be a prophet: If the international Jewish financiers in and outside Europe should succeed...

She decided to buy the wool coat, perhaps look for a nice little hat to go with it, something chic, but practical, have a coffee and a piece of that outrageous looking *nusstorte* and still get back to the office before Eberhardt could miss her. So infused was she by this delicious prospect that nothing further about the Führer's plans penetrated the mind of Frau Hildegard Kube.

> ...in plunging the nations once more into a world war, then the result will not be the bolshevization of the earth, and thus the victory of Jewry, but the annihilation of the Jewish race in Europe!...

Against his better judgment, Bjorn Milfs banked the fires in his shop to hear Hitler speak. He filled a good-sized mug with a sudsy Pilsner, put his feet on the table, chewed on a piece of salami, drank and listened.

> ...At the moment the Jews in certain countries may be fomenting hatred under the protection of a press, of the film, of wireless propaganda, of the theatre, of literature, etc., all of which they control...

"All of which they control? What a lot of horseshit!" said Bjorn Milfs, clicked off the radio, drained his beer mug and returned to the smithy to straighten horseshoes.

> ...If this nation should once more succeed in inciting the millions which compose the nations into a conflict which is utterly senseless and only serves Jewish interests, then there will be revealed the effectiveness of an enlightenment which has completely routed the Jews in Germany in the space of a few years. The nations are no longer willing to die on the battlefield...

In Dortmund, intensely concerned about the fate of her husband and the whereabouts of her stepson, Gretchen Schumann heard Hitler's pronouncements at the home of her parents, Hedwig and Reinhardt Krause. She was deeply puzzled. Listening to the vitriolic fury spilling from the radio, she didn't know if Hitler was right or wrong. For three years now she had listened to Oskar's propaganda and often wondered if his truth was any better than Hitler's when all it got him was a bloody beating. She married Oskar to have a better life, but that didn't work out very well. Hitler talked about how Jews controlled the press and the film and everything else? Well, if her Jew husband was controlling anything it sure wasn't improving her life. Controlling things, hah! Her husband's kid couldn't even control his bladder.

The strange, the incomprehensible truth was that she cared what happened to her sad, confused mate and his sullen, untamed son, cared more than she wanted to admit, even to herself. Of course Oskar was a rotten provider, a bewildered dreamer who would always put the welfare of the people ahead of his own. But a parasite? What did Hitler mean by that? All the Jews she knew worked their tails off, minded their own business and never bothered anybody. Oskar didn't buy her jewels or fur coats, but when she was sick he stayed at her side, nursed her until she was well. When she was troubled, by Horst, by life, by all the hate and turmoil blaring at her from kiosks, newspapers and radios, Oskar remained patient and sensitive, attuned to her moods, always tried to explain, to clarify and to ease her heart. The truth was that she loved him; not in the romantic, passionate way she loved her streetcar Italians, but in a more mature, womanly way. Her parents wanted her to leave Oskar, to come home and live with them. She would not do that. She had made her bed and she would lie in it.

As her mother and father watched in consternation, she gathered her belongings and waved good-bye. As she made her exit, Hitler's voice intruded, followed her out the door.

> ...so that this unstable international race may profiteer from a war or satisfy its Old Testament vengeance. The Jewish watchword 'Workers of the world unite' will be conquered by a higher realization, namely 'Workers of all classes and of all nations, recognize your common enemy!

Horst was anxious to reach Walter's house before the speech ended, before mobs emptied into the streets. He was familiar with Hitler's technique. For the past two years he had heard Oskar rant against the Nazi leader's oratorical deceits. As he rushed in the direction of his neighborhood, he listened to Hitler's speech in the way one views scenery passing fleetingly between telephone poles from a moving train. He ran through the streets cautiously, dodged bullets of venom flying from public loudspeakers, storefronts and through open apartment windows. In need of supplies, he contemplated going into his own apartment, using the back entrance of course.

He found Walter in the alley, playing soccer against a wall. They moved into the hallway.

"Heard anything, Walter?"

"Nothing. They're all listening to Hitler. What about you?"

"We met at school, the Grünbergs, Soli, Lifschitz and I. We decided to go down into the sewers for a couple of days."

"All of you? To that stinky place?"

"Come with us."

"Me? Are you crazy? Uh uh!" Walter shook his head.

Horst laughed, patted his friend's shoulder. "You'll miss us, Walter." He remembered there was no time to waste. "Could you make sure no one's watching my house?"

Walter returned a moment later. "A few people in the street, but no uniforms."

That was good enough for Horst; he would go to his apartment and take what he needed. "Here's the plan. First, I'll check out the bunker and make sure everything's okay. Then I'll wait until the others arrive. You stay here and keep your eyes open. Try to find out what you can, but be careful. One of us will come to see you tomorrow night after dark. Maybe, just maybe, the Nazis will have sent our fathers home by then."

They separated, reluctantly. Horst found the window to his room unlocked. Nobody was home, the apartment musty, abandoned. He was grateful that Grete had recently shopped, took two tins of sardines, a jar of sauerkraut and a package of pumpernickel, added the knitted afghan from the living room couch, stuffed everything into his rucksack along with socks, a shirt and the Karl May book Walter had lent him. He remembered to take the flashlight from the kitchen drawer, candles and a box of matches. A little light would help. He found a roll of toilet paper in the bathroom. Just a couple of days, he reminded himself, don't make things difficult.

Hitler's speech must have ended. Church bells rang out, mingled with band music. He reached the sewer without incident, saw no one around and entered quickly. He was getting better at it. Nothing inside had changed, although a bulb near the bottom had burned out. He spread his things in the alcove, tried to read

Karl May with his flashlight and thought it might be better to save the batteries. Weird. The place was beginning to feel like home.

For the hundredth time he wondered if Oskar was still alive, prayed they would let him go. The last three years had not been easy for father and son, especially when they tried to deal with personal matters. Whenever Horst brought up Liselotte's name, his father stammered something about accidents and careless doctors, then he escaped, acting irritated. At other times Horst tried to tell Oskar about his strange life around Westfalia, about Czerny and Milfs, about Uncle Walter and Norma and Hubert, about crazy places he'd slept in, about the poems of Heine, about the work he had done and how hard it was when the winters came. Oskar listened, his eyes grew moist behind his thick glasses, he fidgeted, then quoted some Russian philosopher, or maybe a Greek, Horst couldn't tell. Then he always had a meeting to run to and Horst never received answers. Since Hitler came to power they talked even less about family. Oskar was one of the first Communists the Nazis went after. They knew he was a Communist because they saw his by-line on numerous KPD pamphlets. The first time they arrested him, they locked him in the basement of the police station, but released him after four days. Horst was there when he came out, a bloodied, puzzled mess who clung to his son and his idealism like a drowning sailor to a leaky lifeboat. Horst saw the torturer staring down from his safe lookout, hated and despised him, for himself as much as for Oskar.

After that they were closer, not good friends, but closer. They knew they had become aliens in their own land, were heading toward a future neither of them dared to analyze or even acknowledge. Now contempt, indignities and malice grew throughout the country, suffocated all hope, distorted everyone's daily life and stripped away personal identity.

Sheer existence was difficult enough. Horst did his best to cooperate, tried hard not to aggravate the eroding relationship between husband and wife. He helped his father sort leather hides in the basement storage room, shopped for Grete and spent most evenings reading books or working on his penmanship. Even on warm nights he stayed in the house, aware of danger in the streets.

Late in the summer of 1934 he had made a bad mistake. He had risked a game of soccer with friends in a small park close to his house, near the Friedenskirche, but his timing was dreadful. The Horst Wessel Realschule let out while they were playing, dozens of Hitler Jugends traversing the park. A boy from his street recognized him, yelled: "There's Schumann, the Communist Jew!" They surrounded him before he could run, pushed him, hit him in the stomach, spat in his face. He looked for help, but his friends had fled.

"Let's show this goddamn yid how much we love him," snarled the one they called Günter, a tall, raw-boned youngster, obviously their leader.

They dragged him to the edge of the park, tore off his shirt, pulled him to a tree stump and pushed him to his knees. Günter yanked his left arm over the stump.

"Hold him," he ordered the others. They had done so.

Without hesitation Günter stepped down hard on his arm, which cracked with a sharp explosion. He screamed like an animal. The pain was overbearing, vomit covered his chest.

"The other arm," said Günter.

"The other one?" mumbled one of the boys, looking pale. "Isn't one enough?"

"The other arm," ordered Gunter. "For Jews there's never enough."

They laid his other arm on the stump and Günter broke it. He was already in shock, didn't feel the pain as much, only dimly aware that he was still alive. They let him lie there, drifted off alone and in pairs, like witnesses slinking from an appalling accident. The smaller boys kept looking back, giggling to cover their fear, for the first time witnessing the monstrous face of brute power disfigured by unreasoning hate.

His friends, aware that he was in trouble, had lingered near the park. They saw what had been done to his arms, bone fragments piercing the skin. Gingerly, they lifted him to his feet and made him take a few steps. It took them an hour to get to Doctor Grünberg's office. He often screamed and sank to his knees in pain.

The doctor had sedated him, set his bones, put his arms in plaster and taken him home. "I can still see patients at Johannes Hospital," he told Oskar. "I want Horst there tomorrow for X-rays. The casts will do until then."

"How is he, Lev?"

"He's young, Oskar. He'll mend; at least his arms will."

Both Oskar and Gretchen had been kind. With both arms in casts, he couldn't do much for several weeks. He often went with Oskar in the Opel calling on old customers, those still willing to do business with a Jew. Several shoemakers asked about his broken arms. He told them it was an accident; that he fell down a flight of stairs. They looked into his eyes and knew better. What could they do? At least they could give Schumann an order, pay him what they owed. When the casts came off Oskar suggested keeping them, to put them back on from time to time. Business, recalled Oskar of that period, had never been better.

Although his arms mended in time, his bruised survival instincts took somewhat longer. Bored, jittery, cooped up in a foul sewer, those instincts were thoroughly tested at this very moment. He tried to read the Karl May book again and despite the terrible light lost himself for a time in the adventures of cowboys and Comanches. Soon it would be dusk. Thank god, he would have company. He thought he might actually rather risk the Nazis than spend another night alone in this hole.

In the Westfalenhalle, Hitler concluded his speech, brought his remarks to a rousing finish with tirades against Jews, Bolsheviks and assorted enemies of the Third Reich. For several minutes he stood at the rostrum, smiling, acknowledging with limp salutes the tumultuous "Sieg Heils", the stiff-armed adoration of an intoxicated assembly. Then, at a nod from Hess, he turned abruptly and disappeared into the Western tunnel, together with his entourage. Within fifteen minutes the hall was cleared and the lights dimmed. A crew arrived, took down the flags, disassembled the podium and, sounding like machine gun fire, slammed shut the metal folding chairs and stacked them against the walls.

Martin Lutz watched the activity, amazed by its military precision. At the exact moment Hitler left the stage, Oldenburg had gathered his things, grabbed his briefcase and slapped on his visored hat.

"Good work, Lutz. I'll send a note to your manager. Tell me, why aren't you in uniform?"

Lutz stared. Why in the world should he, Lutz, wear a uniform?

"Well, never mind," said Oldenburg, "the time will come soon when the Führer will need your skills and not just to record his speeches. Keep learning, Lutz. Heil Hitler." He was gone.

Lutz disassembled the broadcast system, coiled all cables in the proscribed manner, loaded the dolly and wheeled it toward the service elevator's ramp. Something gnawed at his gut. He returned to the auditorium, sat in an empty seat and stared at the scene below. The decorations were nearly gone. Flags had been folded and stored in huge boxes. Only a few sections of metal chairs remained standing. On the main floor an army of sweepers piled up small mounds of refuse.

He made the connection, an uneasy one, but inescapable. When he was a young boy, a circus came to Dortmund and erected a large canvas tent on the Grossmarkt for a two-day engagement. His father took him there and it was very exciting. There was a ringmaster who ran everything, clowns and wild animals and people who walked on high wires and also the first live elephants Martin had ever seen. He was so stirred that he went back the next day, but the circus people were already closing up, the tent was down, the animals were in their cages and the wagons were loaded. He saw no clowns, no ladies in spangled tights and no lion tamers with whips and red coats, only a crowd of workmen yelling at each other. All the magic had disappeared. Finally a very old man had shuffled along with a cart and carefully shoveled into pails the mountains of shit that elephants had deposited on the ground. That had been the closing act of the circus.

Lutz grimaced at the memory, loaded his equipment and drove slowly toward his company's headquarters. He knew that he promised Ursula to celebrate the successful conclusion of today's historic event. He couldn't put his finger on specific reasons, but he didn't feel like seeing her. What the hell did Oldenburg mean by "the time will come when the Führer will need your skills?" Martin Lutz could imagine all kinds of commercial uses for his electronic skills, but he was sure Oldenburg had something else in mind. Troubled, in no mood for love making, he wanted to be alone tonight, have a beer or two, install a new transformer in his radio, maybe finish the mechanical water wheel he'd been fooling around with for weeks.

He simply couldn't leave it alone. What was bothering him so persistently? Shouldn't he be thrilled to have completed his job so perfectly? No, this had nothing to do with the job or with Hitler or with his speech about Jews and Bolsheviks and other assorted enemies. Martin wasn't very interested in politics, had not really listened to the whole tirade. What continued to irritate him was the mechanical way everything was organized. It reminded him of just another day in school. You entered the building when the bell rang, rose from your seat when the teacher appeared, sat down on his command, listened to his yelling for an hour or so, cleaned your desk, waited for the day's final bell and went home when granted permission. One mistake and you were made to feel like a jackass, as useful as that old man shoveling elephant shit into his pail.

On his way back to the office he heard band music receding in the distance, parade sounds fading in the direction of the airport. Realization finally dawned on Martin Lutz and made him grin: School was out and the circus was leaving town.

13

Twice that morning Rollo Pflug nicked himself shaving. He disliked using his straight razor; one had to pay too much attention. Every morning he determined to buy a safety razor, like the kind advertised in magazines, but immediately felt conflicted as he did in most matters involving his late father. The razor was Gustav's gift on Rollo's sixteenth birthday, a proud parent celebrating his son's entry into the fellowship of stubbled men. The silver-plated Solingen instrument was inscribed: "From GP to RP. Stay Sharp!" Despite sentimental misgivings, Rollo promised himself to buy a new razor, but not today. Today, other matters occupied his mind. He needed Rika's reaction to yesterday's events, particularly to his talk with Terhoven. He dabbed his cuts with a styptic pencil, finished dressing, noted his unpolished boots and belt and silently vowed to shine them on the weekend.

Rika and the children were having breakfast in the kitchen. Rollo poured himself a cup of coffee, nervously spilled some on the table. He buttered a roll, then dropped it on his trousers.

"Damn," he muttered, rubbing the fat spot, "just what I needed."

Rika watched quietly and sent Heinz off to kindergarten and Trudi to her room to play. She had lived with Rollo since Freiburg days, understood very well how he functioned. Rollo's mother had cautioned her on the day of their wedding: "Give him time. He's like a cow, chews everything twice before it gets to his brain." Rika discovered that to be good advice.

Rollo wiped his trousers with a dishtowel, stopped, and threw it across the kitchen into the sink. Rika pulled a chair to the table.

"Rika…."

"Hmm?"

"I came home late last night. Didn't want to wake you."

"I was awake."

"I know."

Rika wondered what had happened to him; his face looked drained, his eyes tired. "Aren't you feeling well, my love?"

He shrugged off her question. "What did you think of Hitler's speech?"

"Not so good for the Jews. Such bitter words." Her concern was not about Jews or Hitler. Rollo was deeply agitated. "What did you do after the speech?" she probed.

"Heiko and I, Terhoven, Littmann the *Gruppenleiter* from Essen and an SS guy named Buchberger, we went to the airport and saw Hitler off.

"Who is Buchberger?"

"One of Bormann's people from Berlin. He came out last week to take charge of the Hansaplatz project."

"Is that what's bothering you?"

"He's an unpleasant man, but no, that's not it." Rollo's shoulders sagged. He continued, obvious reluctant. "First we had a meeting in the office, then Terhoven invited me for supper. He wanted to chat; at least that's what he called it. We drank some beer. He chatted a lot. It got late. Forgive me for not calling."

"Don't worry. It doesn't matter. What did Terhoven want?"

Rollo stared at her. "He wants me to…" Rollo took a deep breath before he continued. "He wants me to move to Essen. He wants me to transfer to the SS. He thinks I'm wasting my talents running the Dortmund SA. He says he has a job for me with greater potential. A promotion."

"Why Essen? What would you do in Essen?"

"Terhoven wants to appoint me to Westfalia's branch of the secret police, the *Sicherheitsdienst*."

The butcher's hand, proffering the knife. Rika managed to put down her cup without spilling a drop. Cold chills crept up her spine, matched the frozen look on his face.

"And? What did you tell him?"

"I told him I needed time to think, that I wanted to discuss it with you."

She couldn't move. Her whole life suddenly felt suspended. The hallway clock growled its customary warning, then softly tolled nine o'clock. She despised that clock. It split each day into fragments, repeatedly reminded her of chores yet undone. It was a wedding gift from her parents, so it was kept.

"I have to go, Rika." He put on his coat and cap, kissed her softly on both cheeks. "We'll talk tonight. I'll be home early, I promise."

She sat for a time, her mind a cauldron of conflicting thoughts. Finally, in need of focus, she went to Trudi's room and played with her, helped her dress dolls and polish the dollhouse. Her daughter's high-spirited innocence restored a semblance of equilibrium. Once or twice during the morning she permitted herself to utter the word *Sicherheitsdienst*. It sounded repellant and ominous.

Pflug arrived at his office shortly after nine-thirty, not surprised to see Böhm already waiting in the reception room. He advised Frau Schuster to compile data for Buchberger's impending visit and requested the Stuttgart file to be available in the afternoon. "At two o'clock, please, Frau Schuster. Come in, Heiko."

Böhm sat next to the desk. Pflug walked to the window, gazed at the banner undulating in the light breeze, felt his customary pang at the prospect of leaving for the nearly completed concrete and glass blockhouse. Frau Schuster served coffee in two cups.

"Heiko. It's time to assemble that bunch in the basement and move them into the yard."

"Ahh! We have transport orders."

"No, we don't have transport orders. No orders of any kind."

"Terhoven said nothing about Communists?"

"He said many things. Yes, the Communists came up for discussion."

"So?"

"He told me to deal with the problem as I saw fit. I've thought about it. I'm sure our guests in the basement understand by now that Communism is finished in this country. Nobody pays attention anymore to their gibberish, so I've decided to send them home for the time being."

Böhm was dumbfounded. The sound of the banner slapping in the breeze could be heard through the window. "You what? Tell me I'm not hearing this right."

"Your hearing is perfect, Heiko. I told Terhoven we would release our Bolshevik rabble-rousers and watch them carefully. They are to stop all hostile activities immediately."

"And he agreed?"

"He was cagey. He said something like 'they can run around for now. Soon there'll be changes; they'll be like rats in a maze.' Of course that made me curious."

"I'm curious too."

"We'll both have to wait. Terhoven didn't elaborate. So let's get on with it. I want them in the yard, but first have them use the washroom. No reason why they should look like they've been in an accident."

"No accident."

"I'm aware of that, Heiko. Give them soap."

"Waste soap and water? Jesus, Rollo, kick the whole bunch out the back entrance or send them off to Dachau, if you ask me."

"I'm not asking you, Heiko. Do what I say and do it now."

Böhm was startled. Pflug never spoke this sharply to him.

"Tell me when they're ready. I want a few words with our friends before they go."

The *Gruppenführer* and his adjutant locked eyes. Up to now their association was based on the tacit assumption that Dortmund's disciplinary procedures were best left to Böhm. The arrangement worked well until Hitler ordered Party Chief Roehm assassinated. If Hitler's earliest and most trusted ally was dispensable, who might be next? The time had come to make choices. The color of Party power was rapidly changing from brown to black, Himmler's SS clearly on the rise.

Ever since he escaped the mines and joined the Party, Heiko Böhm had convinced himself that the slogan "Might makes Right," while often dependent on controversial means, was a concept that nearly always led to beneficial ends. Heiko admired power and worshipped results. Vermin like that in the basement should be quickly put out of its misery. A simple solution for a simple problem. Apparently math teacher Pflug thought otherwise, seemed to regard a circle as the shortest distance between points. Terhoven's consent to set those Commie bastards free puzzled Böhm. What did the *Gauleiter* have up his sleeve? Böhm admired Terhoven, an SS hero with solid connections and a leader to appreciate the talents of men who, like Heiko, had clawed their way up the ladder. Future personal contact with Terhoven had to be carefully developed, but not right now. Right now, Heiko thought, it was best to follow orders, to wait and watch, to see which way the winds blew. He nodded to Pflug.

"I'll have them in the yard in half an hour."

"Good. And Heiko…"

"Yes, Rollo."

"I am not your enemy."

That startled Böhm. "Good heavens, Rollo, I never assumed you were. Why would you say such a thing?" Pflug just looked at him, the hint of a smile on his lips.

"Well, okay then Rollo, in the yard in half an hour," Böhm said and walked out the door. "Watch your ass," he murmured to himself as he strode toward the basement. "Pflug is soft as pudding, but stupid he's not. Watch your ass, Heiko, before somebody bites it off."

14

The boys climbed into the foul-smelling bunker with great apprehension. They knew this was probably the best hiding place to be found on short notice. Still, crawling into a hole in the ground was definitely terrifying, nearly unbearable. They understood that they were in this lousy bunker because their fathers were Communists and Jews. The Communist part they knew by heart; Communists had their heads bashed because they were political enemies. But what was so threatening about Jews? Were Jews so dangerous they had to be driven into underground shitholes? Yes, of course their fathers wished for a safer, more decent world but did they truly, endlessly, complacently have to try prodding Germans into more virtuous and open-minded behavior? Wouldn't it be smarter to spend more time suggesting ways to fill hungry German bellies with meat and potatoes? The boys were deeply sympathetic to their fathers, but resented a cause that held them hostage to a life within prison gates like those over their heads, that even now muffled their uneasy discourse.

Each time a truck rattled the iron gates, Solomon Rabinowitz let out a yell, ran into one of the tunnels, complained that the air was bad, that the ground was too hard, that he had to eat cold food for supper, and that crapping into a cess-pool was beneath his dignity.

"I'm leaving, guys. I hate this place."

"Nobody's keeping you, Soli," said David. "Be careful though, could be dangerous out there."

Soli gathered his things, climbed two rungs up the ladder and climbed back down. "Tomorrow," he mumbled, "I'll leave tomorrow. My mother's staying with my grandmother tonight. Too far to walk." He plumped morosely against a wall.

"What time is it, Albert?"

"Eight. Seven minutes after eight. How about some chess? Come on Horst, I brought my portable and a candle."

"I'm a bad player."

"So am I, but I'm bored. Let's just do it."

"I'll take on the winner," David offered graciously.

While they moved pieces, David kibitzed. Karl, who had a deck of cards, played rummy with Soli.

Being together provided some comfort, a comradeship of shared danger. After they tired of chess and games, of exploring dials and electrical connections, after exchanging teases and comparing farts, with Albert declared the winner, they divided their food, good stuff, which even Soli approved.

"Tasty sardines, Horst," he mumbled through a mouthful, "nice and oily. Good pumpernickel too."

With quiet desperation they made believe that it was all normal, merely another glitch in their lives. It didn't work, not for long. David Lifshitz voiced everyone's feelings.

"Sorry, guys, I don't like it. Not your fault, Horst, you meant well. It's okay for tonight, but that's it. I'm out of here tomorrow, real early. Even if the Nazis are after me, I'd rather be where I can run, not in this stinking trap."

"Run where, David?" Karl looked up, hopeful, ready to follow him up the ladder, immediately. His father, the doctor, placed cleanliness ahead of godliness and this place was neither clean nor godly.

"The Den could be safe for a day or two, Karl. Hard to tell. When our fathers come home we'll have to plan more carefully because this whole stupid mess will happen again. You staying, Horst?"

"Only until tomorrow night, believe me."

David hesitated. If Horst could stand it, so could he. Oskar and Dov had always supported each other. "Maybe," he said with a sigh, "it's better if we stick together."

At night their weariness intensified. The pressure of rotten air, dreary light and mounting anxiety, weighed heavily. In the alcove, sitting close for warmth, they traded words of optimism, not quite believing them. Soli was the first asleep, snoring softly. The Grünberg brothers, raised by an orthodox mother, whispered an evening prayer. "*Boruch atoh adonoy, eluhenu melech hoalom*", ancient words floating into dark tunnels. *Praised be Thou, O Lord our God, King of the universe, who hast kept us in life and sustained us, and enabled us to reach this season.*

David peered thoughtfully at his friends. "Maybe God heard," he yawned, "but if he did, he sure is taking his time answering."

◆   ◆   ◆

Böhm's notion of personal hygiene, at least as it pertained to the shuffling, battered assemblage before him, reflected his distaste for Pflug's decision. The prisoners were yanked out of cubicles and herded into the basement's washroom.

"You have ten minutes. There's water. Wash. No towels. Dry your dirty ass with toilet paper for all I care."

The men were prodded into the yard with batons, like cattle led to slaughter. Pflug watched from a ramp, leaning on a railing above their heads.

"I'm letting you go." He raised his voice. "But before you harbor false notions of immunity I want to make something very clear. Engage in activities detrimental to the Reich and you will be caught and punished. What you've experienced the last few days is minor, I repeat, minor, compared to what is in store if you make attempts, any attempts at all, to inflict your Communist philosophy on German citizens."

He studied their faces, determined to penetrate each stubborn mind. Herz and Koerner were broken, surprised to be alive. The priest, Thalmann, was defiant, disrespect spewing from his pursed, pinched mouth. Grünberg, the physician, stood erect, rigid with dignity and aloofness, wordlessly reminding Pflug that it was he who had saved his son's life not long ago. Schumann and Lifschitz most likely meant trouble; they slouched close to each other, eyes hooded, lips curled in mockery. For a brief moment Pflug considered returning those two to the basement, back to Böhm and an uncertain destiny. That would solve nothing, only create martyrs and inflame the rest, the diehards clinging tenaciously to their skewed vision.

"Get them out of here," he signaled to Böhm, pushed away from the railing and went to his office. He watched their torn shapes shuffle to the sidewalk and stagger down the street. Only Schumann hung back, scanned the building until he found Pflug at the window. He glared scornfully, pulled himself as erect as his bruised body allowed, defiantly stuck his hands in his trouser pockets, turned his back and stumbled off.

◆   ◆   ◆

The five boys emerged from the sewer after dark, inhaled the fresh air with immense relief, resolved to go home to hear the latest about their fathers and let that determine their course. Horst found Walter waiting, reliable as always.

"They're out!"

"Who's out?"

"Your father, Gitte's father, all of them."

"What?! Are you sure? How do you know?"

"I saw him. He was looking for you, all excited. I told him you'd be here soon."

Horst rushed through the alley and up the stairs. Oskar and Gretchen sat at the kitchen table, pages of paper scattered in front of them.

For a short, penetrating moment father and son looked at each other. Love, worry and relief intermingled, intensified their feelings and energized their embrace. Under great pressure, they had endangered themselves and those who cared for them, but today's events had renewed their courage. They had endured, at least until now.

"Papa, are you okay? Are your hurt bad?" Horst winced at Oskar's cuts and bruises.

"No more than usual. Don't worry about it. What I have to tell you is more important. Sit down. I have wonderful news. I have such wonderful news I want to cry and laugh at the same time."

Horst caught the excitement. Something extraordinary had occurred to make his father this happy, especially when he had just been released from prison. Grete was grinning too. He quickly jumped into the nearest kitchen chair, hardly able to bear the suspense.

"Papa, what is it? What's happened?"

"I know you won't believe me if I tell you, so you'd better read for yourself." He handed over an opened letter.

Clara's words hit Horst's eyes, invaded his brain like electric currents. He stared at Oskar, bewildered, his heart thumping, not able to absorb the astonishing news. His mouth agape, he looked from the letter to Oskar, to Grete, back to Oskar. Was this the miracle for which he had prayed? Or was it a mirage, a cruel mockery?

"Oh Papa, America! Is it true? Can I go? Can we all go? What do we have to do, Papa? America! I can't believe it. Can we go together? Oh my god, America!!"

Oskar clapped his hands, unsure how to contain his own elation. "I'm so thrilled for you, Horst. No, of course we can't go together. You go first. We'll follow. You see what it says?" He read several lines out loud. "The people who want to adopt you have friends. Important friends. With important friends it's much easier to emigrate."

"But Papa, I'm your son."

Gretchen, sharing the joy, offered advice. "Your father wants to protect your future, Horst. Life in Germany is terrible for all of us. You go first and we'll come later. You can help us much more once you're there."

Horst had never experienced a feeling of such intense happiness. He realized already that he would be leaving his father, but the prospect of going to America overwhelmed him. He couldn't control his feet, leaped in the air. "I'm going to America," he shouted, "I'm going to America!"

The evening became a tempest of exhilaration, a flurry of activity. Hardly able to contain themselves, they composed an answer to send to Clara.

Dear Clara,

We received your letter this morning and we don't want to wait even a day. It has been a dark time. We didn't think we would ever see the sun again. But now you have brought us sunshine and the sky looks blue. Naturally it isn't easy for a father to give up his son…

Oskar barely managed to finish the sentence. He felt Horst's eyes, wide and questioning, saw him hunched forward, kneeling on his chair with desire so urgent he gulped for each breath. Throughout his adult life Oskar Schumann had striven to write truth as clearly as his faculties allowed, to express the roots of human discontent and mankind's continued struggle for mutual understanding. The fierceness of the last few years had eroded his emotions, painfully reminded him that his need to help others often imperiled those near and dear to him. He had to lose his son through heedless passion before he found him again. Never had he loved, or needed, the boy more than now, just as he was about to lose him again. As he consigned Horst's future to others, the pen in his fingers was a knife slicing his soul.

> …but we can read the writing on the wall. It is an act of great kindness that the Malkin family wants to adopt Horst. They sound like wonderful people and I am deeply grateful. Horst is terribly excited about America. It must be a fine country. I don't have to tell you that things have been hard for us. We are hopeful Hitler and his government will realize that attacking Jews and other minorities makes Germany hated in the rest of the world and is a disastrous political road to follow.

Please take this letter as an agreement between the Malkins and us. Horst will come to America and become Horst Malkin. He is a wonderful boy and I believe will be a wonderful man.

Thank you for the money. It is much needed since no one wants to do business with Jews. Business is still good for capitalists, especially if they're gentile. But for Jewish and other unpopular proletarians life is bitter.

We did our best to fill out the form for American Immigration. It is becoming more difficult for Jews to exercise their civic rights and information is harder to come by. Please let us know what else we must do. We will find a way to do it.

Maybe later my wife Grete and I will join Horst in America. Oh, to be in a land and among people where freedom and the rights of workers are more than a hollow lie!

Until we hear from you, please once again, accept our heartfelt thanks for this wonderful offer. We are deeply grateful.

Your loving brother,

Oskar, Grete and Horst read and re-read the letter, made certain that it left no doubt about their intentions. They studied the immigration form at length, not sure what all the words meant. A German-English dictionary helped. Finally nothing remained to be done. Oskar signed the letter and Horst did too; the post office would send it off in the morning. It was late, nearly midnight. The last few days were a visit to hell; now everyone needed sleep, desperately. Still they clung to each other, loathe to letting go of euphoria, of an almost forgotten promise of tomorrow. Then none of them could keep their eyes open any longer.

"Good night, son. Happy dreams."

"Good night, Papa. I'm glad you're home." Horst kissed his father and for the first time in their few years together, he also hugged Gretchen, cheerfully and with ease.

15

On a lovely, late summer night, one thousand nine hundred thirty-five years after the birth of Jesus Christ, the spiritual descendants of that noted Hebrew revisionist were transformed by a profoundly grotesque act. Those Germans who retained a sense of social justice were astounded by its impudence. On that fateful evening Oskar and Horst Schumann went to sleep as bonafide German citizens, as did five hundred thousand others of their religious persuasion.

Oskar Schumann always thought of himself first as a German, next as a Communist. Being a Jew lagged far behind in his metaphysical pecking order. It mattered not at all that he, like three of his brothers, had fought in the German army, was wounded at Verdun, was, in fact, a flag-waving Jingoist. To most Germans he remained apart, a creature known to supplicate God in an exotic, vaguely Oriental house of worship called a synagogue where clusters of bobbing, weaving worshippers, wearing outlandish regalia, mumbled devotions in an alien language. That Oskar's mind-set was fundamentally agnostic, conditioned as it was by Marxist views, went unheeded. When Gretchen once dragged him to a Catholic service, he nearly persuaded her that Latin, altars, goblets, surplices and endless choral hymns served basic human needs no less exotically than similar Jewish ceremonials. They never went again, at least not together.

Oskar Schumann, like most German Jews, made his living by hard work. He bought and sold leather hides, hustled from village to village, from shoe repair shop to shoe repair shop, gave fair value at fair prices. He was also an intelligent person who numbered among his friends a doctor, a few teachers, a scientist or two and several artists, solid professionals, all of them staunch Germans. It made no difference. Centuries of involvement in Germany's economic and cultural affairs would not erase a mystifying stigma of Otherness, the notion that Jews were strange, somehow not quite…well…human. However, not even the most virulent anti-Semites questioned the Jew's right to citizenship. Not, that is, until the night of September 14, 1935, when Oskar and Horst Schumann, along with all German Jews, became, *de facto*, citizens without a country.

"What the hell does it mean?" Oskar asked Dov Lifschitz.

He went to see the lawyer about current immigration laws, potential roadblocks to Horst's exodus. Their appointment coincided with the morning on which Hitler issued his "Law for the Protection of German Blood and Honor." The text, printed in the daily newspaper, the *Dortmunder Zeitung*, lay in front of them.

"Nothing complicated here, Oskar. You and I are no longer German citizens."

"Come on, Dov, don't be ridiculous."

"Quite simple, my friend. While the law doesn't directly disenfranchise us, at least not yet, its intent is clear. Your grandfather, on your father's side, was he a Jew?"

"He was a rabbi in Zeltingen."

"And his wife?"

"What a question."

"And on your mother's side?"

"Sephardim Jews. Totally pious."

"There you have it, Schumann, like it or not. From the peak of his private Valhalla our cherished Führer has hurled down an irrefutable anthropological truth which is that you, Oskar Schumann, are one big, fucking, government-inspected and certified Jew."

Oskar, still puzzled, shook his head. "That's old news, good friend."

"Yes, but in a remodeled context. Now a Jew can no longer be a citizen. It says so right here, see?"

"They're joking."

"They're not, believe me, they're not. It may be madness, but I see a diabolic method to it. You see, laws that deprive us of rights granted to all ordinary German citizens may easily be applied to rights that extend beyond our person." Dov's finger stabbed at the middle of the page. "Look, here's an example. No more screwing gentile women. *Verboten.* By current law that doesn't include your *schikse* wife but you'd better find out what's now legal and what isn't before the Gestapo spies through your bedroom window to see what dirty non-Aryan things you're doing to her."

"Dov, for god's sake."

"Leave God out of this, Oskar. This is devil's work, crude but clever." Oskar fully agreed. He didn't believe in the devil, but if there was one, he surely had a hand in this. He listened carefully as Dov continued his explanation.

"Their next move is predictable. Let's call it confiscation, or dispossession; doesn't matter, just different words for piggishness. If the Nazis can legislate us out of rights as German citizens, they can also legislate us out of rights to be doctors, lawyers and leather merchants. Whatever. They can legislate us out of ownership of property, like your house on Weiherstasse; also out of rights to our bank accounts. What it boils down to is that if this piece of Nüremberg wisdom holds up in the courts, and remember it's their own damn courts, they will take away everything we are and own. They can legislate us to walk into the North Sea stripped naked and drown, for all they care. That, my friend, is what this means."

The lawyer ran a hand through his unruly curls, heaved his bulk out of the swivel chair, looked through the dirty window of his office, lit a cigarette and sat down again, deeply troubled.

"You see, Schumann, we have a basic decision to make. You and I, we've had our heads in the beast's jaws more than once, huh? I like you, Oskar. You're not one of those here-today-gone-tomorrow pinkos learning to sing the Horst Wessel song the moment they threaten you with physical abuse. You and I, we've stared Pflug and his henchmen in the eye. We've performed a miracle by eating their shit without kissing their feet. I don't know about you, but I'm not ready to start doing so now, just because of this illegal Nazi villainy."

Oskar took off his glasses. Without being aware of doing so, he had rubbed them on the sleeve of his coat for several minutes. "It's costing me my family," he said, "a heavy price to pay."

The lawyer understood only too well. "A price has to be paid, Oskar. I don't go free, either. I always meant to write law books, be a professor, teach young Germans how to respect differences of opinion. Let's discuss that later. Right now we must concentrate on getting Horst out of here. I still have friends at City Hall. Not all of them have turned into monsters."

True, Oskar thought, there are decent people left and as long as they remain it's a battle worth fighting. He took a deep breath, seeking to gather strength he no longer possessed, and put a hand on his comrade's shoulder. "Thanks, Dov. It scares me, but I feel like you do. There's a problem. In the future how do we distribute our message? Pflug will watch us like a hawk."

"Hawks don't fly underground. Herz had to quit. They ruptured his kidneys. He's pissing blood. Two days ago, in the dead of night, the poor bastard schlepped the mimeo out of Grünberg's medical locker and brought it here." He opened the office supply closet, revealed the mimeograph machine hidden under old files. "I'm scared too, Oskar, but I also have to live with myself. If I sell out now, I've sold myself to the devil and without even getting thirty years of fun and games in exchange, like Faust. No thanks! As far as I'm concerned the war goes on."

They made arrangements when and where to meet, hugged and parted, feeling righteous, powerful and terrified.

◆   ◆   ◆

From that day on a mist of indifference blanketed Germany's Jews. Following publication of the *Nüremberg Gesetz,* open acts of hostility and bitter personal attacks against them turned to cold-blooded apathy. For many Germans, certainly for loyal Nazis, Jews simply ceased to exist as flesh-and-blood humans, remained only as more or less nettlesome statistics to be sorted, filed and discarded as quickly as disposal methods could be developed.

"I don't understand," Walter said while crossing Bornstrasse. "What did he mean, we're not German?"

They saw Eckert and friends at the corner, skirted around them to avoid trouble. Eckert didn't bother to look, the rest just snickered.

"Hey yids," one boy yelled, "go back to Jewland. You're not Germans. Get the hell out of Germany." They laughed in an ugly way, used obscene gestures and turned away, not interested in further harangue.

"Papa explained it. Dov says the Nazis passed the law so they can take everything from us."

"What for? We don't have much."

"Well, whatever we have, they found a way to take it."

"Can they kill us? Can they take our life, too?"

"Sure. No law needed. When they're ready to do it, they'll just do it."

"I wish I were going to America with you."

"Me too. Maybe when I get there my new parents will send for you and your family."

Walter raised his arms to the sky, a dreamy smile on his face. "Wouldn't that be great?"

School, too, was gloomy. An aura of embarrassment and self-doubt now hung over remaining teachers and their handful of students, a few still earnestly conjugating verbs, assimilating French, wrestling with geometric theorems in damp, unheated classrooms. All felt the change, an uneasy sense of total disconnection from familiar footings.

Their recent brush with terror had molded the sewer mates into a firm unit. During recess, they agreed to meet in the boiler room after school. The Grünbergs hesitated, but came. Soli Rabinowitz shared his chocolate bar. Brigitte Herz and Lisa Koerner joined the group. Brigitte's father, Isador, operated a furniture re-finishing shop in Oskar Schumann's building and, until recently, the Dortmund KPD's mimeograph machine. He churned out what Oskar wrote when there was money for ink and paper, gave his daughter, and whoever else could be persuaded, the dangerous job of distribution. At the moment both Isador and his machine were out of commission, the latter hidden in Dov Lifschitz's office, the former pissing blood, the result of incisive kicks to his kidneys administered by one of Böhm's trained technicians. Brigitte, "Gitte" to her friends, indoctrinated since childhood in Marxist rhetoric, remained steadfast to the cause. She and Lisa Koerner were inseparable, closer than sisters. Lisa's father, August, a skilled mechanic and, like Lifschitz, a disciple of the KPD's *Rote Frontkämpferbund*, the Red Fighters Front, repaired Herz's mimeograph machine when it broke down, which was often. He possessed other talents: how to renovate pistols, rifles, shotguns and explosive weapons. He could also manufacture useful objects such as bullets, fragmenting mines, booby traps, even bows and arrows, should need for those arise. Like Herz, Koerner was feeling poorly. During their recent stopover in Böhm's basement Heiko personally demonstrated the ease with which a person's nose breaks when tapped with a steel baton. Ever since, Koerner's breathing came in fits and starts. While her father recovered, Lisa performed what duties she could for the cause.

"Boiler room," whined Soli, hugging a frayed cardigan, "Nothing boiling in here, that's for sure."

Gitte didn't hide her irritation. "Stop whining, Soli, we have other problems. Horst, is it true? I hear you're going to America."

"You lucky dog," said Albert. "Man, would I like to go on that ship with you. When are you sailing?"

Horst hesitated, self-conscious about his good fortune. Then the excitement he felt ever since Clara's letter came, won out. "Dov told Oskar it might take a while. The American Embassy in Berlin has to send papers to an office in Stuttgart. After that they'll give me a visa."

"You're so lucky. I'd give anything to go to America. Papa could be a doctor again. I could study music at a real music school, listen to some great concerts." Albert slumped in despair.

"Can we still count on you? Until you go?" asked Lisa, her expression serious and all business. She had no time for dreams. Not now.

They wouldn't blame Horst if he quit. He was going to America, why screw it up just to hand out leaflets, scrawl slogans on walls and fences. Look what happened to their fathers, beaten up, put in prison, threatened every day of their lives. For what?

"You can count on me. It's for the cause," said Horst.

"The cause," Dov Lifschitz had once explained to his son David, "has nothing to do with government or politics. The revolution isn't about who runs the bureaucracy, who heads up this office or that. It has nothing to do with campaigns or policies. The real cause is with having and not having. The real cause is money. That's right, David, money. Don't let anybody tell you money doesn't buy everything. In fact, money does buy everything. It's a lot of garbage to say that money can't buy love, or happiness, or good health. Only poor people believe that. Wherever you go in the world, money is considered a great good. The people who have a lot of money are often considered good people because of all the good they might do with their money. It's sad, but these good people often do evil things because of the power their money gives them. They don't admit these things are evil since good people with good money couldn't possibly do evil things. They also insist that having no money makes people less good, makes them envious, leads them to complain endlessly about good people and their good money. That part is true. Few people have the kind of money that creates true power, so not only do they want to hang on to it, but increase it. If they could, they'd own it all."

"But what for?" asked David, unfamiliar with the concept of greed.

"If they owned all of it they would be in total control. Then they could do whatever they want, without any consequences."

"And Communists don't want money?"

"Sure they do. Unfortunately there are some Communists who think they're the only good people in the world and should therefore be entitled to all the money there is. Then, of course, *they* would have total power."

"We're Communists too, Papa. We don't think like that."

"No, David, we don't. Most Communists believe money and power should be spread around. Maybe not exactly the same for everybody, but enough so most people in the world have plenty to eat, a decent home, and some fun. A minority shouldn't control the majority. A lot of us are willing to fight to prevent that. That's our cause." David figured he understood.

"Count on me," said Horst. "The Nazis make things miserable because our fathers are Communists, but the Nazis aren't stupid. They know it's us kids who put up flyers and paint slogans on walls. Pretty soon they'll punish us for it. Nobody in the SA is going to say 'let's not bother Horst Schumann anymore because he's going to America.' It scares me, but as long as I'm still here I want to help."

Not all of them were sure what they would do if they were in his place. He was going to America. Why take a chance? But his explanation made them feel good.

It confirmed that their actions amounted to something. They didn't understand all the slogans they glued on kiosks, but their fathers were kind men, not vicious and cruel like the Nazis. The cause had to be right, worth taking risks for. So they believed.

"My father wants us to meet in his office," said David, stomping his feet and shaking the cold from his hands. He looked at his friends and the two girls. "He said it's important. He also said if anybody is afraid, that was okay, they don't have to come. Nobody will be angry. The time is Sunday morning at eight."

"Why Sunday morning?"

"Because most people are in church or still sleeping."

That made sense; the streets would be empty.

"Can't you tell us anything about the meeting?" asked Gitte.

"Papa thought you'd ask. You know the mimeo machine your father has been operating?"

"What about it?"

"It's in Dov's office now. He and Oskar will run it until your father and Lisa's father are okay again."

They understood. The fight would continue; nobody was quitting.

"I'll be there," said Solomon Rabinowitz.

"Me too," from Horst; then from all of them.

They felt proud. Their fathers were abused and their families threatened; their country said they weren't wanted, but somebody wanted and needed them. They had a cause.

"See you Sunday morning at eight." One by one they departed, turned toward home, quietly prayed they still had one.

16

In 1930, after receiving his Masters Degree, *magna cum laude*, from Georgetown University's prestigious School of International Studies, William Clay Jodel, Jr., Willie to friends and family, was certain he had the world by its tail. Young, reasonably rich and adequately handsome, Jodel was in proud possession of his first job, Administrative Assistant to the Honorable Jason Baggott, First Secretary in Berlin's important American Embassy. Now, only five years later, as he looked out of his fourth floor office window, Willie was convinced that what he had by the tail was a snarling tiger or, more likely, it was the other way around.

Jodel's view from the Embassy's upper floors on Bendler Strasse could be restful. When he first arrived, his eyes had feasted on lush expanses of Berlin's famed Tiergarten and, further on, Bellevue Castle's convoluted pergolas and porticos shimmering like a mirage in early autumn's icy blue. Lately, however, he saw only a desk piled high with stacks of files, each folder a maze of documents, opinions, petitions and demands leading to one objective: exit from Germany, entry into the United States.

He sighed. At the outset he thought of Berlin as sheer heaven, a paradise thoughtfully arranged for a carefree bachelor's earthly delights. The cabarets, the theaters, the romance of gazing at one's companion through *The Volle Pulle*'s candlelight were intoxicating to a young man conservatively raised. Nothing prepared him, or any of the Embassy personnel, for the profound changes of the past two years. Apprehensively, they witnessed the Nazi assumption of power; then, with mounting dismay, were horrified by book burnings, escalating bloodshed on city streets, the menacing attacks on all opposition and the murderous treatment of scapegoats, especially of Jews.

The Embassy noted that Willie's dossier included a "Graduate Seminar in Immigration Policies and Procedures." Secretary Baggott promptly handed him the sensitive job of dealing with high priority exit visas. At first they numbered only a few. Nearly anybody who wished to emigrate simply applied for papers, such applications routinely approved for emigrants with good connections or well-defined purposes. Since 1933, however, nothing was routine any longer. A trickle of visa petitions grew to a stream, became a raging torrent. High priority cases that required special handling multiplied at alarming rates.

Jodel considered himself fortunate not to work on the side of the building facing Matteus Kirche, where State's Visa and Passport Division handled run-of-the-mill applications. There, Jews of every description crowded waiting rooms from the moment doors opened until a sergeant-at-arms forcibly pushed them out in the late afternoon. Willie had no idea where they spent the night. When he passed by after working late, he saw dozens who leaned against building walls, cradled personal belongings, and apparently stood there until morning. He was told that police regulations forbade anyone to sit or sleep on sidewalks. Willie wondered if those regulations were enforced only on Bendler Strasse. The poor bastards, he thought, they don't even understand why they're standing in line. Only when they finally reached a clerk was it explained to them that a U.S. visa was merely a first step.

Last week the Germans had issued new and explicit regulations emanating from von Weizsäcker's Foreign Office. Ambassador Dodd, always deeply suspicious about Nazi edicts, called a meeting to clarify their potential impact on German-American relations.

"Mr. Baggott, I assume you have analyzed this newest remodeling of the emigration process as devised by those political geniuses on Wilhelm Strasse?" the Ambassador asked in his renowned scholarly manner.

"We have, sir, and we believe there is a hidden agenda."

"Which is?"

"If you don't mind," the First Secretary suggested, "I'd like Mr. Jodel to explain. His contacts in von Weizsäcker's office are impeccable. His conclusions appear to be logical and entirely plausible."

"By all means, Mr. Baggott. If you will, Mr. Jodel?"

"Of course, sir." Willie was pleased that he came prepared. "Under these new regulations all entrance visas to the U.S. approved by us must be submitted to Wilhelm Strasse. They want to check them out before they confirm and return them to us."

"This applies only to U.S. entry visas?" The Ambassador sounded disturbed.

"No sir, to all visas."

"To what purpose?"

Jodel hesitated. He was on tentative ground. Still, he believed his reasoning to be sound. He plunged on.

"I am convinced this is aimed chiefly at Jews."

"Ah!" Mr. Dodd sounded as if he expected something to that effect. "And the implications?"

"They are creating special categories. Not all visa applicants are to be treated alike. For example, visas for applicants holding foreign passports may be processed here in Berlin and issued by their own consulates."

"And German applicants?"

"Well, there it is, sir. Berlin has already established numerous regional offices and plans to open more. From now on, most German applicants must file visa applications regionally. A new bureau has also been opened in Stuttgart."

"What's the purpose of all this?"

"The way I see it, sir, is that Berlin is intensely interested in the financial status of everyone who wants to leave the country. It's simpler for regional offices to determine an applicant's assets. I've seen the information these offices request. If you'll pardon my cynicism, they're setting up a system to appropriate all such assets before they issue exit visas."

"Not everyone who wants to leave German is Jewish, Jodel. Not all Jews have money. What about those?"

"Regional offices may approve such visas."

"Then what's the Stuttgart office for?"

Jodel swallowed. "That one affects my desk, sir. Stuttgart was apparently established to administer an entirely separate category, what they call 'Special Visa Applications.'"

"Meaning?"

"Visa applicants with prominent sponsors, with business associations or political connections; anyone who is backed by foreign subsidy or funding; in short, anyone with special affiliations."

The Ambassador was puzzled. "Why in Stuttgart?"

"Nobody in their Foreign Office wants to go on record, but I've heard rumors. We're talking mostly about Jewish emigrants. The Germans think Jews with foreign connections, or those well established in financial circles, will try to remove their assets from Germany."

"A reasonable assumption, wouldn't you agree, Mr. Jodel?"

"Yes sir, precisely why they opened the Stuttgart office. They want to bring Jews with money or influence into what they call an *Untersuchungsstelle.*"

"A what?"

"A discreet place for...well...they call it an interview. Frankly, I see it as a cross-examination, away from the turmoil of Berlin and far less accessible to foreign journalists. The Nazis want to keep this under wraps as much as possible, at least for now. They know perfectly well which Jews have money, in Berlin or in any other large city. Under these new rules all such Jews must now go to Stuttgart and beg for exit visas. One can only imagine what goes on there. I'm sure those who have to go to Stuttgart will be a lot poorer when they leave."

"Hmm. Not much we can do about German internal affairs, gentlemen. Unfortunate, but that's the way it is," said Dodd. "I am deeply concerned, however, about applicants sponsored by American interests. Roughly, Jodel, how many such cases have we?"

"A desk full. As of today about four to five hundred."

"Keep me posted. I'd like a status report on my desk every other Friday. I may be able to exert pressure, especially where political involvement is a consideration."

"Of course, Mr. Ambassador."

"That reminds me, Willie," said Baggott, "would you come and see me for a moment."

The meeting had ended. In Baggott's office Jodel was handed a file, a clean one, obviously recent.

"Hate to add to your pile, but I've heard it said around here that if it's important, just Jodel." Willie grinned perfunctorily. "Forgive me, Willie. Anyway, please put this at the head of your list. It's Warren Luckman's deal. Illinois. Chairman, House Ways and Means, also Foreign Affairs. That says it all."

Willie scanned the documents. Horst Schumann, aged 12, son of Oskar Schumann, leather merchant, Weiherstrasse 4, Dortmund, to be adopted by Richard and Regina Malkin, Chicago, Illinois. Entry visa approved by Act of Congress, House Bill #A 03685083, duplicate enclosed, copy of confirmation from the Honorable Warren Luckman to Mr. And Mrs. Malkin in Chicago. Routine stuff.

"Everything seems in order, sir."

"Fine. Take care of it. Do your best to move it along."

Jodel went to his office, buzzed his secretary and handed her the file.

"Put this on the road, Sharon. A House Ways and Means deal if you want to be paid next month. Send the 'Documents Requested' sheet today, the one in German. Who knows how long it'll take at this point. The Nasties aren't speeding things up any, especially for Jews. Call Spencer in Hamburg. Have him notify Hapag that a draft for ticket disbursement has been issued in the name of Horst Schumann. That's the file name, Sharon, issued by…let's see…by Fidelity Travel, Inc., Chicago, Illinois. The voucher number is in the upper right hand corner. We'll advise Hapag about the departure date as soon as Stuttgart gives a 'go.' Oh Sharon, a brief note please to Luckman in Washington, copy to Baggott, that the Schumann matter is expedited. You know what to say. Thanks."

He sighed, looked wistfully over the city. No time to play. On to the next case.

◆   ◆   ◆

It was a festive time in Chicago. The Cubs had won twenty-one straight games and the National League pennant, a rare, unforgettable feat. Dick Malkin felt great, not just about the Cubs, of course. The Depression was grinding on, but less severely. Business was reasonably good and weather predictions for the World Series most favorable. All that was minor. Of vastly greater importance was the fact that Oskar Schumann had given his approval for the adoption of Horst. The news arrived two days ago.

"It's here," Clara yelled over the phone. "The letter. There's a letter. Come over." She was so excited she hung up immediately.

Dick called Rae. Together they drove to the Weiss place. Clara translated cautiously and with ease.

"Such sad, beautiful words," said Rae, "what a thoughtful man."

"A little *meschuggene*," said Clara, "but thoughtful, yes."

Hermann poured glasses of Mosel to toast the occasion then excused himself. Customers were waiting. Dick and Rae stopped at Luckman's downtown office, left the INS form and a note for Farber: "Dear Bert, We received permission to adopt the boy. Horst's father filled out the papers you requested as best he could. I'm sure you will personally want to send them to INS. If anything is not in order let me know. I'll take care of it. Thanks again. Yours, Dick."

Truly a festive time. The letter had come shortly before the Jewish New Year, Rosh Hashanah, 5696 by the ancient Hebrew Calendar. At Temple Sholom, holding hands, Rae and Dick beamed throughout the service. The Rabbi was solemn, as usual.

> As we celebrate this joyous holiday let us not forget, not even for a moment, that thousands of our fellow Jews are being persecuted by the Nazi terror sweeping over Germany. I know you've heard me say it before. You're probably a little tired of hearing it. There he goes, you're saying to yourself right now, talking about German Jews. Yes, I am, and I will talk about them again and again and again. I will talk about them until you and the rest of America's Jews come to their rescue from Hitler's madhouse and make it possible for them to live in dignity and celebrate Rosh Hashanah with us in freedom.

He had affected everyone, none more so than the Malkins who felt deep satisfaction because they were doing their part. Afterward on the temple steps the Rabbi greeted his congregation, wished everyone "*yom tov*," a happy holiday.

"Congratulations," the Rabbi said, "*mazel tov* on becoming new parents."

"You've heard already?"

"You know Farber. When he does a *mitzvah* he wants the world to be in on it. Anything to elect his boss."

"It couldn't happen without him, Rabbi."

"I'm just kidding. It's great; one less Jew for those *golems* to eat. Congratulations to both of you. Don't forget, Confirmation is in June. I expect young Malkin to give a good speech. And in English!"

On the way home Rae was quiet.

"Penny for your thoughts," said Dick.

"Nothing, sweetheart, just thinking about this and that."

How could she tell him that the Rabbi had lit a bright flame? This and that? Hah! She was thinking about Confirmation, about the reception she would give. Where should they hold it? Where would she buy the boy's suit, at Field's or at Carson, Pirie? What kind of invitations to print? What should she wear, for heaven's sake? Won't it just be grand!! Her sister's children were confirmed already, those events nearly forgotten. She would have the glory all to herself.

"Happy *Rosh Hashanah* Dick," she said, beaming, and in the middle of traffic she kissed him on the cheek.

17

Dov Lifschitz lived and conducted his business in Dortmund's courthouse district. Attorneys with important clients like *Hammerwerk Hoesch, Dortmunder Union Brückenbau*, or one of the prosperous breweries, occupied elegant suites in Victorian-style mansions near the Hall of Justice, the *Landgericht*. Lifschitz's clientele would have been uncomfortable in that milieu. Dov had no objections to attractive surroundings, but a choice address with suitable décor was of no consequence to him. He spent most of his hard-earned resources on food for his family and the best cigarettes that money could buy. Whatever remained went to "the cause." His modest flat on the sixth floor of a worn brownstone on Holzhof Strasse 26 was a refuge and contact point for what remained of Dortmund's left wing community.

Pflug cautiously monitored activities on Holzhof Strasse 26. In his early leadership days, surveillance of Lifschitz's associations resulted in a few denunciations and arrests, but when the lawyer's appointments slowed to a trickle, vigilance was reduced. Pflug sometimes wondered where old Commies met these days. Party intelligence remained unaware of the secret entrance to Holzhof Strasse 26.

Lifschitz's building fronted Martin Luther Evangelist School, a branch of the Church of Peace directly across the street. The school had two entrances, one on Holzhof, the other on Schwanenstrasse. The latter gave access to a basement where, for economic reasons, the school and Holzhof Strasse 26 shared a boiler room, security lockers and coal storage bins. A basement door led to Dov's building, a back stairway to its main hallway. The door could be locked from both sides; keys were available to tenants only.

When he rented the apartment in 1928, Lifschitz stored a few belongings in the locker and promptly forgot them. A janitor took care of the coal. Not until the early thirties, as attacks against Communists intensified, did Dov appreciate the opportunity to meet associates with less risk of detection. The family and his paying clients used the main entrance. A few friends, exercising unflagging caution, entered through the basement and then only when absolutely necessary.

Lifschitz's office, part of his living quarters, featured another convenience. The flat covered half of the building's top floor; the other half was used as attic storage for tenant belongings, for larger pieces like sofas, broken chairs and worn-out mattresses. Spaces were partitioned with cheap lumber and provided with doors, which no one bothered to lock. Dov realized he had never seen anyone in the attic. "The Den," as it came to be known, was used exclusively in dire circumstances, when other hiding places were unavailable.

It was Sunday morning. A chill rain slanted against sidewalks, puddled at street corners and reflected off streetcar tracks, illuminating them like forlorn silver ribbons in a bleak expanse of oil slicks and concrete. Church bells pealed dissonantly in the dank air, a mournful, gloomy summons to worship. Promptly at eight the Grünbergs, outfitted in rain gear, made their cautious way over the courtyard's slickened cobblestones. David Lifschitz went to the basement door, motioned them up the stairway and remained until everyone had arrived. Horst and Oskar brought Isador and Gitte Herz. Isador was ill but wanted to come. They made sure the street was clear, entered the schoolyard one by one. By eight-thirty all those expected were present. Hannah brewed tea, served it in glasses along with a plateful of cookies. Voices were kept low.

"No speech," Dov said. "You know why you're here. They want to destroy civil liberties. Today it's Jews, tomorrow gypsies. Maybe the day after it's anyone left-handed, except left-handed Nazis of course. We don't want to give up our freedom or our beliefs, at least not without a fight. I'm not sure what we can win. Maybe nothing at all."

"Then why are we here, Dov?" asked Lisa Koerner. "My father will want to know."

"Ask him. Why does he keep sticking his neck out? Why doesn't he settle for making a living? No problem, he's a good machinist."

"I guess he thinks just making a living isn't enough."

"That's why we're here, Lisa."

Fifteen of them crowded the room. Most sat on the floor, quiet, thoughtful, uncertain of a commitment to action, but also reluctant to be left out. The Grünbergs huddled together, silent and apprehensive. Dov introduced two strangers, Peter Bergmann and his fifteen-year-old son, Dieter, both on the run for printing and distributing leaflets, but willing to help before they attempted to cross the Dutch border. Schmuel Rabinowitz straddled a chair, nervous, testy, always ready to do battle. Horst, David and Soli sprawled on a rug with the priest, Father Thalmann, casual in an old sweater.

"I outlined a poster," said Oskar. "One page. It tells Germans in simple language why the Nüremberg Laws are dangerous for the country."

"You think anybody cares?" posed Lev.

"Maybe some do, but who knows? Enough to resist? Possible, but certainly not openly."

"Read it," said Schmuel.

Oskar had printed:

FELLOW GERMANS!
THE NUREMBERG LAWS ARE NOT MEANT TO
ENSLAVE ONLY JEWS BUT **ALL** GERMAN CITIZENS BECAUSE
THEY GIVE THE STATE THE RIGHT TO TELL YOU:

* WHO YOU CAN LIVE WITH!
* WHERE YOU CAN WORK!!
* WHO YOU CAN MARRY!!!
* WHAT YOU CAN DO WITH YOUR PROPERTY!!!!
* HOW TO LIVE YOUR LIFE!!!!!

<u>**RESIST THESE LAWS. LET YOUR VOICES BE HEARD.**</u>

SAVE GERMANY! SAY NO TO THE NUREMBERG LAWS!!

Peter Bergman applauded. "Good, really good. Short and to the point."

Restraining his temper, Lev Grünberg got up from the floor. "They'll be furious," he said, visibly upset. "You remember Pflug's admonition? Frankly, I'm sick of being beaten up."

"Lev. Nobody here can make you do anything. You want to quit? Quit! We're not Nazis. There's no punishment if you change your mind. We all know the risk. You get caught, you get hurt. Most of us know what that feels like. Decide fast. Fight for your convictions or leave."

Lev avoided Dov's eyes to stay clear of dissension. A skilled physician devoted to healing, he grew tired of endless political skirmishes and useless sentiments. He and all the men in the room had jeopardized their lives more than once for their convictions, proudly wore their battle scars with a sense of fulfillment. Then their children had joined in, naively attracted to exploits officially forbidden. What was life without a little danger, as long as it was kept in check? The two years since the Nazi rise to power taught them a different, more sobering lesson; the perils were out of control, had become deadly. The children were no longer motivated only by filial devotion.

"Is there a plan?" Schmuel wanted to know.

"Assuming you approve Oskar's poster," said Dov, "we'll run off what's left of our paper, about five hundred sheets. The children will have fifty each and post them after midnight. I'll take Peter with me to cover city center. The whole job shouldn't require more than an hour. It's probably the last time we'll have a chance to do this. Talk it over, friends. Remember, no hard feelings if you say no."

The finality of Dov's remarks struck home. "It's probably the last time we'll have a chance to do this" he had said. No doubt he was right. In the end, after lengthy discussion and voicing of concerns, nobody wanted to be a quitter, not if this was to be a last effort for the cause.

Lisa Koerner cut the mimeograph stencil. The machine was set up on the kitchen table, filled with fresh ink. In less than an hour copies were run off, folded discretely into newspapers and distributed along with glue bottles. They left as cautiously as they had arrived. Afterward, Lifschitz flushed the original down the toilet and dragged the machine into The Den. He hid it under old legal files, recognized the absurdity of the act. No pretext was needed if the Nazis wanted to eliminate him.

That night Horst covered the Burg Wall area, pasted fliers on the Post Office, the Museum, the Petri Kirche and the Olympia Theater. He glued six sheets to the entrance of the Horst Wessel School. He wanted Günter to see the forbidden flyers when he came to school, wanted his warped mind to grasp who had posted them.

◆   ◆   ◆

Paul Terhoven, Nord-Westfalen's *Gauleiter*, was exasperated. The day had degenerated from mere anxiety to intense frustration. Forty-two years old, he had ceaselessly labored on Hitler's behalf since 1926. He had fought for the Party in the streets, spent time in jail and dedicated his life to the movement. He had killed for the Führer, was wounded time and again in brawls with Communists when that scum still showed its face. He had earned his *Gauleiter* stripes. The Party owed him plenty.

Like most *Gauleiters* in the country, Terhoven established lucrative fiscal relationships, not difficult to manage in his highly industrialized district if done cautiously. Such special compensation merely followed precedent. Göring had Benz and BMW connections, not to mention rake-offs on all aircraft contracts. The fortune old comrade Ley skimmed from Labor Front funds was no secret. Where was the harm? As long as the Party maintained public trust, no one got hurt. It was only important not to be greedy. He thought he was fair with the local daily, the *Essener Nationalzeitung*, had steered advertising its way and secured its publisher favored status on the cost of newsprint. In return, he demanded only a miniscule percentage of gross receipts and a decent donation to the Winter Relief Collection, fully half of which he forwarded diligently to Party headquarters. Who, then, was the troublemaker?

This morning he received a distasteful note to advise him that as of this date and on Reichsminister Göring's orders, all the newspaper's financial documents were to be forwarded to, and approved by, accountants at *Reichwerke Hermann Göring*. Terhoven controlled several other enterprises, so the loss of revenue didn't bother him. He was more annoyed at losing face with Göring, not a man to provoke in matters of money. Best to send Hermann a note, apologize for unwarranted conjectures and suspicions and suggest that this was merely an unfortunate mistake. Not that it would fool Hermann for a minute, but protocol had to be served. However, this latest mess in Dortmund was something else, an annoying, worrisome situation. He would have to go to Dortmund and talk to Rollo. He decided also to see Böhm, but confidentially. He rang for his secretary.

"Ask Otto to bring the car. I'm going to Dortmund. Phone Pflug and tell him I'm coming. Also call Böhm, but make sure he's alone. Tell him to meet me at Café Grafenhof at eight this evening and to keep our meeting confidential. Let me know when you've confirmed arrangements."

When Terhoven arrived in Dortmund's Party headquarters in the late afternoon, Pflug was waiting for him.

"You wasted no time, Paul."

The Gauleiter did not remove his black overcoat and visored hat.

"Let's go where walls don't have ears, Rollo. I could use a schnapps and a decent beer, if you don't mind."

The SS chauffeur drove them to the Rathaus, polite amenities exchanged during the ride. The dimly lit Rathskeller had small, cozy alcoves, available to preferred customers. Pflug was well known, taken immediately to quarters reserved for dignitaries. The waiter served quickly and withdrew, closing the door.

"So, Rollo, please explain what this is about."

"You've heard, I assume."

"I didn't come for the beer."

"Who told you?"

"What's the difference? The damn things were apparently posted all over Dortmund." He slammed the table with his fist. "You promised there would be no more Communist shit. You've embarrassed me, you've embarrassed the Party and you've embarrassed the Führer, not to mention yourself. Goddamn it, Rollo, if Himmler hears about it we might both wind up with a can in our hands, collecting for Winter Relief. What the hell is going on with you?"

Pflug licked his lips. "My mistake, Paul. After Hitler left I let them go with a strong warning. I thought they understood, but they don't give up easy."

"Those bastards have a death wish. High time we accommodate them. Because of certain policies I won't go into, we can't afford noisy incidents right now, but next year is different. By the end of January I want that entire pack of rats off the street, in fact off the face of the earth. Do I make myself clear?"

"Yes, Paul."

"Good!" Terhoven emptied his glass, leaned in, his eyes cold and probing. "My next question. You've given some thought to my offer? In light of this stupid episode I'm not even certain you're qualified."

"Then why offer it to me?"

"I'm not sure; maybe because you're Gustav Pflug's son. Gustav was my friend, a true comrade in arms. Gustav and I went through a lot together."

"I've heard the stories, Paul. It doesn't mean I'm the man for the job."

Terhoven studied him thoughtfully. "O.K., let's be honest, Rollo, you don't want it, right? You want nothing to do with something as…how shall I put it…as disciplinary as our Security Service, the *Sicherheitsdienst*. Correct?"

Pflug searched for the right expression, aware that he was on dangerous ground. "My training goes in other directions."

"Your training? Ah yes Rollo, naturally, your training. You still want to be a teacher, right? A mathematics teacher?"

"Some day, when things have settled down, I'd like to go back to the classroom."

"Of course, when things have settled down. However, I don't believe they will settle down, my friend. Not in the foreseeable future. In the meantime we must practice vigilance. Vigilance, Pflug! You want schools to teach in? Better destroy the enemies who work hard to tear them down, along with everything else in our country. Can you understand that?"

"I hear what you're saying, Paul. Please don't misinterpret about the *Sicherheitsdienst*. I appreciate your offer. I want to serve the Führer, but I truly believe many fellow Party members, *Parteigenossen*, are more suitable."

"Aha, I see. Well, you're right, you're absolutely right of course. You should stay exactly where you are. You're doing a good job. Except for little mistakes like this, a really fine job. I'm sure I'll find someone else." He glanced at his watch. "I'm so sorry. Wish we could talk longer, but it's late, I must go. I have another appointment. Please get your Bolshevists off the street. I don't want to hear about them again."

"I'll take care of it."

"Yes, Rollo, I'm positive you will."

On the way back to headquarters they pretended to be old friends, but their relationship had changed. Pflug was keenly aware that Terhoven had dismissed him as a future ally and would immediately search for a replacement. For the briefest moment he wondered how he, in Dortmund, and Terhoven, in Essen, had learned about the flyers simultaneously. That insight dawned effortlessly, along with the probable identity and nature of Terhoven's next appointment.

Böhm arrived at Café Grafenhof before Terhoven. He recognized that this impending meeting was a turning point in his career. The uneasiness he had experienced when he telephoned Terhoven earlier had disappeared. Pflug was warned about releasing those contemptible misfits. By now Rollo would have the flyers ripped off and forgotten the whole episode, at least until the next incident; then he might, or might not, do something. In the meantime, Bolshevists laughed up their sleeves, probably planned a new assault already. He was certain Terhoven would want to know.

"Böhm, good to see you. Thanks for calling so promptly."

"I thought it was important."

"It was, believe me, it was."

Terhoven secured a table in a quiet alcove. They ordered dinner, made small talk until served.

"I'll get to the point. This is bad business. Communist activities must stop. Too many enemies of the Reich still running around."

"I agree."

"Yes, well. Pflug is a fine man, Böhm, a devoted Party member, a patriotic German. You are not to forget that."

"Of course."

"He has a problem with…well, let's call it corrective discipline. Isn't that true?"

"Yes, it is."

"Here's my proposal. I hereby appoint you to Nord-Westfalen's *Sicherheitsdienst*. You will remain in Pflug's command and work for me under cover, at least for the time being. You will report all actions against the State, compile a list of suspected enemies; in short, anything that might damage our Führer."

"I appreciate your confidence in me. I want to thank you."

"Fine. I think you'll do just fine. Your first assignment is to supply the names of those Bolshevik Jew traitors, the ones who posted that filthy propaganda."

"I know most of them. Do you want them…taken care of?"

Terhoven smiled. "Not yet, not quite yet. Westfalen will celebrate the holiday season harmoniously. After the holidays, the latest by the middle of January, I want those names on my desk. When I send word, you will deal with them properly. I don't want us to be bothered with them again. I will give you a private number where one of my staff can be contacted at any time. Don't mess this up. I want it taken care of before the pause."

Although Heiko was well informed, he had never heard of "the pause." Terhoven explained. "There's talk in Reichsminister Himmler's office about restricting procedures until the Olympics are finished. We're hosting foreign visitors, newspaper and magazine writers. Those writers would like nothing better than to spread their ugly lies about the Third Reich in their Jew-controlled press. For a few more months we'll deal with local trash as quietly as possible. I'm sure you understand."

"Perfectly."

Terhoven claimed another appointment and left before he finished his meal. He had accomplished his aims. His friend Gustav's son kept his job, but under close supervision. Böhm was an invisible hammer, precisely what the Dortmund office needed. Terhoven despised Böhm for betraying a comrade. Not like it was done in the old days, but that was then, this was now. Now the stakes were higher, much higher. There was a world to be conquered. No misguided collection of Communist Jews was allowed to get in the way. Terhoven leaned back in his car seat and smiled with self-satisfaction.

"When we come to Essen, Otto," he said to his chauffeur, "let's stop and have a beer."

◆   ◆   ◆

The posters were removed within twenty-four hours, but not before thousands of citizens read them and wondered how they were distributed without detection. The conspirators braced for retaliation, exercised extreme caution before they entered their homes. Oskar decided to conduct out-of-town business. He needed money for life's necessities and for fuel for the Opel so he could reach customers. Horst gladly kept him company, hoped the trip would bring them as much luck as the last one, the time when his arms were broken. School was out of the question. He was too vulnerable there. With funds depleted, supplies and heat were no longer affordable. Whoever wanted an education pursued it on his own.

They drove to Hörde and called on Reinholt Bechtel, a long-standing customer.

"Schumann. I see you brought your helper. How's business?"

"Not good, Reinholt. You're an old friend. I don't have to tell you why."

"Right, Oskar. The problem is what to do about it? What can I tell the sons of bitches? What's the answer when they warn me not to deal with Jews?"

"I'm not sure what to tell you, Reinholt. I understand your position. On the other hand, you and I have done business together for…well, for over fifteen years. Doesn't that count for something?"

"Yes, it does, Oskar, but things are different now. Take a look at Schmidt's butcher shop on the other side of the market. Schmidt is watching us right now. See him making notes? Tonight he'll tell his pals that Schumann the Jew came around to visit old Bechtel. Sure as hell tomorrow I'll get a visit, depend on it; maybe a stone through the window. Who knows?"

"As bad as that? Even in a town as small as this?"

"It's worse. Lefkov had to close, the only decent tailor around. I think he went to Holland. There's a sign on Meyer's hardware store, "Store for Sale.""

"Isn't anyone in this community willing to speak out for old friends and neighbors?"

"Speak out? Against the Nazis? Come on, Oskar, you know better than that. They do what they want. Last week they fired the two sisters, the teachers, the Rubens women, Leah from the Realschule, the other one, I don't remember her name, from the Volksschule. Both my children had Leah for math. They're gone. I don't know where they went, either."

"It's not just Jews, Reinholt. They're getting rid of anybody who doesn't fit into their plans, you know that."

"They're getting rid of a lot of things, like my money, Oskar. If it's not a collection for Winter Relief it's for the Workers' Front or the War Veterans. Always something. Since Hitler arrived in the picture I work twice as hard for half the money."

"Speaking of money…"

"Oskar, I know. You've been patient. I appreciate it. I'll buy two hides. If you don't mind, deliver them around the back. The less that butcher bastard knows, the better. I'll pay what I owe you, I think it's sixty Marks. Then I'm afraid we have to say good-bye. I'm sorry, old friend, but I have to think about my family."

"A sad ending, Reinholt. I hope it's not for long."

"Me too, friend. I'll keep my fingers crossed. For all of us."

Before he headed home, Oskar called on customers in Schüren, Berghofen, and Wellinghofen. Bechtel's money was all he collected. The shoemakers were courteous, but ill at ease. They busied themselves, asked him to please come another time, avoided looking at him, and said it was the holidays, that they had spent all their money.

Horst couldn't stand it, felt miserable watching his father rejected again and again. The Opel's heater died, adding more discomfort. In Hacheney they stopped at Ludwig Holzer's repair shop, but found it closed.

"Too bad," said Oskar, bravely trying to hide the day's disappointments. "You would have liked Ludwig, a strange man, a dwarf, but an artist and a gentleman. Well, maybe some day. You know what? We've worked hard. I think we deserve a treat. How about something sweet and hot?"

"I'd like that, Papa."

They found a small café, ordered hot chocolate and cake, topped with whipped cream. The table was covered with linen, the service gracious, a holiday feeling warming the winter chill.

"It's nice to be here with you, Horst, with a clean tablecloth and a pleasant waiter." He watched as his son ladled dollops of cream into his cup, delighted in the luxury.

"I used to have hot chocolate at Café Corso."

"I wondered if your would remember."

"How could I ever forget, Papa?"

Oskar felt the blow. He knew his son was furious with him for putting him into the orphanage. That was to be expected, but at this moment, after their long, strenuous day together, he heard something else, a deep need to breech the awful desolation of their past. Oskar never intended to cause his children pain. Despite his obvious neglect of them, he never doubted that he loved them, deeply. Yet he had lost his daughter and abandoned his son. During frequent bouts of melancholy he often lingered on his failure as a parent and tried to understand the reason for his blunders. Was his such a relentless, overwhelming need to ameliorate mankind, no matter what the cost? Oskar resisted an urge to undermine his sense of duty, but deep down he suspected a different motivation: his emotions were so crippled by Toni's death that all he yearned for, from then on, was a cause, intellectual gratification, abstract political rewards. Even at this very instant, as he regarded his responsive, thoughtful child, he didn't know the answer, not absolutely. The moment was precious; he knew he must not let it pass.

"Your mother, Horst, do you remember her?"

The boy looked at him, his dark eyes huge, his lips compressed, holding back tears.

"Yes, Papa, I remember her. She was beautiful."

"I loved Toni very much."

"Yes, Papa, I believe that. We both did."

To invoke Toni's name, for the first time acknowledging her presence, if only in memory, genuinely moved them and no longer did they feel quite so apart. A weight began to lift and their hearts felt lighter. Nothing could change the pain of their past or alter their uncertain future. They had performed only a small act, a pulse beat in their seasons, but they had finally reached out to each other and found a response.

When they came home, a letter from Stuttgart had arrived in the mail. It bore the imprint of the Ministry of Foreign Affairs beneath an engraved eagle, clutching a swastika.

Stuttgart, 15 November 1935

Horst Schumann
c/o Oskar Schumann
Weiherstrasse 4
Dortmund

Re: Horst Schumann

On 2 November 1935 this office received from the Embassy of the United States of America notification of your request to emigrate to that country, together with an entry visa granted under provisions of an action originated in the Congress of the United States of America.

Exit documents and passport may be issued only on receipt of the following:

1. A notarized copy of the applicant's Certificate of Birth.

2. A notarized statement, by a licensed physician, that the applicant is free of communicable diseases. This statement is pursuant to agreements between the government of Germany and the government of the United States of America and, if not furnished, will invalidate the application.

3. Six copies of Horst Schumann's photograph, regulation passport size, headshot only, 6X6 cm.

4. An original, notarized statement, signed by the director of the *Krieswirtschaftsrat,* (Kreis Dortmund), certifying total personal assets (bank accounts, real estate, personal property, and so forth) of the applicant.

5. A notarized statement by the guardian/s of the minor, Horst Schumann, that they are in full accord with the emigration of that minor to the United States of America.

On receipt and approval of the above documents, a request for the personal appearance in this office of said applicant, Horst Schumann, may be issued. Following that appearance, the applicant may be issued a valid German passport and a certificate entitling the applicant to an exit visa. Arrangements as to the date and location for issuance of such exit visa are made at the applicant's personal appearance in this office.

All documents listed above must be received in this office on, or before, 15 December 1935. Late delivery will invalidate the application.

A copy of this letter has been sent to Mr. William Jodel, The Embassy of the United States of America, Bendlerstrasse 18, Berlin. That office has guaranteed passage to the United States of America on receipt of exit approval.

Heil Hitler,

Dietrich Hartung
Office of Special Visas

The precious letter in front of them, father and son beamed at each other across the kitchen table.

"I'm so happy for you, Horst. It's going to happen. You're going to America!" Together with his happiness, Oskar felt a terrible sadness in his heart, already dreaded the loss, but vowed not to voice those lonely feelings. The boy's safe departure was all that counted. Nothing else mattered.

Much remained to be done and precious little time left to do it. They knew that arousing authorities with yesterday's agitating flyers acutely endangered Horst's exodus. "We shouldn't have put them up," Oskar said worriedly, "not at this time."

Horst, full of anticipation and excitement, objected. "I'm glad we did, Papa. Later, it wouldn't have meant anything."

That was true. Yes, it was important. "Still," Oskar said ruefully, "if I had considered more carefully…well…it's done. Only the future counts now. We need to see Dov. He has experience with documents."

They talked into the night, planning, wishing, and supporting each other. It had been a special day, a wonderful, meaningful day.

18

As a child, Pflug was attracted to symmetry, responded most vigorously to balanced and stable environments. He could walk a tightrope before he was three and juggle small chairs at the age of five. His wood block buildings, delicately proportioned, always towered above those of kindergarten playmates. He was drawn to science by its insistence on empirical evidence, to higher mathematics by its inexorable assertion of principle. He met Frederika at a Freiburg student party. While others ate and drank, she tinkered on a small spinet in an adjacent room, earnestly scanning the sheet music, a Bach fugue. He was instantly attracted to her looks, the elegance with which she bent her slim body to the keyboard. He found irresistible the way she shook black bangs from her eyes, as he loved the discernible harmony between the woman and her music, strong, complex, profoundly compatible. Until recently the fabric of their common life remained unimpaired, had withstood the strains of social and political unrest. Not until Rollo exchanged the classroom for a slot in the Party bureaucracy did an occasional uneasiness, a disquieting shadow, intrude on their relationship. Rollo had been in a foul mood since yesterday.

Tonight's dinner was particularly cheerless as both children picked up on their father's sour disposition. Rika knew Rollo approached a crisis. The posters about the Nüremberg Laws had made him furious. She sensed that he came to a decision about the *Sicherheitsdienst*, but right now all he needed was a sympathetic ear. He sat in the kitchen, distractedly polishing his boots.

"Terhoven was in Dortmund yesterday."

"About the flyers?"

"Yes. He heard about what happened at the same time I did. I'm not positive who told him, but I think it was Heiko."

"Oh god, I hope not."

"Who else would have the temerity to call Terhoven?"

"But Rollo, I don't understand. Why would he do that? Terhoven has always been your friend. Why would Heiko take a chance? What's in it for him?"

"How about the job Terhoven offered me? The *Sicherheitsdienst* appointment?" Rollo hesitated. He meant to erase all doubt from his mind before giving her the news, but he also didn't want to keep her waiting. "I turned it down,

Rika. Terhoven didn't say much, but I think he knew I would." He held his boots to the light, admired their shine. "Actually, I think he had already picked someone else."

"Oh god, Rollo, you can't mean what I'm thinking."

"If you're thinking Heiko, I'm afraid you might be right. My good buddy, Heiko. 'Every pot finds a lid', as the saying goes. Fits the job perfectly, wouldn't you say?"

Rika despised Böhm. He represented the worst of the new order, narrow-minded, brutal, an enforcer. She also understood why Rollo chose him as adjutant. He performed chores his boss couldn't stomach.

"Has Heiko said anything to you?"

"No. I'm not positive I'm right. Just a feeling I have. Something about him was different today, an attitude, a kind of cocksure strut. My guess is he'll be working under cover. Heiko has always considered me soft on Communists. If he had his way they'd all be dead long ago. After the flyer thing I think that's going to be his job, hatchet man for Terhoven, keep an eye on Pflug and kill Commies."

"Without telling you?"

"If he's working for Terhoven he doesn't have to tell me anything. To whom would I complain?"

Each day Roland and Frederika Pflug understood more clearly the direction in which their government moved. In the beginning they trusted the Führer, in the belief that Germany's pride would be restored, the country returned to political stability and economic greatness. Rollo abandoned his career, his place in the classroom, to make that dream come true. Despite misgivings, Rika stood by his side. Had they done the wrong thing? The dream eroded all too quickly. Now military parades and saber rattling, corruption and murderous denunciations, rampant killing and torture raised their ugly heads and, most likely, the specter of war.

"Be careful, my dearest man. Please, for our sake, be very careful. For me, for us."

"I'd better be careful," he agreed, and quietly thought "or Heiko might send me to Dachau."

◆　　　◆　　　◆

Dov Lifschitz could not be reached. Oskar telephoned him relentlessly, but for two days and nights no one answered. Oskar grew frantic. Without the lawyer's know-how and connections the task of putting the documents together in a short time would be overwhelming. Two precious days had gone by already. He stayed close to the phone. Lifschitz called on the third night.

"Oskar? Dov."

"Dov! God, am I glad to hear from you! It's two in the morning. Are you all right? Where are you? What's happening?"

"Not now, Oskar. Meet me in an hour at my place. Use the basement. Be careful. Don't let anyone see you come in." He hung up.

Oskar parked the Opel a block away. Schwanenstrasse looked deserted. He scurried into the basement. Dov locked the door behind him, hurried up the stairway.

"In the den, Oskar."

An oil lamp made a tiny pool of light.

"For god's sake, what is it, Dov?"

"They picked up Rabinowitz. I took Hannah and David to Bonn for a couple of days. When we came back I called Schmuel. Wanted to know if he'd heard anything. They arrested him."

"Oh my god!"

"Emma answered, hysterical. The Nazis broke in, caught him naked. He fought. You know Schmuel. They knocked him cold, smashed the furniture, hit Emma and Soli and dragged Schmuel into a car.

"Oh god! Why Schmuel?"

"I don't know but I'll find out tomorrow. Not just for Schmuel, for all of us."

"Who's going to tell you?"

"I know somebody at police headquarters. Jessen, Hans Jessen, a Civil Service inspector. Used to be politically active in Weimar days. Now he's just an old guy with a gambling habit. Wrote some bad checks to cover debts. I had his case killed a month ago. He owes me. Lay low until I find out more. Send Horst out of the house, any place where it's safe. Call Grünberg, Koerner and Herz. Get their kids out, too, and find a safe place for them. Who the hell knows what's on Pflug's mind."

Oskar realized his timing was terrible but he had to tell Lifschitz about the letter from Stuttgart.

"No problem with the birth certificate," said Dov. "So far they don't deny we've been born. As soon as it's safe I'll make a copy. I'm a notary, or at least I was yesterday. Grünberg will issue the health certificate, assuming he's still alive to do it. What else?"

"The pictures."

"Easy. No passport studios for Horst. Too public. I know a kid, Avram Levi. His mother was a client. He's terrific with a camera. He's done work for comrades. I'll arrange it. What else?"

"A statement about what Horst owns, some kind of document from the District Economic Council.

"Aha, that one! The bastards. Exactly what I predicted. They're going to strip us naked before they let us go. If they let us go."

"Horst doesn't own a penny."

"Let me see what I can do. You have money?"

"Fifty Marks."

"Right, Schumann, you're a regular millionaire, like the rest of us. Anything else?"

"A statement that I agree to his emigration. Notarized."

"I'll write and notarize it. When does the whole *megillah* have to be in Stuttgart?"

"On or before December fifteen."

"Oy, so soon. We'll make it. One of us has to be in America to let them know what's going on here. You're too dumb, Schumann, better it should be your son. Go home. Watch yourself. Call our comrades; send the children out of the house. I don't know where, but someplace hidden. I'll be in touch tomorrow, assuming they don't find me first." He turned out the lamp. On Schwanenstrasse, Oskar headed toward the Opel. Lifschitz hurried in the opposite direction, toward the ghetto.

When his father told him the news, Horst was shaken, but calmed down immediately. He knew exactly what to do. "Call them, Papa, call them now. We can go to the mines. I've been there more than once." He described the abandoned colliery he and Walter had investigated. "It's not great, Papa, but it's out of the way. Safe enough until you find out what's happening. Believe me, we will be fine."

Oskar telephoned the others early in the morning. They refused to believe his story, yelled and cried over the phone. Precious time was wasted until all parents understood that it was vital for the children to be in hiding and that the mines might be a useful solution. He instructed all of them to be in the parking lot of the Heilige-Geist-Kirche at six in the evening. "It's not far from there to the Zcheche Tremonia mines," he told them.

When Walter stopped by to see Horst later in the day, he begged to go too. "Nobody is at school anymore. It's too cold. Please, Horst, I want to come with you."

"Why not?" Horst asked his father. "Maybe we'll need a messenger. The Nazis don't know Walter. His father isn't a Communist. It's a lot safer for Walter than for us." To have an innocuous messenger for the next few days was valuable for them all.

Oskar turned to his son's friend. "We leave shortly before six, Walter. Clear it first with Yetta, she might not approve. If you come, bring warm clothes, a blanket and food."

"You know what it's like," Horst added, "we've been there."

Walter had not forgotten their last visit. "Remember what you said, Horst, when I asked you why we were going?"

"Yes, I do."

"You said, 'I think it's coming. I've seen it coming for a long time.' That's what you said."

Horst fingered his pocketknife, Czerny's image clearly in mind. "I hate to say it," he answered, "but it looks like it's here. Look what happened to Schmuel. We're all in danger now."

◆   ◆   ◆

Dove reached Hans Jessen at noon.

"Hans. This is Lifschitz."

A long silence. "Dov? Just a moment." The sound of the phone being moved, then Jessen's voice came on, lowered. "Where are you?"

"A pay phone."

"You know the *Kneipe* on Inselstrasse, right behind Schüchtermann?"

"'Zum Jäger?' Yes."

"Meet me at twelve thirty."

"I'll be there."

They took a booth at the back, out of earshot of other customers.

"Thanks for coming, Hans."

"Least I can do. You saved my ass."

"What's going on at headquarters? They snatched one of my friends."

"I know. Rabinowitz. I asked around. But first, Dov…"

"What?"

"I'm up for retirement. If they find out who told you…"

"I'm not stupid."

"No, of course not." Jessen tugged nervously on his gray mustache. "It's Böhm. Somebody from the office saw Terhoven and Böhm together at the Grafenhof. Real close, in serious conversation."

"When?"

"The day after you…after somebody put up those Nüremberg posters."

"Does Pflug know?"

"Not sure. I think Böhm ordered Rabinowitz arrested without asking Pflug. One of the guys on the SA detail bragged around, said it was high time a few Bolshevik Jew heads were broken."

"You think he's after all of us?"

"I don't know. Böhm is unpredictable and he's vicious. We know that, so yes, sure, but right now? I just don't know."

"Why not right now?"

"The word around headquarters is that rough stuff is called off until after the Olympics, when the visitors are gone."

"I see. Makes sense, except what about Rabinowitz?"

"I can only guess. I have a hunch Terhoven put Böhm on *Sicherheitsdienst*." Lifschitz went cold. *Sicherheitsdienst* was Böhm's kind of work all right. "I think they'll take it easy on Jews for the time being," Jessen continued. "Communists? That's another matter. Jewish Communists? If I were a Jewish Communist I'd get the hell out of the country. Rabinowitz may be an example, a warning. A tough guy, everybody knows that, so Böhm is showing his power. When you people…when somebody put up those posters, a rock got tossed into a hornet's nest. That was stupid, Dov."

Dov ignored the comment. "What will they do with Rabinowitz?"

"Böhm sent him to Dachau this morning."

The lawyer's heart stopped. He closed his eyes, absorbed the blow. He knew it would happen sooner or later. They were soldiers in a battle and in battles soldiers died. He forced air from his lungs through a pursed mouth, rubbed his eyes, and composed himself. Later, alone, he would mourn his comrade.

"I'm sorry Dov."

"Yeah. The day will come…Oh Hans, just one more question. The son of a friend wants to go to America. Stuttgart asks for a statement from the *Kreiswirtschaftsrat*. Know anything about it?"

"Yes, it's new. I suppose he's Jewish. How old?"

"Twelve."

"Shouldn't be a problem. He can get a form at the Finance Department. A twelve year old doesn't own much. They have a civil servant working on these cases full time. Naturally. More and more people trying to leave, a real money-maker. The file goes to Pflug."

"Pflug? Why Pflug?"

"If a Jew escapes with a fortune, somebody will be held responsible." He looked behind him, made sure nobody was listening. "You can bet it won't be Adolf."

"You've been a big help. Many thanks."

"You stuck your neck out for me. Let's call it even. And Dov, please, I've told you nothing."

"Understood. Happy retirement, Hans."

Dov paid for the beer and drove his Citroen to the office. Perhaps it was intuition, nothing more, but he felt reasonably safe. The Nazis had their sacrificial lamb. He knew they'd be back for more, but not today. He dreaded the call to Emma. Solomon would be of small comfort to her. Hannah might stay with Emma for a few days, at least until the shock wore off. Schmuel, tough, handsome Schmuel at Dachau. Shit! He slammed a fist into the front door, mounted the stairs, his heart heavy with sorrow.

At Heilige-Geist-Kirche, the low, threatening clouds intensified the children's dark mood. Soli Rabinowitz, always a part of the gang, stayed home to comfort his mother. Dov's information was a severe blow. Everybody was gloomy and scared. Oskar drove Horst, Walter, Gitte, and David in the Opel. Lisa came with the Grünbergs, both Karl and Albert dressed for the North Pole. The children said quick good byes to their parents, reassured each other that this was a safety precaution, a few days only.

They carried their belongings in rucksacks and their food in shoulder bags and walked the short distance to the open gate at the north end of Tremonia Strasse. Horst led the way into the deserted mine area. Although frightening, it still felt like an adventure. Toughened by circumstances, no strangers to danger and oppression, they had somehow learned to sustain a measure of optimism. Tomorrow would be better, the sun would shine, and they would be alive. Horst's explorations paid off. He brought the group directly to the crumbling wooden shed of the colliery, which loomed against the sullen sky, its entrance door hanging from rusty hinges.

"This is it?" asked Karl. "Schumann, you really know how to pick 'em. At least it's above the ground for a change, not like the last one."

"Unless you fall into the mine, Karl."

They used their flashlights only when necessary, carefully entered the structure. The main shaft, its broken wood ladders leaning against mine walls, was covered with planks.

"Removable in an emergency," said Horst.

"How about water?" asked Gitte, "I just brought one bottle."

Horst pointed toward the nearby shed. "There's a faucet on the outside. The handle is hard to turn but there's plenty of water."

"What if someone comes?" Albert wondered.

"We'll take turns standing watch. If we have to, we can hide in the woods."

"What woods?"

"Fifty meters outside the fence, Albert. Big hole in the fence on Lampe Strasse."

"You really checked this out, didn't you?"

"Lots of practice."

"I can see that. Probably comes in handy in America."

America! Horst was glad to be reminded. He had nearly forgotten, it seemed so far away right now. Dov had called earlier, told Oskar about the documents. He was encouraging, except for the paper Pflug had to approve. No point to worry about that paper now. It would all work out. They huddled under coats and blankets against the cold. Albert passed chocolate around. It tasted great.

"Imported from Holland, guys," he said. "The last bar we had."

"Soli would have loved it," said Gitte, tears in her eyes.

Poor Soli. They were not fond of Solomon Rabinowitz; he was a glutton and complained a lot, but yesterday the Nazis took away his father. Soli might never see him again. If it happened to Solomon it could happen to them. The girls moved closer under their blanket.

"In America, Horst," said Karl, "what do you want to become when you grow up?"

"Old! Right now, I'd settle for that, Karl."

They giggled, whispered more, mostly silly things, tried hard to cheer each other up. The rucksacks served as pillows when it came time to go to sleep and one by one they dozed off, restlessly. Just as in the sewers, David and Horst were the last ones awake.

"Horst? Want to talk?"

"Yeah. Outside."

The fresh air felt good even though it was cold. Careful not to wake the others, they kept their voices low.

"If we had to do it over again," David asked, "would you put up the flyers?"

"I don't know. Yes, sure, well, who knows but maybe not. Everybody thought it was the right thing to do. But I don't know."

David insisted. "If you had a choice, I mean if you could do it again, or not do it again, what would you do?"

"I don't know. I can't figure it out. Oskar and Dov, they've been beaten up so many times, you'd think maybe they'd try some other way."

"What other way is there?"

Furiously, Horst responded. "Some way they don't get the shit kicked out of them!"

"You mean stop being Communists? You think they could do that?"

"Why not? I don't get it, David. I've been in a lot of little towns in the last six years. There were always some Communists, or Socialists, or whatever they called themselves. All they ever did was fight in the streets, throw bottles, run around screaming at people."

"At the Nazis, you mean?"

"Sometimes at the Nazis, sometimes at each other. Sometimes, I think, at nobody at all. Just screaming."

"You ever talk to Oskar about it? Dov thinks Oskar is brilliant. Dov says Oskar has read more books than anybody he knows."

Horst slumped against the rotten wood. The acrid smell of moist anthracite invaded his nose, dried up his throat. He was supposed to go to America. Maybe the secret to getting out of this terrible place was in one of Oskar's precious books. He wanted so bad to be in Chicago. He loved using the word Chicago. Chicago. Maybe he would meet real Indians there like in the Karl May books. He had read someplace that Chicago had gangsters. Or was it Mendel, the history teacher, the one who visited his sister in America who had talked about gangsters with machine guns in that city and some kind of train running over the top of the streets? He couldn't wait to see it all.

"Right, David, my father's good at reading books. Big deal!"

"What's going on with you? Aren't you with us anymore?"

Horst wasn't sure, not entirely. "Yes. No. I want to go to America. I want to be in Chicago. I want to go to school and do something else besides hiding from Nazis."

David Lifschitz shared his father's convictions, but Horst's longing got through to him. "I wish I could come with you. And you know, maybe it wasn't the right thing to do."

"What?"

"Putting up the flyers."

It had been a long, difficult day, too late now to figure it out and they were tired. Earlier, Horst had volunteered for the first watch.

"I'll wake you in a couple of hours, okay, David?"

"Okay." David crawled into the darkness. "Shalom, Horst."

"Shalom, David."

19

Hans Jessen's information was both enlightening and disconcerting. If accurate, Jews were off the hook for the time being, at least until expected large crowds attending Berlin's Olympic Games, had departed. Oskar was sufficiently astute to recognize Hitler's need for a peaceful-looking Germany, a semblance of social harmony and good will designed to assuage international rumors about atrocities and renewed militarism in the Fatherland. Perceptive minds in Goebbels' ministry advised strict control over Westfalia's public relations. The probability was strong that do-gooder journalists would snoop around the region's blue-collar workers looking for discontent and snippets of barbaric behavior.

Oskar also understood that a hiatus in the harassment of Jews was no guarantee for his own safety. As both a Jew and a Communist, his life was in double jeopardy. Stern measures would be taken against the mere hint of a Communist presence. Schmuel Rabinowitz's swift destruction served as an unmistakable warning. No one knew if that tragedy was the result of official policy or Heiko Böhm's personal vendetta. What difference did it make, thought Oskar; a trip to a concentration camp was a trip to a concentration camp, no matter who sponsored the journey. He deemed it wise to delegate visits to official agencies to Grete, who dreaded dealing with bureaucrats but became a reluctant, although relatively risk-free courier.

The truth for Gretchen Schumann was palpable, once she acknowledged it. Put bluntly, she was sick and tired of the whole business, disgruntled with endless poverty, fed up with being the beleaguered, semi-legitimate, Aryan wife of a wholly endangered Jew. Oskar could be such a dumb ass. Considering the risk, she thought his latest caper, what she called "that Nüremberg nonsense," to be an act of sublime idiocy. Euphoria over Horst's emigration had worn off. She vaguely hoped his son's imminent exodus might inspire Oskar to consider emigrating to America. She would have liked that. She loved American films and fashion magazines. They were romantic, the women beautifully dressed, the men charming and sophisticated. She supposed not everybody on that side of the Atlantic was rich and lived in beautiful houses with swimming pools, but some of it had to be true. In fact anything would be better than what she had today. At thirty-six, most of her adult life ahead, she felt she deserved some pleasure and fun, yet here she was, waiting around a dreary old records office. Well, soon it would be finished, one way or another. After the boy was gone Oskar might come to his senses and think about the future. If not, she would seriously consider a new beginning for herself, perhaps in Italy or Spain. She was attracted to those places. On her way to the bureau she thought about her streetcar romances, about meeting young men named Luigi or Enrico. Well, first things first. She had to get a copy of Horst's birth certificate. She watched the bald-headed clerk as he tried, unsuccessfully, to look busy and important before he condescended to call her.

"Yes?"

"I need a copy of a birth certificate."

He gave her a form. "Fill it out. In ink."

"I don't have a pen."

He pointed to a wooden stand that held an inkbottle and a pen. The form asked for name, address, birth date and the number of copies requested. She filled in the information, waited at the window while the clerk continued to shuffle papers. She hated him for making her wait. He never even looked up.

"Four Marks."

She handed over the money, resenting it. "How long do I have to wait?"

He scribbled a receipt. "Tomorrow. After two."

Damn, she thought, another trip to this awful place.

◆   ◆   ◆

Walter left the mine, skirted bustling Westfalenhaus and turned north on Kückelke, towards home. He brought with him several requests. Everyone needed soap and only Horst remembered to bring toilet paper. Albert felt a sore throat coming on and asked for medicine. Lisa and Gitte would appreciate two more towels, if that could be managed. All parents were to be told that their kids were fine and not to worry. Walter located Oskar in one of his basement's storage rooms, grading cow hides with chalk marks. Together they made the telephone calls. Lev brought over a bottle of red syrup and two rolls of tissue. Lisa's mother delivered towels and soap and Yetta Pariser added rock candy and a bag of mandelbrot to her son's bulging rucksack. Dov sent a written message: "Horst! Be at Avrom Levi's house, 36 Zimmerstrasse, just north of Steinplatz, tomorrow at midnight; passport pictures to be taken. Wash your face, comb your hair, come and go quickly." After Oskar added a few magazines and a piece of salami to his pack, Walter left, anxious to be back at the mine before school let out. At the edge of West-Park he bumped into a group of youngsters in uniforms rushing out of the Rittershaus. Walter, with his strong Semitic features, was eyed suspiciously and subjected to insulting remarks as he walked quickly toward busy Sonnenstrasse. He didn't feel safe until lost in traffic.

◆   ◆   ◆

Horst found the Zimmerstrasse address without difficulty. Avrom Levi, a slender, pimpled youngster, was waiting for him, equipment all set up. Avrom was the proud possessor of a Zeiss-Ikon camera, a *bar mitzvah* present from his now deceased father. He posed Horst against a piece of gray paper, turned on a spotlight and took twelve pictures. The session lasted ten minutes.

"I'll develop tonight and deliver prints to your house tomorrow. I have your address," said Avrom. "Your father will pay me. Good luck. Where are you going?"

"Chicago."

"Ah, America. Great. I'm going to Palestine."

"When?"

"When I get papers. Maybe soon."

"Mazel tov."

"You too. Be careful."

"I will. Thanks, Avrom. Thanks very much."

"Shalom, Horst."

◆   ◆   ◆

Oskar visited Grünberg's office on Beurhaus Strasse, near the Johannes Hospital. Lev worked at the hospital for sixteen years until its staff and Board of Directors grew uneasy with a bearded, Jewish, left-leaning orthopedist. He now practiced in two small rooms, sent his x-ray business to a clinic. Referrals still came from former colleagues, doctors who understood that a superbly trained specialist was hard to replace. In the reception area Oskar nodded to a gray-haired man, one arm in a sling, waited until Lev ushered him in.

"Dov said you need a health certificate for Horst. It's made out; a secretary next door notarized it. Just see to it he doesn't break out with something before he leaves."

"Like what?"

"Hitleritis," said Lev, "the Böhm Disease, whatever. When is he going?"

"When the documents arrive in Stuttgart, they'll let us know."

The two men regarded each other. "It was stupid," said the doctor, "ill-timed and risky, especially for the children. We should have known better."

"Too late now, Lev. Maybe we did some good. People read them before they were torn down."

"Hope it was worth it. Anyhow, I'm planning to get out. I have relatives in London. It's important for my boys to have a decent education."

"You sure you can do it?"

"Sure? What the hell is sure these days? No, I'm not sure at all. If they don't let me go I'll make a run for it. How about you?"

"First Horst, then I'll see."

"Do it, Oskar. I think we're finished in this country. Here's Horst's certificate. Let's be careful. Maybe Dov is right and Schmuel was only a warning. I want to bring the children home soon."

They embraced. "Thanks Lev. Not the way we thought it would be, is it old friend?"

"We had a vision, Oskar. I remember Dante said something, I think it was in the *Divine Comedy*. 'He goes seeking liberty, which is dear, as only he knows who renounces his life for it'."

"Take care, Lev. We'll talk soon."

Oskar tucked the certificate into his coat pocket, nodded to the elderly gentleman on his way out. One step closer to liberty, my son, he reflected and exited quickly into a rush of pedestrians.

◆   ◆   ◆

Promptly at two, Grete picked up the birth certificate at the records office. The same dour little clerk handed her a manila envelope. She turned at the exit sign, caught him looking at her legs. One more place and I'm done, thank god, she thought and loudly banged the door shut. Oskar had telephoned the *Kreiswirtschaftsrat*, learned it was located in the north wing of the Finance Department. Grete crossed Gerichts Strasse and found the building, a squat brick structure that looked like a fortresss. At an office suite on the second floor she stated her business.

"Jew?"

"Who? Me?"

"The person who wants to emigrate."

"Oh. Yes, Jewish."

"Your relationship?"

"Stepmother."

"One moment."

The receptionist walked off, a sneer wrinkled her face. She peeled a form from a stack, whispered to a clerk behind a desk. The young man glanced at Gretchen, grinned and looked away. Gretchen blushed with fury and humiliation.

"Here," grunted the woman and shoved the required form across the railing. "An *Erklärung der Besitztümer*, a declaration of ownership. It must be signed by the applicant, notarized and returned to this office. If I were you, I would mail it."

Gretchen stuffed the paper into her purse and hurried out of the building, shaking with anger.

◆   ◆   ◆

The spirit of adventure wore thin. The group was restless, all of them anxious to see their parents. At first, living in an abandoned mine together brought them closer, but after three days they bickered and teased, gradually lost the sense of purpose that had united them so far.

"How much longer in this hole?"

"Not much, Albert," said Horst. "I'll try and find out what's going on tonight, after midnight."

Horst's promise cheered everyone up. In the meantime they tried to keep busy. Gitte, who wanted to be a teacher, organized a school session in English. Her father had learned many English words while he was a prisoner in an American camp and had taught them to her.

"Schumann," she said, "you're going to America. Better learn to speak some American. Maybe we'll all go to America, so pay attention. Now, everybody, repeat after me: This is a door. I open the door. I close the door."

By nightfall, after they had learned all the words Gitte knew, Horst made a second list of things they wanted; toothpaste for the Grünbergs, fresh fruit for everybody.

Albert's wristwatch, their common link to the outside world, hung on a nail. Albert took the evening's first lookout, woke Horst at midnight.

"Will you be back before morning?"

"Yes, I think so."

"Call my father. Tell my mother I'm feeling good. Just lonesome. Be careful."

"I will."

Horst slipped through the gate into the cold, starlit night. He found Weiher-strasse as asleep as the rest of Dortmund, but to be on the safe side he used the drainpipe opening to enter his house. Gretchen never stirred. Oskar, still awake, met him in the kitchen.

"What's wrong?"

"Nothing Papa, except everybody is restless."

"I can imagine. Thank god you're okay. Up to now they haven't bothered us. You shouldn't be here, you know, but I'm glad to see you. You have to sign papers."

Oskar called Dov, also still up, reading.

"Horst is here. The children want to come home. What do you think?"

"Maybe a couple more days. The kids can stand it. Grünberg and Koerner called too. I haven't heard anything. What about Horst's papers?"

"I have them with me."

"I'll notarize the whole batch in the morning. Come in through the front, like we're not worried, just in case they're watching. You never know. Let me talk to Horst."

"Dov?"

"Tell David I miss him. If it's still quiet the day after tomorrow you can come home. How is everybody?"

"Lonesome."

"Naturally; a couple more days, to be on the safe side. Will you tell them that?"

"I will. Good night, Dov."

Oskar poured a glass of milk for Horst and brandy for himself. Together they worked on the ownership declaration, amused by some of the questions.

"How much real estate do you own, Horst?"

"A chalet in the Alps and a castle in the country, Papa."

"List the stocks and bonds you own."

"Thousands. Can you say thousands?"

"How much cash do you have?"

Horst turned his empty pockets inside out.

"We can't say 'nothing'." Oskar fished a coin from his pocket. "Let's put down *one groschen*. Maybe somebody has a sense of humor."

Perhaps it was the late hour or an easing of last week's stress, but for the first time in days they relaxed a bit, then lingered over the Stuttgart documents longer than necessary. Horst signed the forms and hugged his father good-bye.

"Walter will be here in the afternoon, Papa. We'll stay until we hear from you."

"Be careful." That caution was on everybody's mind.

"I will. I promise."

He circled the city center and arrived at the colliery moments before sunrise. Gitte and Lisa, standing watch, welcomed him with relief. In low tones he answered all their questions, told them that everything seemed quiet.

◆   ◆   ◆

Oskar felt strange when he entered Dov's place through the front door. He couldn't remember when he had last used the Holzhof Strasse entrance. Dov's office reeked of coffee and strong cigarettes. "Believe it or not," the lawyer said, "I still have clients. You don't smoke, do you?"

"No. Never been tempted."

"Yeah, well, I'm filing a lawsuit for Leffler, the poor schnook who runs the tobacco shop in the Grossmarkt."

"What happened?"

"Bunch of Hitler Youth hoodlums broke his windows, cleaned him out, cigarettes, pipes, cigars, whatever they could schlepp away. Left the shop in shambles."

"Are you suing the Hitler Youth?" exclaimed Oskar,

Lifschitz chuckled. "A good one, Oskar, a real good one, suing the Hitler Youth, that's great, man. Nah, I'm suing the insurance company. They don't want to pay damages because they figured if I take them to court, by the time the case comes up I won't be allowed to practice anymore. You know what? They're right. Talk around the courts is that soon no Jew will be allowed to practice law. Damn it, Oskar, its time to bid farewell to Germany. Horst is lucky he has papers."

"Can you still notarize?"

"Until they say otherwise." Dove examined the forms. "Scratch out that *groschen* bit, put in 'nothing,' then initial it. These people have no sense of humor, so don't piss them off. Deliver the financial declaration personally. Mail has a way of getting lost." He used his seal, added the date and his signature. "Take care of it fast, Oskar. You know they don't give a damn about our deadlines."

Although he felt vulnerable in official surroundings, Oskar personally delivered the declaration to the finance office, aware of Gretchen's distaste for anything to do with bureaucracy. He empathized with her. Since the Nüremberg Declaration her self-esteem, not high to begin with, suffered a damaging blow. She couldn't grasp what had happened to her in a few short years. Despite their different backgrounds, Oskar knew she married him with reasonable prospects for a secure, middle-class life. Instead, she now found herself scrounging for basic necessities, an unwilling stepmother and a social pariah in her own country. Oskar knew that neither Gretchen, nor the marriage, could withstand such stress much longer. From numerous remarks she had made recently, he suspected that leaving him was on her mind. He could hardly blame her.

A clerk approached him, took Horst's papers. "Write your address on this postcard. We'll notify you. Good day."

For now he had done what was needed. The task completed, Oskar's elation turned to letdown. He felt empty as he walked toward home. Home to what? Home to whom? His livelihood was gone. His faith in his political mission was battered. His son was leaving for a better life on the other side of the world. Unfocused, he drifted toward the city's center, ambled along the South Wall. Without exactly knowing why, he suddenly found himself in front of the synagogue. He had not been inside since Albert Grünberg's *bar mitzvah*, nor did some spiritual force now impel him to enter; he was simply tired and dispirited. The doors stood open, the sanctuary was empty. Oskar sat on a wooden bench in the last row. A thin old man, wearing an embroidered yarmulke, listlessly swept an aisle.

"You're early," he said in a cracked voice.

"Early for what?"

The caretaker continued to gather dust, deposited it in a paper carton. "Shabbat service. Not for another hour."

"Thanks, I'm just resting."

The old man stopped sweeping, looked him over, nodded, went on with his work, stopped again and heaved a deep sigh.

"Resting. Resting is good my friend, but don't stay too long."

"Why not?"

"The young trouble makers, sometimes the old ones, too. They come before the service. Throw things. Sometimes trash, sometimes stones. Not many people attend anymore because they get hurt. The rabbi sleeps in his office. Rest if you want. Plenty of seats." He chuckled to himself. "Plenty of seats."

Oskar lingered a few minutes, experienced no shafts of tranquility beaming at him from the arc containing the torah, no wisdom descending from stained glass windows depicting ancient prophets. On his way out he passed the old janitor who continued to sweep. It had grown dark; a biting chill tore at his face. Loathe to go home, he stopped at Café Lüchtemeyer, genuinely enjoyed the taste of coffee and pastry, then felt guilty spending the money.

A note awaited him, thumb-tacked to the kitchen door. He dropped it on the table, took off his coat, hung it in a closet with forced effort and sat down with a heavy heart to read the dreaded message:

Dear Oskar,

I'm sorry I have to write this. I'm very unhappy and I'm going to my sister's house. She said she would let me stay for a week or two until I decide what to do next. It's better if you don't call me right now. There's nothing to talk about anyway. Maybe after a few weeks we can figure out what to do. I don't know how else to do this, so if I have made you sad, please forgive me. This is a bad time for both of us. Good luck with Horst's papers. I hope everything works out for him.

Gretchen

He stared at her familiar handwriting, then swallowed some bitter tears. He would miss her. 1935 was turning into a dreadful year and the new one held no greater promise. His life was in danger, his wife had fled and in a few weeks his son would be gone. He would be alone.

20

Pflug could point to no specific incident or overt protestations, but since last week he sensed subtle changes in his bureaucratic environment, an elusive weakening of his authority. The SA cadre charged with regulatory tasks, such as security enforcement, propaganda material distribution and Winter Relief, seemed more casual in his presence, unconcerned with routine civility. Frau Schuster was tight-lipped and impatient, outwardly less agreeable. This morning he requested files that dealt with subversive activities in his district, sensitive documents not to be divulged without his approval.

"They are in Herr Böhm's office, Herr Pflug."

Was she sneering at him? Herr Böhm, indeed! It used to be "Heiko" and uttered not too graciously, either. When he made Böhm adjutant she threatened to quit, said she was afraid of Heiko's gruffness. She generally dealt with him at arm's length. Now it was "Herr Böhm."

"Please ask Herr Böhm to join me, if he can spare the time."

"He left with Herr Buchberger. They went to the Hansaplatz project."

"When will he be back?"

"He didn't say."

A taste of bile welled in his throat. "When Herr Böhm reappears send him to my office, immediately." He turned away, did not want her to see his frustration. "In the meantime, we have paperwork to do, or is Herr Böhm taking care of that, too?"

She flinched at the tone of his voice. He wasn't being fair. It wasn't her fault that lines of authority were muddled.

"Frau Schuster." His voice became softer. "Let's clear emigration files this morning, they've piled up. And may I have a cup of coffee, please?" He smiled pleasantly.

"Of course, Herr Pflug." She rushed out, somewhat relieved.

He cradled his cup as he stared out the window. Random snowflakes eddied around the undulating banner, its swastika twisted black against a gray sky. Christmas was two weeks off. He had always enjoyed holidays with his family, delighted to share with them the robust games of winter. It was different this year. Even now he felt chilled with apprehension; a spasm of foreboding erupted in his right temple, the dreaded onset of a migraine.

Frau Schuster stacked his desk with papers that required his attention and signature. The documents from the *Finanzamt* would occupy the rest of this morning. He understood the pitfalls lurking in these files. Dortmund's Jews were not renowned for their wealth, certainly not compared with the fortunes of leading Jewish businessmen in Berlin and Frankfurt. Nevertheless, caution was advised. Who really knew the treasures buried in those fetid warrens of the ghetto, that garlic-reeking precinct behind Mallinckrodt Strasse's slaughterhouse? He scanned the cover sheet of an *Erklärung der Besitztümer*, thankful that his office was spared the investigative work and responsible only for sifting out politically dangerous elements. Six months ago there were a dozen applicants. The number had now grown to nearly a hundred.

He scanned the list. Abramovitz, Ahronson, Berliner. Fact-finding was the Dortmund Economic Board's responsibility, but Pflug clearly understood that final accountability was his. He would double-check everything. Levy, Moskovitz, Nachmann and Nussbaum. Unfamiliar names. Oberheim, Oppenheimer. That one deserved scrutiny. Simon Oppenheimer had his fingers in many enterprises; in fact, Pflug thought his mortgage payments were made to an Oppenheimer bank. Riskin, Roth, Schwartz, E., Schwartz, S., Schuler, Schumann.

Schumann? He drew back in astonishment. Impossible! Not *that* Schumann, he wouldn't dare. Pflug flipped through the files, found the one marked "Schumann, Horst." Ah, the son wanted to leave, not the father. The file contained nothing of interest. Of course not, the boy was twelve years old, owned zero. Pflug stared at the endorsement clipped to the application. "Investigated. Approved." The department's seal, a swastika wreathed in the eagle's claws, the bureau chief's signature in black ink, dated, slightly smudged. Official. A blank space awaited Pflug's signature as District Dortmund's *Ortsgruppenleiter*, the Party's chief local administrator.

The document in hand, Pflug moved to the window, stared at the leaden sky above the drooping banner, its background now muddled to a crimson smear against the deepening snowfall. Not long ago the Schumann child had been on the sidewalk below, supporting his beaten, broken father. Pflug vividly recalled the two wretched creatures and how their fierce loathing had penetrated the short distance to the window where he now stood, holding in his hand the instrument that could surely decide the boy's life or death. For one agonizing moment he envisioned Horst Schumann's fate should he consign him to the mercy of Heiko Böhm, resident booking agent of Dachau's re-education center. The shade of

Rollo's father, Gloomy Gustav, beckoned to duty, but Pflug ignored it, took the file to his desk, carefully dipped his pen in the inkwell and signed the Schumann *Erklärung* with crisp, clean strokes. The commitment thus made, he grinned from ear to ear. He would deal with the probable consequences some other time.

That morning, Roland Pflug, in high spirits, approved all applications, each and every one, from Abramovitz, Abraham to Zeitlin, Felix. At lunchtime, feeling fine and delightfully hungry, he stacked his day's work neatly on the corner of his secretary's desk.

"Please return these to the *Wirtschaftsrat*, Frau Schuster. Send someone from the transportation pool. And could you please do it now?"

"Immediately, Herr Pflug." She lifted the pile into her arms.

"Oh, Frau Schuster?"

"Yes, Herr Pflug?"

"Christmas is almost here. Surely you must have shopping to do. Get the files on their way, then take the rest of the day off."

Astonished, she watched him grab his winter coat, slap on his hat and stomp out the door, smiling all the while. She wondered briefly what had happened to him. Well, never mind; an afternoon off was welcomed indeed. In the same carton in which they were sent, she brought the files to Transportation. Her desk in order, dressed in her warm coat, she exited the front door and waved to the driver just as he pulled away from the curb, on his way to make the delivery.

◆   ◆   ◆

"I want to go home," said Albert Grünberg, "I think I have a fever. My throat is sore."

It was their fourth day in the mines. Their mood had spoiled thoroughly. It was much colder now. In the morning they found the water tap frozen, their food supply nearly gone.

"I told Papa that Walter will check in today," said Horst. "Papa promised to call around for signs of trouble. We will know more when Walter returns."

"If it's safe," suggested Lisa, "Dov or someone else can drive Walter back to the church and wait for us there. Maybe they can take us home right away."

"We might fit into two cars." Karl sounded more than ready to go. "I'm sure my father will also come."

"Only if it's safe," David warned. "If it isn't, I'd rather stay here."

Dressed in borrowed sweaters, his rucksack empty, Walter took off from the mine in the middle of the afternoon. He hurried all the way, encountered no trouble and arrived home in less than an hour. He ran up three flights of stairs to see his parents, then went to Weiherstrasse and Oskar.

"How is everybody?"

"Cold and tired and hungry and Albert has a fever."

Oskar called the families before connecting with Dov.

"What do you think, Dov?"

"Looks more and more like Schmuel was a warning. If they really want to put us away they'd have done it by now. Let's bring them home. Meet you at six in the Heilige-Geist parking lot.

"I'll be there."

Walter told his mother what was happening. He was anxious to deliver the good news so he ran back to the mines and told everybody to pack up. With great relief and profuse cheers they gathered their things and left a few minutes before six, not once looking back at their hiding place. Dov hugged David, loaded the Grünbergs and Lisa into his Citroen. Church bells pierced the bleak winter night. Horst, Walter and Gitte sang folk songs, their exhaled breath frosting the Opel's windows with wintry designs. Oskar listened to the young peoples' voices with deep satisfaction. Such spirit, such a powerful will to live! Soon they would all go elsewhere. He would miss them terribly. His eyes were moist as he drove cautiously on the glazed streets toward the bleak flat on Weiherstrasse. He wished Grete were there to greet them. He missed her. If he could be more mindful of her needs in the future, perhaps she would reconsider and come back. He would talk to her soon. Meanwhile, he felt happy to have Horst home, aware it would not be for long.

◆　　　◆　　　◆

Only a week before all papers were due in Stuttgart, the *Kreiswirtschaftsrat's* promised postcard arrived in the mail. Oskar and Horst picked up the registered one-page document, signed and notarized, which attested that as of this date Horst Schumann, aged 12, Weiherstrasse 4, City and Kreis Dortmund, possessed no property, bank accounts, savings accounts, real estate liens, interest in mortgages, or any other transferable fiscal assets. Furthermore, according to directives from the Reichministry of Finance, the fiscal, commercial, investment and management organizations in Kreis Dortmund jurisdiction were ordered to report all future changes in the financial status of said Horst Schumann. Oskar paid the fee and accepted the receipt.

He went with Horst to the main postoffice, all documents bundled in a large, sturdy envelope boldly addressed in black ink. He checked the papers once more and made absolutely certain nothing was omitted, sealed the letter and took it to a counter. Mindful that the envelope's contents were the key to his son's freedom, he paid extra for registered protection.

"This must be in Stuttgart by the fifteenth," he told the clerk, "a matter of life and death."

"What isn't?" came the laconic answer. "Registered mail takes three days."

Hugely relieved, father and son walked toward home. Horst was very proud of his father, aware how much love and care had gone into this troublesome assignment, and under extremely difficult circumstances. Dortmund's streets were crowded with holiday shoppers, the Hansaplatz bratwurst stands doing brisk business. Money was scarce, but Oskar, irresistibly tempted by the aroma that surrounded them as well as by their mutual happiness, needed to celebrate. They bought bratwursts, dipped them in mustard, ate slowly and with gusto, comfortably lost in the crowd. Amidst smiling faces, a sprinkling of brown and black uniforms seemed miraculously less menacing

"Oh Papa," Horst whispered as they left the square. "Maybe, just maybe, everything will be all right."

Oskar walked on, an arm around Horst's shoulder. "From your mouth to God's ear, my son," he said softly.

21

Winter in a gray, industrial city is bone-chilling, but on this twelfth day of December even Dortmund's weather couldn't match the frozen grip that imprisoned the soul of Roland Pflug as he drove home to his wife and children. Yesterday, without warning, Terhoven had sent a memo demanding a meeting with Kreis Dortmund's entire staff, to take place the following morning at the new NSDAP headquarters, promptly at ten o'clock, no exceptions allowed. The memo stated the occasion to be a visit by SS-Commander Theodor Eicke, currently on a national tour enumerating SS security measures to be implemented in the coming year. All group leaders, organizers and department heads were ordered to attend, failure to do so considered insubordination and to be dealt with appropriately.

Terhoven phoned in the late afternoon. "Rollo, I assume you received my memo. Any problems?"

"Only minor ones, Paul. We're still short on chairs and the walls won't be painted until next week, but everyone will be present."

"Good. Let's meet briefly in your office beforehand to write down the agenda. You will preside of course. And I'd like to see you afterward to clarify a few matters with you and your adjutant, Böhm. Heiko, isn't it?"

"That's right, Paul. Heiko."

The preparatory meeting was short and to the point. Frau Schuster took notes and typed the agenda in time for their entrance into the auditorium, the first use of the new facility. Terhoven and Eicke marched at the head of the procession, followed by Pflug and Böhm. Terhoven led the singing of the Horst Wessel song and the traditional salvo of "Sieg Heils." From a dais decorated with banners, Pflug introduced the speakers. Frau Luetzke of the National Socialist Women's Union attested to the readiness of Westfalia's women to serve Reich and Führer, followed by a representative of the Union of German Girls, equally willing to do its duty. Both the Hitler Youth and the Students Union pledged their troth. Pflug made a failed effort to be attentive. There was a time when such rallies excited him, when he listened to every word, but by now Nazi catch phrases were too familiar and their uncomplicated propaganda too repetitive to be endured. Party fledglings, however, strained to heard Eicke, a squat, dour-looking man, seated motionless beside Terhoven. Everyone present knew it was Eicke who had murdered Ernst Roehm, their former boss. Afterward, Hitler had appointed him chief inspector of concentration camps and director of the SS Death's Head guards. The Führer rewarded his friends.

Commandant Eicke's message was unmistakable. Slowly, proudly, he described Dachau's facilities, apparently greatly improved since he established the camp in 1933.

> "Our Death Head Squadrons are trained to deal with enemies of the Reich. We show no mercy to those who seek to undermine Germany's future. You are all good Party members. Beginning at this moment, I want you to feel the Dachau spirit in your hearts, in your minds, in the marrow of your bones. No sympathy for our enemies. They are to be hunted down and imprisoned. We must rid ourselves of the rats of subversion. Not tomorrow, but today."

Pflug sensed the rising emotions of the men and women around him, the young ones eager with excitement, their eyes glowing with ardor.

> "Our Führer is a man of peace. Our Party is a Party of peace. Bolshevists and their Jewish leaders are the enemy of our Führer and our Party. Therefore, they are your enemy. They want to destroy you. As citizens of the Reich it is your duty to seek them out and help us rid our Fatherland of this evil. All else is treason."

Pflug knew he wasn't being addressed personally. By no conjury, however fiendish, could Eicke be aware of his signature on Horst Schumann's declaration, clearly an act of treason by Eicke's definition. Still, one never knew. He glanced at Böhm, saw him staring back from slitted eyes. Something unpleasant was going on. Why did Terhoven want to meet afterward? What was that little game, not remembering Böhm's first name? Well, he'd find out soon enough. Eicke was wrapping it up.

> "You are the guardians of the land, defenders of our faith. Together we will triumph over those who wish to destroy us. We will not let them. Let that be our pledge to our Führer, Adolf Hitler. Sieg Heil!"
>
> "Sieg Heil" roared the assembly, arms outstretched.
> "Sieg Heil" cried Eicke, twice more.
> "Sieg Heil," they answered him.

Again, they sang the Horst Wessel song, of banners high, of ranks of marching feet, of knives and blood and battles to be won. Then Eicke left and it was over.

"We'll make this brief," said Terhoven minutes later, seated on a hard chair in Pflug's office, not bothering to remove his coat. "I've given a lot of thought to our last conversation, Rollo. Regional needs have changed. I believe my district would be better served with a…different…ah…approach to Party matters in Dortmund. We need improved leadership in the area of education. The Teachers Union has been sadly neglected. I know that's where your interests lie. You understand these matters better than anyone else. I want my…ah…associates to be enthusiastic about their work."

"What are you telling me, Paul?"

"Ah, well, fine. Good. Let's do it your way then. On the first of the year you will take over Westfalia's Teachers Union. For the time being Böhm will assume your duties as Dortmund's *Ortsgruppenleiter* until a…suitable…yes, suitable replacement is found. Please help Böhm in any way necessary. And Rollo, understand this is not, I repeat, it is not, a demotion. It is a…well, a more effective use of Party personnel. I'll leave you gentlemen to work out the details. Heil Hitler." Without further ado he walked out.

What an abrupt departure, mused Rollo, feeling dazed. He was well aware how much Böhm distrusted him, but immediately dismissed that concern as a waste of time.

"You can begin running things today, Heiko, right now if you want."

"Terhoven said first of the month. That's soon enough."

"Good. Fine." Feeling oddly detached, he called Frau Schuster and told her the news. "As of January one Herr Böhm will be Dortmund's *Ortsgruppenleiter*. I'm sure you will give him the same efficient support you have always given me." She listened, mouth agape, then fled the office.

Pflug waved an arm. "Make yourself comfortable, Heiko. I'm taking the rest of the day off. Christmas shopping for my family. Unless you really need me, of course." He put on his warm, heavy coat. Böhm sat unmoved, silent. "Well Heiko, congratulations." It was surprisingly easy to smile.

"Rollo? You said something to me once, here in this office."

"What was that?"

"You said Heiko, I am not your enemy."

"Yes, I remember."

"Rollo. I am not your enemy either."

Pflug wanted to slap Böhm's face and express his contempt for Heiko's insolence and dishonesty. Instead, he smiled as amicably as before. "Christmas is just around the corner, Heiko. Peace on earth, good will toward men. Try to remember. Heil Hitler." He waved to a wide-eyed Frau Schuster and escaped the building.

Böhm was relieved to see him go. Christmas nonsense. Terhoven had made the right move.

"Frau Schuster," he called through the open door, "We may as well begin. I want the files dealing with Communist subversives and the list we made several months ago."

"They are on the…on your desk, sir."

"I also want the new emigration materials from Stuttgart. We need to make procedural changes, not now but promptly at the beginning of the year." He paused, tried to remember what he meant to ask. Ah yes. "Frau Schuster. Do you want to stay on after Pflug leaves? Will that be difficult for you?"

This was her moment to get out. She was always uneasy with brute force. Could she possibly work for a cruel man like him? A warning thought struck her. Böhm was just the kind to be vindictive. Perhaps it was wiser to bide one's time, leave later when things had cooled down.

"No, it won't be difficult at all, Herr Böhm. I'll do my best."

"I'm sure you will." He watched her close the door, settled comfortably behind the desk and stared out over the swastika roiling in the winter breeze. He picked a file, randomly, from the stack in front of him. "Herz, Isador. Aha," hummed Böhm, "the mimeograph artist and his bitch daughter." Bolshevist Jews, enemies of the fatherland, Commandant Eicke had called them. The perfect place to start. He lifted the intercom phone.

"Gajewski? Heiko here. Come up right now to Pflug's office. I have a little project." He tapped his knuckles with the file. "Herz. How appropriate. Let's give these yids a Christmas present they'll never forget."

◆   ◆   ◆

The Lifschitz phone rang late in the afternoon.

"Yes?"

"Dov? Jessen. I only have a moment. Pflug is out. Böhm is in. It's Dachau for all of you after the first. For God's sake, get the hell out while you can." He hung up.

◆   ◆   ◆

No one was home when Dov phoned Oskar. Oskar, desperate for money, had loaded the Opel with hides. Together he and Horst called on every customer he thought might still risk doing business with him. Two hides were sold, an old debt collected, a welcomed eighty Marks. In the ghetto Hershl Auerbach closed the shutters of his repair shop at four o'clock.

"Finishing early, Hersh?"

"Some Jew you are, Schumann, worse than the *goyem*."

"How so?"

"First night of Chanukah, at sundown, you dummy. What's the matter, you don't light candles?"

"I have no wife to light candles."

Touched by Schumann's sadness and the disheveled look of his son, Auerbach made a quick decision. "So come home with me. My Friedl makes the best latkes in Dortmund. Plenty for you. Your kid there looks like he could use a square meal."

The Auerbach apartment was small, but warm and comfortable. Hersh's young daughters said the prayers and Friedl lit the *shames*, the candle representing the oil lamp that burnt for eight days, according to ancient legend.

"They know the story by heart," Hershl pointed at his girls, "but maybe now its more important than ever. The Maccabees had to fight for their lives. It could happen again. You agree, Schumann?"

"The truth, Hershl?"

"What else?"

"Take your wife and children and leave."

"And the shop? How do I make a living?"

"People wear out shoes all over the world. Get out. Get out now. Get out as soon as possible."

The children spun a dredl, used hazelnuts and candy for prize money. Friedl knew the Chanukah songs and they sang while wolfing down mandelbrot and sponge cake. Auerbach, his eyes lovingly on his family, hugged Oskar when the time came to say goodnight.

"I appreciate your warning. It's hard to tear up everything and start over. Were you serious, what you said earlier?"

Oskar put a hand on Auerbach's shoulder. "The Dybbuk has sprung to life again, Hershl, only this time not as an ugly dragon. This time he's dressed in a brown uniform and wears a mustache. Leave Germany, my friend, leave before it's too late."

They drove home in a somber mood, Horst vaguely humming Chanukah melodies, Oskar in deep thought. As they turned onto Born Strasse they saw ugly, gray smoke rising from one of the buildings. Weiherstrasse was blocked off. They parked the car, pushed through the crowds and past fire engines. Ruhmann, the grocer, sat on the curb, his shirt smudged, his eyes sooty.

"Max, what in god's name is going on?"

"Oh Jesus Christ," the grocer sobbed, "don't you know?"

"We just got here."

"You don't want to know."

"Max, what is it?"

"It's Herz. Herz and his girl."

It happened at sundown, at the same time when Jews lit candles of freedom, of deliverance from oppression. The timing was surely accidental; nothing could have interested newly appointed *Ortsgruppenleiter* Heiko Böhm less than details of Jewish ceremonials.

"I was sweeping out the store," lamented Ruhman. "I saw them through my store window. Two cars. They parked that way, toward Brügman, about fifty meters. Six of them. Four went in Isador's shop, carrying a box. Oh God in heaven. It isn't fair."

"Max, what happened? Where are Isador and Brigitte?"

The grocer stared at Oskar as tears trickled down his cheeks.

"I heard Isador scream, then Brigitte too, but just for a moment. The four men came out and walked to their cars. It took them only a minute." He buried his face in the apron, rocked his head as if it had come unhinged.'

"Where is Herz, Max? And Brigitte?"

"Don't you understand, Schumann? Don't you understand anything?" Ruhman hovered on the edge of hysteria, his expression contorted. "Can't you see? Are you so stupid I have to draw you a picture? They bombed the store. Blew it up. Herz and his daughter were inside."

"They were both in the store?"

"The girl made it to the door, screaming through the shattered glass. I saw her! Oh God, Schumann, how will I ever forget? She was on fire, covered all over with blood. Then she screamed 'Papa' and went back into the flames. I ran to her. I swear to God I ran to her but everything was on fire. There was nothing to do."

"Oh Papa," Horst stuttered, crying hard. "I'm so scared, Papa, I'm terribly scared."

"Then the two cars passed me," Rohman wailed, more to himself than to anyone listening. "The beasts were laughing as they looked out the car windows. They just blew up two people and they were laughing, Schumann, laughing, like they were having a wonderful time. Do you know what I mean?" He folded his hands in his lap, stared blindly, unable to cope with the horror of his vision.

"Oh Max. No! I don't know!" Oskar clasped the grocer's shoulder, felt him shiver, held him for a while. Then he took Horst's hand and led him off the street. A policeman barred the way to their house until convinced they were residents. They made it to the kitchen table, sat numb with grief for a long time, helpless with fear, frightened by their own rage.

"Papa?" Horst raised his head and Oskar saw the terror in his son's eyes. "We could be next."

Oskar knew lies were foolish. "Yes, it's possible. We must find you a place to hide until the notice from Stuttgart comes. Immediately. And we must warn Dov." He telephoned the lawyer, but received no answer. "I'll try again later. There is something else I need to do. Stay with me. I need you." He found paper and ink in his living room desk and wrote hurriedly, reading each sentence aloud:

Dear Clara,

It looks like Horst will get his notice to leave very soon. Please tell the Malkins everything is on schedule. I know this will be trouble for you, but I must leave Germany too. I can't tell you the unspeakable horrors being committed here, the kind you probably don't hear about in America. You know what my politics have been. I am doomed if I stay. If you can help me quickly I would be deeply grateful. If you can't help right away, let me know because then I will try to escape before it is too late. I could use a little money. I don't have enough to see us through.

Your loving brother,

"Papa, they won't let you go."

"I don't know. Maybe they'll be glad to get rid of me." Oskar felt near the breaking point. "They can have whatever I own. I want to start all new. How about in New York? Or even in Chicago."

Writing the letter, doing something constructive and hopeful, brought a small measure of comfort, but not for long. Emotionally drained, they stumbled around the apartment. Isador and Brigitte's fate followed them into every room, haunted them with images of horror and pain, made them cling to each other out of dire necessity as fire trucks roared away in the night.

22

As was his custom, Dr. Becker was last to enter the conference room. Fräulein Grimm had attended to details in routinely brisk fashion, oak table dusted and oiled, pads of paper, pencils, clean ashtrays distributed at seats carefully arranged to reflect the current status of Stuttgart's fluctuating pecking order. At the moment, Anton Schirardi, in charge of the "re-deployment" of Jewish property, a Byzantine scheme labeled "Aryanization," sat at Becker's immediate right. Not too close, of course; Becker considered distance, physical and emotional, requisite to effective governance. Dietrich Hartung sat at the very end of the table, across from Hofmeister of "Race and Resettlement", adjacent to Fräulein Grimm who would record the proceedings in minute detail. Schweiger of "Transportation and Logistics" and Deppmüller of "Security" were comfortably positioned in the middle. At precisely two minutes after ten Becker strode to his winged chair, fit an English Oval into his mother-of-pearl holder, accepted a light from Schirardi, inhaled deeply, glanced cheerfully about the room, eyes glistening a mere fraction as they met Grimm's and exhaled smoke in Hartung's direction, as if to obscure him from view.

"Gentlemen, let's not waste time. Fräulein Grimm has placed today's agenda at your disposal. Last week's directives from our Chief Councilor should make you aware of certain delicate...shall we say...adjustments...in dealing with escalating emigration." He tapped a growing ash carefully into his ashtray, gracefully brushed a fleck from his immaculate uniform. "I am interested in your interpretation of Minister Neumann's administrative modifications. Schirardi?"

The muscular, balding ex-soccer player carefully arched his back, mostly to buy time. Like everyone present he was inured to his superior's methodology. Becker rarely made small talk. Questions were never asked idly, judicious answers always expected. "My impression," he said cautiously, "is that Minister Neumann's and Doctor Goebbels' offices have joined to...agreed on the...wisdom, perhaps foresight is more appropriate, of using...hmm...caution in the...in dealing with...in protecting...yes, protecting certain emigration information, especially during an expected influx of foreign press in the near future. Yes, exactly. That's my impression." He exhaled sharply.

Becker smiled. Schirardi is learning how to walk through mine fields, he thought to himself. "Does everyone agree with that assessment?" he asked aloud.

They concurred, under no delusion about revisions to strategies pertaining to the expulsion of Reich enemies. The policy of appropriating Jewish possessions would continue. That was, in fact, their clear understanding of "Aryanization," an intricate, wholly appropriate procedure of alchemizing Jewish gold into thin air, then making it reappear later in the form of tangible assets under Party control, both State and private.

"We have another problem," said Becker. "This morning's dispatches had an announcement. We will be visited on..." he peered at Fräulein Grimm.

She consulted a memo. "On December twenty-eight, at ten in the morning in the Great Hall. The entire staff."

"Make a note, gentlemen. Our visitor is Theodor Eicke, SS Commandant Eicke on a national tour. No need to tell you what his message is likely to be."

"Excuse me," said Schweiger, "how does one reconcile Berlin's new directives, what Schirardi a moment ago called...what was that word, Anton...caution?...with Commandant Eicke's more, well, I think it's appropriate to use the term...aggressive...techniques?"

"Interesting question, Schweiger. Ask him when he gets here."

The meeting lasted until lunch, most urgent business disposed of, lesser items postponed until after the holidays. They slowly began to leave. Note pads and documents were stuffed into briefcases, a few hearty pleasantries exchanged. Hartung was about to exit when Dr. Becker addressed him.

"Oh Dietrich, a moment please."

Damn, thought Hartung, it's always 'Oh Dietrich, a moment please.' Why not 'Oh Deppmüller' or 'Oh Hofmeister, a moment please.' What the hell does he want now?

The room emptied. Hartung remained in his seat. Becker paced, smoked, and sat down.

"You're doing a good job, Dietrich. However..."

It's always 'however,' thought Hartung. I need a drink.

"...there's still too much backlog. Your files are piling up. Frau Zeidler showed me the numbers yesterday. I assigned you two more people, assumed that would get the job done. Was I wrong?"

Hartung fumed inside. Why didn't Zeidler tell him Becker checked up on him? Or maybe she did tell him and he forgot. Unfortunately it was true; things were piling up.

"With all the new directives, there's been a bit of confusion, Herr Becker. Not here of course, not in Stuttgart, but in some of the district offices. I've been making phone calls. It's improving. It's speeding up." Damn it, why did his neck always sweat when he talked with Becker? He was sure the bastard noticed. "Right now I'm scheduling trips to a dozen districts."

"When? Where?"

"Immediately after the holidays, starting in Westfalen."

Becker stubbed out his cigarette, carefully put the holder in a side pocket of his jacket. Both elbows on the table, he cradled his head in cupped hands and smiled at the perspiring Hartung.

"You know, I like you, Dietrich. You have humor. You're not what I would call...well, dynamic, but many good people lack...forcefulness. That's just the way they are. It's pleasant. I can always count on you for a good laugh. So, let's put our heads together, you and I. We need to be totally clear with each other. Point one. Eicke arrives in Stuttgart on the twenty-eighth. Eicke works for Himmler..." he crossed the first two fingers of his right hand..."who is like this..." he crossed the first two fingers of his left hand..."with Hitler. Eicke's job is to fill his camps with enemies of the Reich. Used to be just Dachau, Dietrich, but apparently there are now two or three more such places. In fact, I have it on good authority that some of our own people, I mean SA and SS people, have been invited to use those facilities. From what I understand they're mostly fellow Party members who...how shall I put it...didn't get the job done?"

"But Herr Becker..." Hartung interrupted, rivulets of sweat coursing his spine.

"Allow me to finish. We have to understand each other completely. Point two. Here is what you *will* do, beginning the moment we conclude this conversation. You *will* go to your office. With your secretary's assistance you *will* set up appointments between tomorrow and Christmas in as many districts as possible. That still leaves you the rest of the day and tonight to deal with those special visa requests that have been overflowing, obviously for some time, in your 'To do Immediately' basket." He leaned forward and his face hardened. "You *will* do them immediately. Before you leave tomorrow, Hartung, I assure you that basket *will* be empty. I don't wish to interfere with your decision-making process. For all I care you can consign the whole basketful to the spirit world, as long as they leave their worldly goods behind. When Commandant Eicke pays his visit, I am only concerned that he tells Berlin how incredibly efficient we are, how brilliantly we separate filthy Jewish Bolshevist chaff from golden German wheat." Becker smiled, relishing his metaphor. "I'm sure you comprehend my meaning."

"I'll get it done, Herr Becker," ventured Hartung.

"Oh, undoubtedly. By the way, I meant to ask you, how are you doing with your little problem?"

The silver flask burned in Hartung's pants pocket. He thought it might melt and spill single malt Scotch down his leg and all over the floor. Was it his imagination or was Becker staring at it straight through the fabric?

"Completely under control, sir," he lied. "A couple of beers with dinner and that's it."

Becker's eyebrows arched perceptibly, a brief chuckle rumbled in his throat. He focused on Hartung's eyes. "Let me tell you, Dietrich, and I don't intend to bring up this subject again. Ever. Please listen carefully. I do not, I repeat, I do not wish to be victimized by your craving for alcohol. Is that absolutely clear?"

"Yes sir. That's clear."

Without further word Becker walked briskly out the door, slammed it behind him. Hartung wiped sweat from his neck and forehead, lurched down the stairway to his office. Frau Zeidler was out to lunch. He shut his door, thankful for her absence, and emptied his flask. Then, generously lubricated, he attacked the overflowing 'To Do *Immediately*' basket. What the hell difference does it make, he mused. Why bother with all the details? The lousy yids have to come here anyway, then we'll damn well make sure they get away with nothing, so what the hell? Knots of tension loosened up. Each folder contained a blank appearance notice that required a department stamp and his signature. He found the stamp on Frau Zeidler's desk, started at the top, barely glanced at the files as he rapidly worked his way toward the bottom. Rosenbaum, Herbert: stamp, signature. Rotman, David: stamp, signature. Saltzmann, Mordecai: stamp, signature. Samuels, Peter: stamp, signature. Schumann, Horst: stamp, signature. Schwartz, Leah: stamp, signature. A few more and the basket was empty. There, that would show Becker!

When Frau Zeidler returned from lunch, she understood perfectly what had happened. She would affix passport photos to notices, emboss them with ministry seals.

"Frau Zeidler! Why didn't you tell me Becker was here yesterday?"

Oh god, she thought, he's loaded already. She smiled. "Routine check, Herr Hartung. No problem. Grimm tells me you're visiting districts tomorrow. I'd better start with the reservations. You go home and pack, get some rest. You're going to be busy. I'll put the itinerary and train schedules together. You can pick them up in the morning. I'll be here at eight. Okay?"

He nodded, grateful for her efficiency, and lost no time making his departure. She consulted her appointment book, filled in blanks on appearance notices, entered dates on her chart. At the proper time the files would be parceled out to rigorously selected interrogation teams. The Schumann letter was one of twenty recorded and readied for pick-up.

Stuttgart, 15 December 1935

Herr Horst Schumann
Weiherstrasse 4
Dortmund

Dear Herr Schumann,

It is hereby ordered, in connection with your application for emigration, that you appear in person in Suite 422, The Rathaus, The Ministry of Foreign Affairs, Division of Special Exit Visas, Department of Immigration, Stuttgart, on January 21, 1936, at 10:00 a.m. Failure to appear at that time will result in the forfeiture of all exit priorities. For purposes of identification, you will present this notification at the reception desk. Loss of this document or any other reason for failure to present it, or yourself, at the specified time will result in immediate cancellation of your application.

Heil Hitler,

Dietrich Hartung
Office of Special Visas

She stamped his signature, addressed envelopes, carefully stuffed them with correct notifications and made sure a mail clerk picked them up promptly. Greatly relieved to finally have these notices on their way, she determined Hartung's most effective itinerary and called appropriate offices to confirm appointments with selected *Ortsgruppenleiters*. She arranged reservations of railway tickets with a transportation clerk in the Party's finance bureau on Büchsenstrasse and, pleased with a job well done, exited into the crisp autumn air. She remembered seeing notices of a Mozart concert at the *Hochschule für Musik*. Well, why not? Maybe a bite to eat and a short walk to Kanonenweg. She felt at peace with herself. She had been loyal to Hartung. Church bells pealed as she skirted the Schlossgarten.

◆   ◆   ◆

Whatever doubts lingered in the minds of Dortmund's nearly extinct left-wing community about Party intentions were erased by the violent murders of Isador and Brigitte Herz. Heiko Böhm was clearly in charge, with an unmistakable mandate to eliminate them. The time had come to run immediately, no matter where. Even under a threat of death, however, to disappear entirely from the face of Germany was a difficult task, more so for some than for others.

Lev Grünberg thought it best to book accommodations as quickly as possible. He telephoned Ruth Bender, widow of a former colleague, who managed a small hotel near Tegel. He had stayed with her whenever medical business took him to Berlin.

"The place is full," Ruth said on the phone, "Jews from all over trying to get out, hanging around embassies, any country that might take them. How urgent is it, Lev?"

He recounted the disasters of the last two weeks. "I'd be grateful for whatever you can manage, Ruth."

"For you and your family I'll make space, Lev. You can stay in my own apartment. The guest room will be crowded with the four of you, but I have extra beds."

He sold his office equipment and supplies at a considerable loss to a young doctor at Johannes, made similar arrangements about furniture with his landlord, pretended he was moving to a new medical assignment. Within a week he was ready to leave, personal belongings packed tightly in his old, well-maintained Mercedes. He called Oskar the night before departure.

"Some country will welcome a skilled orthopedist, Oskar. Maybe even one with a social conscience."

"That's not the question, Lev, you know that. Böhm, Terhoven, maybe Adolf too, they want our hide. You really think you, or any of us will be allowed to leave Germany? I think we'll have to sneak out like thieves in the night."

"Who knows? Meanwhile, it's easier to get lost in Berlin. If I have to, I'll escape as best I can. Anything is better than waiting for Heiko the Hun to ship us to Dachau. It's no longer a matter of right or wrong. I must do for my family whatever is possible."

"I'll miss you, old friend. Let me know what happens."

"I'll try. Good luck with Horst. Shalom, Oskar."

"Shalom, Lev."

◆   ◆   ◆

Dov and Oskar held a strategy meeting in a quiet corner of the zoo, near the aviary. The day was cold, but sunny.

"You know, Oskar, the real beasts are out there. The wrong creatures are kept in cages."

Oskar nodded agreement. Dov, too, would go soon, just as Lev had fled to Berlin. They regarded each other with affection. "You have plans?"

"I sent Hannah and David to my sister's."

"Böhm knows where you live."

"Most of the time I stay in the ghetto with friends and old clients. I only sneak into my flat when I have to. Believe me, old friend, as soon as I can, I'm leaving."

"Where to?"

"Not sure. It depends on how well old contacts work out. Maybe Russia."

"You can get a passport to Russia?"

"It's not easy, but there are ways. I must find money. For money there's always a way."

He dragged deep on his Turkish cigarette. The incongruity of the moment was not lost on these two middle-aged warriors: decades spent on causes won and lost, careers up in smoke, a future putrid with emptiness; a litany of despair accompanied by hundreds of birds chirping melodiously in the wintry chill.

"What about you and Horst?"

"I sent Horst to Walter's house. I'll hang around until we hear from Stuttgart. Then? I don't know, Dov, I honestly don't. My French is pretty good. Maybe Belgium, I have friends in Liege, but right now? I just have no idea."

The lawyer reached into a pocket. "Here's the key to The Den. Use it. For a week or two it might be okay. You'll find food in the apartment but be careful. Böhm might look for me. Who knows what that bastard will do!"

"I appreciate this, Dov. I really do."

"Don't be ridiculous. If you need The Den, better go at night or you might run into the janitor. Not a man to be trusted. Listen, might not be so bad if Horst joins you. After Herz and Brigitte, your building isn't too safe either."

"When are you leaving?"

"In a week, on the twenty-fourth. Even Böhm doesn't kill on Christmas. Here's a suggestion. Why don't you, Horst and I meet at my place on Christmas Eve? You guys can help me pack. It also gives us a chance to say a decent good bye."

"We'll be there."

There was nothing more to say, no plans to hatch, no faith to share, no principles to debate. Oskar left first, Dov soon after, pinching the tip of his Turkish, saving the butt. One never knew; his supply was getting low, as were his resources.

◆   ◆   ◆

The Pariser apartment on Neue Strasse was barely large enough for two. Now it housed four. George Pariser earned a meager living as a fill-in typesetter. Publications in town were reluctant to keep a Jew on their permanent payroll, but Pariser was experienced and quick, welcomed as an extra hand at print time, especially since he came at bargain prices. When he wasn't working, George read Talmud, devotedly studied the Hebrew commentaries. He also embroidered, mostly landscapes and animals, delicate and true to life which Yetta, his wife, fashioned into pillows and antimacassars and occasionally sold to the ladies for whom she made dresses.

Horst did his best to be unobtrusive. Walter occupied a tiny alcove near the bathroom, not large enough for two beds, so Horst slept on a mattress in the living room, stored it on Walter's bed during the day. They knew it was a short-term arrangement; the Stuttgart notice would come soon. Brigitte's death disturbed the boys deeply. She had been so smart and helpful, so full of energy, a true and sincere friend. Now she was dead, burned alive.

"They're killing people, Horst. I hate it here. I hate it so much. I want to go to America with you. Everybody is leaving. Karl and Albert are in Berlin. David is at his aunt's. Soli and his mother are…I don't know where. Lisa says her father talks about going to Sweden. You'll be in America. What am I going to do alone?

"Maybe George will take you to Palestine."

"I wish! He doesn't want to leave his *schul*. Says he's the only one who can read Torah. Besides, he thinks everything will be fine. When he heard about Isador and Gitte, he prayed. Said Isador was a bad Jew, so what could one expect."

Being cooped up made them feel worse. After Horst checked his mail they walked to the zoo. Walter tried to sketch but quit right away.

"Not in the mood," he said. "Why did they have to kill Gitte and Isador that way? Oh Horst," he repeated, "What am I going to do when you go away?"

"Come on, Walter, it's not the end of the world. Many Jews are leaving for Palestine. Sooner or later George will change his mind. Lots of good *schuls* there, they say. What's the expression? 'Next year in Jerusalem'? I'm willing to bet you."

"You'd lose your bet unless Mama makes him do it. She can't find work anymore, not after Nüremberg."

"Listen, Pariser. Some day they'll have a big art show in Chicago with signs on all the kiosks: 'One Man Show by World Famous Artist, Walter Pariser. Now at the Art Museum!' And you'll be dressed in a tuxedo and the ladies will admire you and they'll say 'oh, isn't he wonderful?' And they'll brag about their nice little Pariser hanging in their living room. They'll say 'It's not a big one, of course, nobody can afford a big one. It cost me only a million Marks—oops, I mean, dollars.' And I'll stand in a corner and watch you because I'll be the proudest person in the world. Besides, I'll be the only one who knew you before you were old enough to wear a tuxedo."

"You can have one of my paintings, Schumann, for nothing."

"Don't do me any favors, Pariser. I'll be able to pay for it on my own. How's that?"

They laughed, forgot the real world for a few moments, watched monkeys swing in trees, and visited Ali, asleep in its cave. As always, in his mind Horst set Ali free, but this time the image was different. He pictured himself clinging to Ali's back as they flew through the air and rode like the wind until they came to the sea and…well…they would figure out something, maybe swim to England or stop a ship going by and they would sail to America together.

"It's late, Horst. We'd better go home before school is out."

They took a shortcut past South Station, hurried when kids started to crowd the streets. From Schwanenwall they crossed over to Weiherstrasse, intending to use the alley. They didn't quite make it. Eckert and five of his buddies, on their way home from school, spotted and surrounded them a few feet from the burned-out entrance to "Herz Furniture," its charred sign still dangling lopsidedly from a remaining hook.

"Hey, look what we've got here, friends," sneered Eckert, "its Abraham and Jacob. Coming to visit Izzy?" They roared with laughter. "Haven't seen you around, Schumann. How come?"

"Busy."

"Busy. Busy, he says." He flexed his shoulders, moved in on Horst. "Busy with what? Putting up posters?"

"Leave me alone, Eckert."

"Or maybe you've come to see what's left of your little girlfriend. Is that it?" Horst clenched his teeth, said nothing. "Take them inside, fellows. Let's show them what happens to Jews who put filthy Bolshevist literature on clean German walls." They were pushed and dragged into the burned-out store. People passed by, studiously avoided involvement.

"Take off their pants," Eckert ordered. They were no match for six of them, were knocked to the sooty floor, their pants pulled off. "Turn them over, hold them down." Eckert ripped a blackened piece of board from a burned-out counter. "Let's whack the faggot birdman first and listen to him sing. Then we'll hear from the poster boy."

As Eckert lifted the board to strike, Walter twisted around and raised his arm to defend himself. He did not see the nail, blackened by fire, sticking out of the board, invisible against the charcoaled wood. Eckert swung hard. The nail penetrated Walter's palm and protruded between the knuckles. Walter's scream was like an animal's, fierce and unbearable.

"Let's get out of here," said Eckert, "That's enough for today." They rushed into the street without looking back. A man stuck his head in, walked away quickly.

"Oh god, Walter, please, it will be okay. Oh god, Walter, what can I do?"

Horst yanked on his pants, kneeled next to Walter who lay curled on a pile of ashes, whimpering with pain, nearly unconscious. Horst didn't know what else to do, held Walter's wrist down, gripped the board hard and ripped the nail out of his hand in one swift move. Walter screamed and collapsed. There was blood, but not much.

Beside himself with anxiety, Horst cradled his friend's head and urged him to stand up. "Try, Walter. Please. Just try. Please, you can do it. We have to get you home. Come on, Walter. I know it hurts, but you have to try. It's not far. We have to get you out of here. You have to see a doctor." He tore off his shirt, tied it around Walter's hand and finally managed to drag him down the alley and up the stairs to the Pariser apartment, stumbling on every step.

Yetta bathed her son's hand, which had swollen a great deal already. She gave him aspirin to ease the pain. George came home an hour later, heard the story and beseeched God for mercy before pursuing ways to find medical help.

"Can you get Grünberg, Horst? The one who fixed your arms?"

"He's gone to Berlin."

"I'll try Schwartzbart, Yetta, the Polish doctor who treated you when you had stones."

"Hurry George, Walter looks sick."

Pariser went to the ghetto, to Schwartzbart's run-down office. The doctor was out, making house calls. When he returned two hours later he was exhausted, but willing to see one more patient.

"Who else is there," he said. "I'm the only one now."

By the time they returned, Walter's temperature had risen sharply. He had great difficulty moving his jaws. His back and neck seemed strangely arched and stiff as steel pipes. Schwartzbart examined the hand, peered into Walter's eyes and tried, without success, to look at his tongue and throat.

"Tetanus," he said, shaking his head in despair. "Lockjaw. Worse case I've seen in my whole life. I can give you medicine, but I don't think it will do any good. Prayers might work better."

"You mean my son is going to die?" Yetta cried, her eyes enormous with terror. "There's nothing you can do?"

"Only God does miracles," the doctor answered, closed his bag and fled.

The three tended to Walter through he night, cooling his burning forehead with wet towels. They forced medicine through his clenched teeth until that, too, became impossible. His arm was now swollen to the elbow, his body wracked by endless spasms. Toward morning he went into a coma and just before sunrise he died.

Yetta bathed his body, dressed him in clean clothes. They would arrange for burial later. Now they could only cry without tears.

"There should be a *minyan*," said George, trying desperately to hold himself together, "but where in this accursed city will I find nine others to share my grief? May God forgive me for committing a sin." As if in a trance, he put on his prayer shawl, lifted the bible to his lips and recited the mourner's *Kaddish*, that ancient Hebrew prayer which for centuries had rent the hearts of Jews, even as it was meant to heal.

Yisgadal v'yiskadah sh'mei rabbaw.

The glory of God? Horst muttered to himself. Where were you, God, when they killed my friend? You're never there when we need you.

B'allmaw dee v'raw chir'usei v'yamlich malchusei,
V'yatzmach purkanei v'kareiv m'shichei.

Oh, right, his kingdom. Some kingdom! Horst was furious. What a laugh. The enemy is on the throne, George. Before he gets pushed off a lot of us will die, not just Walter.

B'chayeichon, uv'yomeichon, uv'chayei, d'chol beis yisroel, ba'agawlaw u'vizman kawriv, v'imru: Amein.

Amen. Amen, my friend. Amen to birds and beasts. Amen, wherever you are. You broke your promise, Walter. You promised to meet me in Chicago. Not fair. You were going to be famous and wear a tuxedo. I want one of your pictures, not some dumb, stupid Amen. Not fair, Walter. It's not fair, damn you."

Y'hei sh'mei rabbaw m'vawrach l'allam u'l'allmei all'mayaw.

George bobbed back and forth, Yetta stood frozen, Horst licked tears from his lips.

Yis'bawrach, v'yistabach, v'yispawar,
V'yisromam, v'yis'nasei,
v'yis'hadar, v'yis'aleh, v'yis'halawl
Sh'mei d'kudshaw b'rich hu.

The prayer droned on to its bitter end. Horst wanted to leave before it was over; what did it matter? Papa was right. Prayers were only good for people without hope or for those with full bellies, he once said. This one sure wasn't going to bring Walter back, so what was the use of it? Horst couldn't wait to get out of there.

Oseh shawlom bim'ro'mawv,
Hu ya'aseh shawlom awleinu,
V'al kol yisroel v'imru: Amein.

"Amen," said Horst. "I have to leave now."

"You were a good friend." Yetta hugged him fiercely. Horst was a last connection to her dead son and somehow his leaving would further diminish her life.

He had nowhere to go except his apartment. Dangerous? Yes, but he was beyond caring. What's more, if Papa was willing to risk it, so could he. He checked the mailbox automatically. Nothing. No sign of Oskar, either. He stared out the window. Slowly tears came, then sobs that seemed to last forever. Finally, exhausted by grief and a raging need to be given back his loss, he sank onto the old living room couch and stared, unseeing, into the descending dusk.

23

MEMORANDUM

---

6 December 1935

TO: Hapag Ticket Agents
FROM: Gottfried Eberhardt, Chief Controller
SUBJECT: Revised Procedures, Emigrant Tickets

There will be a meeting in the conference room of our main office on Friday, 13 December 1935 at 1600. The purpose is to instruct ticket agents in revised proceedings mandated by the Ministry of Transportation and taking effect 1 January 1936. Attendance is obligatory.

Hildegard Kube read the memo again to make sure she had the time right. Printed on Hapag's distinctive stationery, it was already a week old. In the crush of holiday travel she had nearly forgotten the details. Yesterday, Eberhardt's secretary called to remind her.

When Hildegard arrived, ten ticket agents were already seated in folding chairs, exchanging company gossip. Eberhardt entered only minutes later with a smiling, portly SS officer whom he introduced as Dr. Ritter of the Foreign Ministry's political section.

"I won't take much of your time." Dr. Ritter's voice was surprisingly high-pitched. "It's important that new security procedures are completely understood. Yes, completely. Emigration has sharply increased. Nobody knows that better than you. Yes, nobody." He smiled without parting his lips. "Unfortunately, some who want to leave are enemies of the Reich and want to steal what rightfully belongs to the State. Yes, rightfully. Others are traitors who spread Bolshevist lies about us. We must find them and deal with them in an appropriate manner. We need your help."

He reached into his briefcase, extracted a stack of printed pamphlets and gave one to each agent. "These are new procedures. Everything you need to know is there. Yes, everything. Let me go over it with you. If you have questions, I will answer them." He leaned toward Eberhardt. "Or do you want to do this?"

"No, quite all right. I'll visit my agents personally, starting tomorrow."

"Splendid." Dr. Ritter scanned the faces before him. "So. Perhaps you are not aware that the emigration process has shifted. Yes, shifted. How? Toward greater local authority. The reason? Simple, it functions better. I'll explain. We believe you'll work better if you know why." He took a handkerchief from a coat pocket, delicately wiped his brow.

"From now on certain emigrants will always be routed through Stuttgart. Their exit visas are approved there, but not until they've been interviewed by our Security Service." He smiled his thin-lipped smile. "I see some of you understand already. Good. Very good. Yes, of course. Stuttgart knows when, and from where, these emigrants are leaving. Directives are sent...that's point three in your pamphlet...we want to be sure you understand the process...they're sent to SS Internal Affairs in the appropriate city of departure, in your case, Hamburg, of course." He looked almost cheerful.

"You see how it works? Internal Affairs forwards the names of the emigrants to the proper ticket control." He glanced amiably at Eberhardt. "In Hamburg, Herr Eberhardt's office. He checks his passenger manifest against those from your ticket offices. Clearly explained on page five. We printed a copy of the form Herr Eberhardt uses for his notations. Look on page six. You see, it's called the 'Approved Passenger Manifest.' It has the name of the ship, the date of departure and the list of those who have cleared Security. Notice the columns called 'In Order' and 'Not in Order?' These columns quite concern you. Yes, quite. On the evening before a ship leaves you are to remove all those tickets stamped 'Not in Order.' Of course Security will be present on departure day. You know better than I that, well, certain people, well, Aryans, I mean decent people traveling abroad usually pick up their tickets weeks before. Yes, weeks. But these subversives almost never show up until the last moment. Why? Yes indeed, why? We discovered why! Herr Eberhardt was instrumental in solving the puzzle." He grinned toward Eberhardt who smiled in return. "Yes, indeed. They thought that with almost a thousand passengers boarding they could sneak all kinds of things aboard; illegal goods, stolen jewelry, money, subversive documents." Ritter's smile became beatific. "Well, that's finished. No exit visas until Security checks them out on 'Sail Day.' You remove all tickets marked 'Not in Order.' That's all you'll need to do. Security takes care of the rest." He grinned, enormously pleased with himself. "Very good care. No more illegal escapes. No more stealing from German citizens. Officially, the procedure goes into effect on January first. That's it. Now then, any questions?"

None were asked. Frau Kube, like everyone else, knew Eberhardt would leave nothing to chance. He would inundate them with memos and visits until every agent had memorized the routine.

Afterward coffee and cake were served. Dr. Ritter, smiling affably, congratulated the men and women on their fine record and keen understanding. "You," he addressed the entire group, delicately wiping crumbs from his black uniform, "are bastions of Reich security. The job you do is urgent and useful." He laid a soft, manicured hand on the shoulder of a young female agent and now his smile finally reached his eyes. "Yes, useful," he said, "very useful indeed."

◆   ◆   ◆

To Oskar's considerable surprise, Gretchen telephoned before Christmas. "Are you all right? I thought maybe you would call."

"You said not to."

Yes, I know. What's happening to Horst? Have you had an answer from Stuttgart?"

"Any day now, I hope."

He told her briefly about the Herz tragedy, heard the gasp in her voice. She and Isador had not been close but had liked each other. Walter's death shocked her terribly.

"Oh Oskar, I'm sorry. I'm so terribly sorry. If you don't mind, I'd like to call you back."

She called back in an hour. "I asked Ilse if you and Horst could visit for dinner. She said it would be okay if you come after dark. You understand, don't you?"

"Yes, Grete, perfectly. It's kind of you to ask. When do you want us?"

"Tomorrow evening? Is tomorrow evening all right? At seven?"

"We'll be there, Grete, if we're still alive."

"Oskar, please don't say such things."

Horst dressed as neatly as possible. Oskar spent the last of his money on flowers and a few gallons of gas for the Opel, which needed repairs and was barely running. Erich and Ilse Koch and four year-old Katje lived in a pleasant apartment on Uebelgönne, near the Ritter Brewery.

Ilse, two years younger than Grete, was in training to be a nurse. A kind and happy person, she had no concern about Grete's marriage to a Jew, or to anyone else, as long as he was a gentleman. To Erich, Oskar was something of an enigma, the only Jew he knew personally. When they first met, Oskar noticed Erich's furtive glances.

"I assure you," Oskar had pointed out, "that Jews don't have a tail or horns." Since then they got along well, but invitations to the Kochs diminished after nineteen thirty-three.

Ilse made a fine dinner, a roast with boiled potatoes and cabbage and a dessert of rich chocolate pudding and a splendid poppy seed cake. Horst played with Katje while Oskar and Erich talked and the sisters washed dishes. When Ilse put Katje to bed, Erich offered Horst a chess lesson. Grete, feeling comfortable, invited Oskar to go for a walk. It was cold outside, a clear, moonlit night. Tentatively, Oskar put an arm around her shoulder. She didn't shrug it off.

"I'm sorry it turned out bad for us, Grete. I understand why you left. I don't blame you."

She didn't respond, quietly walked in step with him. At the corner of Ritterstrasse they passed a tavern, laughter cascading through its walls.

"Grete, can we sit and have a beer or a glass of wine?" He looked through the tavern window. "No uniforms. I'm sure we'll be all right."

In a quiet booth near the back, a bottle of Mosel between them, he told her about last week's tragedies. She listened in mute horror.

"What will you do, Oskar? You know Böhm is out to get you. Maybe not today, but it won't be long. What are you waiting for?"

"For Horst to leave, then I'll go too." He took her hand, heartened by her concern. "I wrote to Clara to send me the papers for America."

"Oh Oskar, why couldn't you have done that sooner?"

"You know why. I had a cause. I was stubborn. I don't have to tell you."

She understood him all too well. Now was not the time to deal with the reality of their relationship. The reality of survival was much more important,

"Oskar, I want to help. I talked to Ilse. It's okay with her. I'm not sure about Erich, but I think she can persuade him."

"About what, Grete?"

"I think Horst should stay with me, with us, until he hears from Stuttgart. He can sleep in my room. There's an extra cot. And you should find some place away from the apartment, too. At least until you hear from Clara. I'm really worried, Oskar, for both of you."

He was surprised by her offer, but he respected her for it and for herself, more than ever before.

"Grete, thank you. You are quite tremendous. I'll talk to Horst. I'm sure he'll be happy to accept. He needs to get away from Weiherstrasse and its memories."

When they returned to the apartment in Uebelgönne, Erich had gone to bed, Ilse and Horst were reading. Horst immediately said yes to Grete's offer. The thought of spending another night in his old home was awful. His friends were dead or gone, Oskar out most of the time. At least here he was comfortable, safe until his notice came.

"Papa, what will you do? Are you sure you don't want me to keep you company?"

"No, son, I'll be fine. Hershl will put me up for a few days. So far they haven't attacked the ghetto. I'll call you tomorrow about the mail."

Horst and his stepmother walked Oskar to the car, hugged him good night and watched him drive away.

"He missed you."

"Your father is a nice man. I wish him the best. I also pray he allows some sense into his head and leaves."

The street was deserted. A distant church bell tolled eleven times into a flurry of snowflakes. They walked into the warm house together.

◆   ◆   ◆

Hershl Auerbach understood Oskar's reluctance to spend another night on Weiherstrasse.

"Just a few days, Hershl, only until the boy leaves. I can sleep anywhere, doesn't matter, the couch, the floor, it's not important."

"Stop worrying. Friedl will make room. That's what friends are for. I'll take it out in leather."

He slept on a mattress in the kitchen. It was warm and smelled good, but he was uneasy burdening these kind folks. Each day he stopped at Weiherstrasse, hoping to find the longed for notice from Stuttgart.

It came on the twenty-third of December. He tore it open, devoured its contents, rushed upstairs and telephoned Horst.

"Horst, it's here! The letter! They are letting you go."

"Papa, Papa, is it true?"

"Yes, my son, it's really true. I'll meet you at Café Lüchtemeyer in two hours. We'll celebrate with hot chocolate."

Next he called Dov, who answered the phone cautiously.

"Dov, listen to the good news. The letter from Stuttgart arrived this morning."

"Oskar, that's wonderful. *Mazel tov*. Here is what I suggest. You come tonight at eight, both of you. Where is Horst now?"

"Staying with Grete. I'll explain later."

"With Grete, eh? Well, we'll send your son off tomorrow. It's almost Christmas Eve, so he should be safe. Let's have a good-bye party, just the three of us. Why not? We're all we have left. May as well enjoy it. And Oskar…"

"Yes, Dov?"

"Be careful. Take absolutely no chances. Not now, please."

"I promise," said Oskar and meant it. "Thanks, good friend."

At Café Lüchtemeyer Horst experienced a light-headedness that accentuated even the most ordinary incidents. At this moment nothing seemed ordinary to him. The café's hushed voices, the pungent smell of fresh-brewed coffee, the flow of incandescent lamps, everything was different, almost unfamiliar. Even his father seemed to exist at a distance, in a space without present, future or past, a confusing, wonderfully exhilarating new experience. They ordered hot chocolate and pastry, unable to control a slight hysteria in their voices. Oskar felt his son already slipping away, stretching toward America, reaching toward a new life. A wave of envy surprised him, but the misery of being left behind soon mingled with his joy for Horst's happiness. He took out the Stuttgart letter, laid it on the table.

"There it is, Horst, what we've been waiting for."

Horst, almost afraid to touch the paper, his heart pounding, ran a finger over the seal embossed in his picture, then slowly read the short page, twice. Only the second time did the letter's dates become meaningful.

"Papa, I have to be in Stuttgart on January twenty-one?" Oskar nodded. "But Papa, that's less than four weeks from now. How will I get there?"

"We'll talk to Dov tonight. He knows about such things."

"Papa? I would like to stop at Weiherstrasse first."

"Today?"

"Just until we go to Dov's? If I have to get to Stuttgart in three weeks, I'll have to leave right away. Maybe this is my last night in Dortmund."

Hearing the words, Oskar's throat tightened. Against his will he began to cry, struggled to hide his tears by wiping his glasses, but Horst saw through the effort. Within seconds he was also crying. They made a futile attempt to stop their weeping, but their tears just kept flowing. Oskar's handkerchief had to serve them both, to wipe eyes and blow noses. Only when Horst's sobs began to mingle with embarrassed giggles did they regain a semblance of composure.

Not since he left Liselotte at the edge of the Paderborn forest had Horst felt so bewildered. Then and now he was torn by the anguish of leaving a loved one behind, but there was also a difference. When he fled Paderborn his goal was unclear; now he knew exactly what he wanted. He desperately wanted to go to America.

"Oh Papa, I'll write to you, I promise. I'll write to you all the time. And you'll come later, right? I know you will. You have to promise me you will."

With wonder Oskar stared at his son. He realized that since Toni died he had not felt truly close to anyone. He bitterly rued a truth, not willingly admitted until now. Six years ago he had sacrificed his son. He had sacrificed him for a commitment to Marxism and its power to emancipate the enslaved people of the world, or so he had believed. His training had come early.

Oskar was only five when his father, Rabbi Jakob, taught him how to read, huddled on benches in Zeltingen's vineyards, hard on the banks of the languorous Mosel. The boy watched his father cobble shoes while humming the workers' truculent melodies, like a cantor caressing a psalm, was nourished by him on the prolix assertions of Marx and Engels, Fichte and Hegel, Lenin and Trotsky. Oskar's heart ached when he saw young women and old men toil under loaded hods to harvest the valley's precious grapes. Jakob admonished: "Don't weep for them, my son. Neither tears nor laughter will sustain them. Speak to them of their needs, listen to them of their wants, write to them of their power." That was the gospel according to Rabbi Schumann, the radical cobbler of Zeltingen. Not until the last few years, not until recently, perhaps not until this very moment, did it occur to Oskar that an essential human element was missing from his father's social ecumenism. The rabbi rarely spoke of love. "Ideas may move mountains," he was fond of saying, "love merely invites praise of their beauty." Oskar believed his words, thereafter harnessed his considerable intellect to this cerebral, bloodless ideology. Well, Sister Clara was right. He recalled her favorite anecdote, one of many she told about her brooding, baffling brother. "Oskar," she had cried, running to where he sat at the river, reading of course. "Oskar, it's Susi, your cat. She fell into the water tank and drowned." She never tired of re-telling his reply as he reluctantly looked up from his book. "*Und was hat die Katz dazu gesagt?*"—And what did the cat say to that?—he had asked. Only sixteen years old, he had already begun to sever connections with sentiments and sympathy, leaving in their wake a residue of dryer passions: anger, zeal and, occasionally, satisfaction. True, he had been deeply in love with Toni, that dark beauty who bore him two children, but he was also exasperated by her demand for orthodoxy, parental ardor, and domestic stability. Toni died in childbirth, radiant in her twenty-ninth year. Oskar mourned her loss and buried the only piece of his heart that had been truly alive. He married Grete for companionship. After Toni, he believed himself incapable of loving again. Until recently. Until now.

"I love you, Horst," he said, "I love you more than I can say. Forgive me for not saying it sooner or more often. Forgive me for my clumsiness. I've had so little practice saying I love you since Toni died."

"I love you too, Papa. Even in America I will love you. I'm sure of that."

Oskar leaned over and kissed Horst on the forehead. What a feeling, he thought, what a wonderful feeling.

When they entered their old home it was damp and cold. The heat was turned off; all human warmth had faded as well. Horst selected a few cherished belongings; an unread Karl May book, his treasured pocketknife—he thought of Czerny—a picture postcard of Ali the panther, purchased at the zoo. He found one of Walter's sketches, a yellow-breasted bird, choked up as he packed it carefully under a shirt. He decided against the English-German dictionary. Too heavy. Oskar found photos of Toni, one of Opa and Oma Schumann in front of their house holding him and Liselotte in their laps, another of Liselotte and himself hugging. He had never seen these pictures and he nearly wept again. The photographs found a safe place between pages of his Karl May book, buried under a sweater, a pair of socks and the one extra pair of pants he owned. He strapped everything down and tearfully pronounced himself ready to go to America.

Church bells rang to celebrate the night before Christmas Eve. At Dov's house, Oskar and Horst found he had prepared a feast, a wonderful spread of cheese, bread, and sausages, topped off by a glorious whipped-cream cake.

"Who can afford it?" Dov said, "but nothing's too good for an American. We don't want you telling everybody in Chicago that we starved you to death. Believe me, young man, we expect you to return the favor. Maybe sooner than you think." Horst drank wine as they toasted him.

"To a safe trip!" said Dov. "In America, please remember who bought you your last meal in Dortmund. Now, let's plan for tomorrow. Show me what they sent from Stuttgart, Oskar."

After having walked a tightrope for weeks, Oskar and Dov decided to throw caution to the wind for this one special night. Both men drank immoderately, became nostalgic and overemotional and finally collapsed from fatigue. Horst, too excited to sleep, tossed fitfully on the sagging couch, tried to shut out the snoring, counted minutes and seconds and eventually dozed off toward morning. Church bells woke him in time to watch the sun struggle in a snow-laden sky.

Breakfast consisted of leftovers washed down with hot coffee. Oskar had dressed, but Dov wore a flannel robe frayed at the elbows. Already the smell of his Turkish tobacco drifted through the apartment. A perplexing apathy hung in the air, a conspiracy to postpone the inevitable, somewhat like people on railway platforms delaying good-byes until the train starts moving. Reluctantly, but with determination, Dov pushed away from the table.

"Let's not be stupid," he said. "Just because they're celebrating the birthday of an eccentric, underground rabbi tomorrow, doesn't mean they'll give Horst a hug and a kiss if they meet him on the street. We can sit here all day, friends. Doesn't matter to me, but it sure as hell won't get the boy to Stuttgart."

"I've given that some thought," said Oskar.

"I bet you have," snorted Dov. "Horst, your father is a fine writer, one of the best I know, but I wouldn't let him arrange a trip for you from here to the bathroom. You'd end up taking a shit in the kitchen."

Oskar grinned self-consciously. He knew Dov had a point. "I'll be happy to listen to your plan, Herr Tour Guide."

"Glad to, but first things first." Dov rummaged around in his bedroom until he found a small leather toilet kit. "Thank heaven Hannah is at her sister's. She would have a fit if she saw this," he said, cutting strips from the linoleum table-cloth and converting the small bag so that Horst could tie it around his midsection. "Stylish it isn't, but it'll work." He snatched the appearance notice from Oskar's hand, wrapped it neatly in a square of linoleum, secured it with rubber bands, zipped the case shut and fastened it to Horst's waist. "Voila," he beamed "I should have gone into the bag business. I warn you, Horst, don't take it off, for no reason. Sleep with it. It's your ticket to freedom."

"I like it. It'll hold all my valuables."

"Sure, and your bundles of money, too."

"I don't have any money, Dov."

"Surprise. How much you got, Oskar? Your son needs funds to travel with."

"I have twenty Marks."

"Same here. Talk about the lame leading the blind."

They gave the bills to Horst, emptied their pockets and added the coins.

"There you are, boy. You cleaned us out."

"How's he going to travel?" asked Oskar, "what's the fastest way?"

Through the dirty window Dov peered into the sky as if seeking the answer from a higher authority. "Tough question. When Horst's notice came I thought what the hell, we'll put him on a train. He'll be in Stuttgart in a day and a half. Big deal."

"Agreed. Seems like a sensible way."

"Wrong, Oskar. We're forgetting who we are; even worse, where we are. We're forgetting who's out there. Human nature, I suppose. Two days go by, nobody gets killed and we pretend we're in paradise.

Oskar sighed, nodded ruefully. Dov was right; this was still Germany, 1935.

"I took a chance yesterday and called Jessen", said Dov. Poor bastard didn't want to talk to me, started to hang up. Scared shitless about losing his pension. I told him this was it, the last time, just to give me a couple of answers, sort of as a Christmas present." He fished the last Turkish from his pack, plopped into a chair, lit up and blew a perfect smoke ring toward the ceiling. "I found out a few things. Item one. We're not the only city in Germany with a Heiko Böhm. Almost every city has a bastard just like him. Jessen is convinced that Böhm is *Sicherheitsdienst.*"

"Shit!" Oskar bellowed.

"My feelings exactly, but knowing Böhm, why should it surprise us? Item two. Jessen is sure that Böhm is involved with Terhoven's security network. He's heard rumors about a high-priority assignment."

"I bet I can guess."

"Of course. Everybody they think is politically dangerous will be arrested and shipped to a concentration camp by the end of January. Communists must not be roaming around when hordes of foreigners come in the spring. We're noisy. We make trouble. They want us dead."

"Maybe us, Dov, but surely not twelve year olds."

"Don't be so naïve, Oskar. They blew up Gitte; do I have to remind you? According to Jessen, the SS is watching train depots, bus stations, adding guards at borders. It's not only Jews they're after. Their turn will come, you can count on it, but not right now. Right now political dissenters like us are the number one enemy. I'm not sticking around. As soon as I can put a little cash together, I'm leaving; tomorrow, if possible. Jessen is right, Oskar, there's absolutely no time to waste. Horst must be on the road today. Three weeks to get to Stuttgart? He'll make it easy. He's a smart boy."

"Dov! Why didn't you tell us yesterday?"

"What for? Why spoil our last night together."

For a minute or so they sat motionless, dreading to take the unavoidable step, to say the final good-bye. Lifschitz moved first, found a pair of David's old mittens and a wool cap.

"Cold out there, boy. You'll be glad to have these. Your father takes lousy care of you. Come on now. Time to go."

"Papa?"

"Yes, Horst?"

"Where is Stuttgart?"

The men looked at each other and broke into a grin. "It never occurred to me. I always thought you'd be going by train or by bus, or…"

Dov found a ragged old map under a stack of legal papers and pointed out Stuttgart. "Nothing to it, Horst. Your father will drive you past Volkspark and put you on the road to Hagen. Then you go to Cologne, then to Koblenz, then to Stuttgart. Easy. You've been on the road before. You'll do fine. Try to stay away from trains and train stations as much as you can. Don't forget us in America. Now get out of here!"

Horst was already bundled in his winter coat, the wool cap and mittens, had slipped on his rucksack and walked to the door.

"Dov, thank you for everything. I'll always remember you."

"Have a great life, young man. Say hello to America for us." He hugged Horst and urged him out the door. "Come back later, Oskar, I'll be here." He closed the door behind them. "May God be with you, Horst Schumann," the lawyer whispered. He smiled ruefully at such blatant orthodoxy, but also, in an unexpected way, felt good having given the blessing.

24

Ever since Terhoven appointed Heiko Böhm to replace him as Dortmund's *Orts-gruppenleiter*, Pflug felt as tight as a drum. His body ached. Rollo knew the replacement was not just a change of duties but a demotion, a display of power intended to warn those who failed to deliver expected results. As the incoming head of Westfalia's Teachers Union he went through the motions, arranged larger offices in the Hansaplatz, held meetings with school principals and even scheduled his own calculus class in the Bismarck Real Gymnasium, but his heart wasn't in it. During the first week with the Union he rarely came to bed before midnight, often stared into space or brooded in his reading chair.

Tonight the children had gone to bed at eight. Trudi fell asleep clutching her doll. Rollo read Heinz a story while Rika straightened the kitchen.

"Can I help?" he asked, looking distracted.

"All done. You want coffee?"

"Not right now. Could we go for a walk?"

Holding hands, they crunched through new-fallen snow. At the Süd Wall promontory one could overlook the old city, mysterious and romantic in the glow of streetlights. Rollo cleared an iron bench. They sat silently, arms linked.

"Rika."

She didn't move, waited for him to go on, sensing her life was about to take a dramatic turn.

"It's hard for me to say this." He searched for words, for courage.

"Say it, Rollo. You'll feel better."

He took a deep breath, exhaled in a white puff.

"I want to leave the Party, Rika. I want the children, you and me to leave Germany. I want to go where we can be human again. I want to do honest, useful work and live a decent life."

There it was! Rika was startled, not by the declaration, but by its scope. She had perceived something coming for weeks, fervently wished for a resolution to her husband's ethical dilemma. Moreover, she was certain Rollo courted disaster. Although he retained his natural reserve in public, he was increasingly outspoken among friends, disgusted with the spreading violence and corruption, the Party's promiscuous exertion of power. He railed endlessly against patronizing attitudes toward women, voiced his resentment about unequal treatment they were accorded in his teachers union, placed responsibility on what he termed "those malicious bureaucrats in the Ministry of Education." Sooner or later his discontent would reach Terhoven who would put Böhm on guard. Böhm! She trembled merely thinking the name.

"You wouldn't mind, Rika? You would come with me?"

That query took her by surprise. "Oh Rollo, my dearest, dearest man. What a question! You and the children are my life. We go wherever you go. I would be amazed if you didn't already have some place in mind."

Rollo kissed her, immensely relieved by her response. Yes, he had a place in mind, had thought about it for days. "Remember an instructor named Fischer? Joachim Fischer?"

"Sounds familiar."

"Freiburg. Von Halen's assistant in Physics. I took his seminar. You met him at a party at von Halen's house."

"And? Have you been in touch with Fischer?"

"Yes. I read his paper on quantum theory. Interesting, but too experimental for my taste, He publishes regularly in Swiss journals and elsewhere."

"Rollo, it's getting cold. What's going on?"

"I called him a few days ago. He's a professor at the University of Zürich. I asked him point-blank if his department could use a trained mathematician. He said jobs at the university are scarce, but occasionally there are openings at the Gymnasia. He asked on whose behalf I was inquiring."

She knew there was more. She waited, aware of her own anxieties, but also trusting his decisions for their future.

"I told Fischer we might take a ski vacation in Switzerland, the whole family. I proposed a meeting in Zürich after the first of the year."

"You asked Fischer to meet us in Zürich? Did he understand what you were after?"

"Not at first. Physicists are not mathematicians, Rika. Their approach is less direct, but he finally got it through his head." He smiled for the first time that night.

"When are we going to Switzerland, Rollo?"

"I made train reservations for the thirtieth. I booked a room at the Hotel du Parc, near the station. The travel bureau said it's a nice family hotel. Not too expensive."

"Oh Rollo, you are incredible! This is all happening so fast." She turned to him, surprised she could feel so elated when they were about to confront the unknown. "Have you told Heiko?"

"No! I assure you that Heiko is not a problem. I'm still in charge, at least until the first. I'm giving myself a well-earned vacation. I'll tell him I'll be back early in January to take up my new duties."

"I see. So the kids and I will stay in Switzerland?"

"You'll be busy looking for an apartment and good schools while I quietly close up the house, our bank accounts and take with me what I can. I'll join you at the latest in the middle of the month. Swiss schools start in February. Maybe I can hook on. If not, I'll tutor, sell chocolate, learn to repair watches. Who cares? I only care about leaving Germany."

She brushed snowflakes from her lap and tears from her eyes. She wished she could brush away her fears as easily. "It's a big step, Rollo. We're Germans. I know how you feel right now, but this is our country. Our friends and families live here. If people like us desert who's left to slow them down?"

"They're in the driver's seat, Rika. Nothing will slow Hitler's people down, not soon. Whoever gets in their way will be crushed. Hitler is going to war. Everybody knows that. Frankly, I want no part of it."

"You've always been proud of being German. Going to Switzerland means living in exile."

"It won't be forever. Remember *Macbeth*? You can kill and kill, and kill some more, but finally there's a MacDuff. There's always a MacDuff. We'll come back some day."

Snow was falling when they walked home. Rollo's step was lighter, his body free of pain. Rika would go with him, was prepared to give him total support. In all the surrounding misery he was still a lucky man.

That night they dreamed of mountains and meadows, forests and lakes, of streets full of people pursuing normal and free lives.

◆   ◆   ◆

Oskar drove with utmost caution. The streets were as slick as his tires; snow still fell hard. He skirted the city's center, turned onto Hohe Strasse, a wide, tree-lined avenue leading South.

Church bells resonated through the whiteness, diminished as they neared Hagen. The car's heater had not been repaired; frost gathered on the glass and obscured their vision. Horst found a rag and furiously wiped the windows every few minutes. When they came to the Westfalenhalle, Oskar suddenly stopped under an access ramp clear of snow and out of the wind.

Father and son sat very still. How could they manage to look at each other? It was impossible. They tried desperately to control what they felt, to grasp the inevitability of these final moments, a word, a phrase, a gesture, anything that suggested hope, that evoked caring, to soften the pain of separation. They were about to part lives, to move into uncertain futures, perhaps never to see one another again. What did one say at such a time?

"What will you do, Papa?"

"I'm not sure. I know an old comrade who lives in Belgium. I'll try to get in touch with him later today. He'll help me cross the border if he's still there."

"Papa."

"Yes, Horst."

"Papa, we have only a moment left. Maybe this is a bad time to say it but I'd better say it anyhow because I've thought about it so often, but you never want to listen. I used to be angry at you, really angry. I used to be so angry I wanted to die." Horst looked at Oskar, his eyes big and pleading. "When I ran away, you know, when I was a little kid, I wanted so much for you to come and find me. I hated that place. I really hated that place. Why didn't you come, Papa?"

Oskar had no answer, no instant remedy for years of pain. "That was so long ago," he said. "Everything has changed. I was a different person then."

It was getting colder; the car's windows almost totally frosted. Its interior was rapidly becoming a confessional, the atmosphere rife with phantoms of blame, guilt and contrition. Oskar knew this had to stop now or they would linger for hours, harrowing old wounds. The boy had to start on his way. America was a promise on the horizon. To sit in a refrigerated automobile and inspect the scars and scabs of their relationship would not get him there. Oskar started the engine.

"Horst, I don't want to avoid your questions. I'm sorry. I'm truly sorry. I did things in which I believed. If I had to do them again I probably would, but not the same way; that much I know. For one, I'd never, ever, bring you to a place like Paderborn again. I have always felt terrible about that." He exited the ramp, peered into swirls of whiteness. "But listen, my dearest son, now is not the right time to settle things between us. We'll do it together in America, I promise you."

He drove past the Volkspark, skirted the bicycle velodrome and brought the car to a stop at the end of the Steinerne Brücke. A sign read "Hagen, 20 km." Horst checked his leather kit, hoisted his rucksack and stepped out into the cold. Oskar joined him, his heart heavy, and his throat tight.

"I'll write to you in Chicago, at Clara's. I'll come as soon as I can. I'll miss you."

"Papa. Be careful."

"I will. You too. Now go."

He hugged Horst hard then gently pushed him on his way. Horst looked back several times and waved, but soon the snow caused them to lose sight of each other. Oskar stood under the sign for a minute, then two, then three, not knowing what to do. He wiped off his windshield and quite unexpectedly thought of his dead wife.

"You would have liked our son, Toni," he whispered into the numbing cold. "He's a good boy, a really special person."

It was Christmas time in Westfalen. Church bells loudly proclaimed peace on earth and good will toward men, but Oskar didn't hear them.

25

Heiko Böhm's office in the new Hansaplatz complex reflected his general attitude toward excess baggage. It featured a chair for visitors, a file cabinet, a telephone and on the wall facing a steel desk a photo of his Führer in full uniform, leaning on a shovel. The image of austerity precisely suited Böhm's taste. When Pflug called for an appointment, Böhm couldn't resist a gloating smile.

"Of course, Rollo, why do you ask? Come over. I'm in the process of organizing." He surveyed his domain with satisfaction. Marvelous, he grinned, Herr University Professor himself, asking for an appointment. Wonder what's on his mind.

Rollo allowed Böhm to usher him to the vacant chair. "How's it going, Heiko? Looks to me like you're ready for business."

"Simple tastes. What can I do for you?"

"I'm taking my family on a short vacation. Sorry I won't be able to help you at the beginning of your new job, but I'm sure you won't need me until I get back to start my new duties."

"I see."

"I wanted to clear it with you." Pflug used his friendliest manner, was gracious and accommodating.

"What for? You're still in charge."

"Not after the first. That's only a week from now. We both know that part of me is gone already." His tone was polite and only slightly patronizing.

"Yeah, of course. You're coming back when?"

"On the seventh or eighth. We'll be in Switzerland. Skiing. They say the snow's terrific this year."

Apparently Pflug couldn't wait to begin his trip. Heiko felt a twinge of suspicion. "Sounds nice. Have a good time. Leave an address where we can reach you."

"I'll write it down for Frau Schuster." Rollo held out his hand, took Heiko's with a firm grip. "Well, Heiko, much luck. You'll be a fine leader."

"Thanks. Call me when you return." Böhm stood up and watched his former boss saunter down the long hallway. "Oh Rollo!" he shouted, "Heil Hitler."

"Heil Hitler," Pflug yelled, smiled and stepped into the elevator.

Heiko felt uneasy, but couldn't put his finger on why. Pflug just seemed too damn happy about going. Best to keep an eye on the man. He wrote a memo to Frau Schuster and left it on her desk. "Pflug is going to Switzerland on vacation. Find out the name of his hotel before he leaves." He signed the note, locked the office and went home to his rented flat for a beer, a sausage and endless dreams of magnificent possibilities—merely a week away—when he would become the boss.

◆   ◆   ◆

Trudging along the road, Horst knew he couldn't get far. The wind piled snow drifts everywhere, stung as it clawed at his face. He wrapped the muffler over his mouth, grateful for its protection. He was thankful that his feet were warm in his high tops with hooks and leather laces, donated by Hershl only a week ago. They fit perfectly. Were Hershl and Dov already out of Germany? Had they safely escaped?

He tried to maintain an even pace, to ignore the bad weather. His steps made pleasant, crunching sounds, the warm woolen socks keeping snow from sliding into his boots. Those last minutes with Oskar, sitting in the cold Opel, their breath creating patterns on the frozen windows, had been dispiriting. "I would never send you to a place like Paderborn again." At least Papa had finally admitted his mistake. As a little boy, when he was hurting so bad, waiting for Papa to find him, he had often wondered if running away had been the right thing to do. Maybe he had just imagined Paderborn's terrors. Maybe he would have made friends. If he had stayed, Liselotte might not have died. Oskar always avoided talking about Liselotte. Maybe it was just too hard for him. But in America Oskar would answer his questions and clear up everything, tell Horst what really happened to his sister.

A sign at the side of the road said "Hacheney, 8 km." If he walked quickly he could reach Hacheney before dark. He had forty Marks, which had to last all the way. He knew he couldn't walk every kilometer to his destination; in spite of Dov's warning he might have to take a train sometime. Stuttgart. What kind of questions would they ask there? Would they know that Oskar was a Communist? If they found out that Horst was the son of a Jewish Communist they would not let him go to America. He would have to be very careful not to say the wrong things. There was so much to think about. Right now he had to think about where to stay tonight, although that didn't scare him. He had always found some place to sleep. Maybe Herr Holzer would take him in. He remembered the name of the shoemaker, the strange small man that Papa used to talk about. Well, even if Herr Holzer wouldn't take him in, it would be all right. He had food in his rucksack, plenty to eat for at least two days.

In the distance he saw farmhouses, but no people. Grete always celebrated the day before Christmas, what she called Holy Night. Tomorrow was Christmas and the day after was Christmas again. Grete never explained why she celebrated the same birthday twice but that's what the Christians did. Grete was probably at Oma and Opa Krause's, having dinner.

A car drove by, a man, a woman and two children. For a moment he thought they would slow down, maybe pick him up and give him a ride to Hacheney, but he was wrong. In Hacheney—was it only two months ago—he and Oskar had hot chocolate and cake and maybe for the first time came to know each other a little better. He remembered the whipped cream and their talk and nearly cried at the happy memory. Better stop thinking about Papa or Gretchen or Dov. Better start thinking about Hacheney, about someplace to stay tonight.

He walked faster, started to run, slowly, and imagined Ali at his side. The panther would be a great protector. They would run as fast as the wind. They would come to an enormous wall, but would find a way to get over it. He had no idea what was on the other side except that he was sure it would be all right.

He walked at a steady pace, sensed the nearness of people. Thoughts about what he left behind grew dimmer. If Herr Holzer remembered Oskar's son, he would most likely help. First Hacheney, then Stuttgart and then America. He wished Walter were still alive. Walter would have been proud of him.

26

In Chicago, Rae Malkin dropped a stitch, furiously unraveled a few inches of her knitting. Dick sprawled on the couch with the Trib, half listening to Fred Allen's twangy jokes on the radio.

"I can't concentrate, Dick. How can you read and listen at the same time? I'm trying to knit a sweater for the boy, but I haven't even finished one sleeve. I don't know his size." She stomped into the kitchen in frustration.

Dick sighed and turned off the radio. Rae needed him. She was growing more irritable daily, was often upset without reason. He heard her slam the kettle on the stove and rattle the cupboard. He understood her nervousness and shared her distress. Nine months already and the boy wasn't here yet. Then that terrible letter came right after Christmas. Clara had called him at the market.

"Dick, there's mail from my brother."

"Trouble?"

"Kind of. Maybe nothing."

"I'll be right over."

As always, the Weiss shop smelled of cleaning fluid and dry steam. Clara finished with a customer and joined him in the apartment. She translated the letter, dated December 15, word by word. He asked her to translate it again.

"I could do that, Dick, but it's not going to get any better."

"Horst hasn't received his notice? What notice? What does he mean by 'everything is on schedule?' What schedule? What the hell's his schedule?"

"Calm down. I think you should have Farber talk to Luckman."

"Easy to say. Luckman's running for office; he has other things on his mind. What are these 'unspeakable horrors?' Clara, what's going on? He has to escape? Clara, I have really bad feelings!"

"Don't panic, Dick. Let's find out."

"I'll try Farber."

Farber returned the call an hour later. Clara translated Oskar's letter for him.

"Scary news, Dick, but it sounds like the one in trouble is the father, not the boy. Let me get on it right away. Be patient, it might take a couple of days. I'll have our Washington office wire the appropriate German desk. Berlin should be able to help. The minute I get confirmation, I'll be in touch with you. No trusting the Nazis, but the boy's father says everything's on schedule. That's encouraging. Let's keep our fingers crossed. You'll hear from me." He hung up.

"What about the money, Dick?"

"When I hear from Farber, I'll wire money. Damn, everything was going so smoothly."

"He'll make it, Dick. He's a smart kid."

"I believe it. Now go and convince Rae."

Four days later and still nothing was heard from Farber. Dick didn't want to pester him. Bert had always kept his word; no reason to doubt him now, but the waiting was nerve-wracking.

"Let's not drive ourselves *meschugge*, sweetheart," he cautioned Rae. "It's the holidays. We'll know more after the first. You'll see."

"Where can he be? They have no money and the father's in trouble. What's happening to the boy? I'm scared, Dick."

He embraced her and kissed her gently. She cared so deeply and was so genuinely concerned. He loved her for it. This had been such a strange year, sometimes exhilarating, sometimes stressful. He hoped they could be spared more of this kind of anxiety. He was optimistic. 1936 would be memorable. Horst would surely come to them. He simply had to.

Winter winds howled against their bedroom window. Without touching her, Dick sensed Rae's tension, the way she clutched herself when troubled, as if defending herself against unseen enemies. He knew she was pleading for assurance.

"Listen, sweetheart. Nobody ever said it was easy becoming a mother. What month did we decide to bring Horst over?"

"In March," she whispered.

"Well, this is December." He tapped her shoulder as he counted on his fingers. "Exactly nine months, kiddo. That's how long it takes to make a child. What you're having is labor pains."

She had to laugh. He was such a dear, understanding man. She nestled close to him, comforted by feelings of tenderness. She thought about becoming a mother. It scared her a lot, but Dick would be there. He would share the problems and also the joy. She was sure there would be a lot of that.

◆   ◆   ◆

Horst reached Hacheney moments before dark. Street lamps cast pools of light on sidewalks. Two months earlier he and Oskar had called on Ludwig

Holzer, proprietor of "Schuh Haus," a plain shop with a secret. Together with two assistants, Holzer delivered quality work at moderate prices and the village burghers admired his craftsmanship. Nobody in the community commented any longer on his physical appearance; they were used to dealing with a dwarf.

Only a few close friends knew that Ludwig Holzer was once a celebrated artist who created for Europe's most elite shoe salons until a drinking problem drove him into the streets. At age forty he sobered up and on a Sunday drive through Hacheney noticed the town had no shoemaker. The following eighteen years brought considerable prosperity to the reformed alcoholic. Although his shop became increasingly busy, he found time to begin designing again for the few who could afford him. His clientele included a well-known opera singer, the president of a Belgian bank and numerous entertainers. For these special clients Holzer required the finest of materials. Oskar Schumann knew how to supply it and the misshapen craftsman of Hacheney and the Dortmund leather merchant formed a gentle friendship, recognizing the creative souls in each other.

Horst had no trouble finding the shop. Holzer was still there and hardly looked up when the doorbell rang merrily.

"Sorry. Closed for Christmas. Come back the day after tomorrow."

"I won't be here then. I need a place to sleep, Herr Holzer. I hope you remember me, I'm Oskar Schumann's son."

Holzer was startled. "Where's your father? In the car?"

"No, I'm alone."

The shoemaker thoughtfully regarded Horst, cautiously swept a handful of beads into a leather pouch and climbed off his specially designed workbench.

"In the middle of winter and all alone? Something new every day." His head was far too big for his tiny body, but his face was expressive and attractive. "Let me sweep the place, then you can tell me what this is all about."

"May I help?"

"Of course. The broom and trash can are in the closet."

The shop sparkled in less than half an hour. Holzer led Horst up a stairway to his simple, well-furnished apartment. He filled the kitchen table with food and a bowl of fresh fruit and poured water into crystal glasses.

"Used to serve good wine in these," he said proudly.

"Papa told me."

Holzer offered a toast and smiled. "Good man, your father. Now tell me what's going on, young Schumann."

Horst delivered a short version of his story. His eyes kept blinking as he tried to keep them open. They finished their meal quickly and then Holzer fixed a bed on the living room couch.

"I appreciate this, Herr Holzer. I really do."

"Tell me, I'm curious. What would you have done if I hadn't been here?"

"I don't know. Maybe sleep in the bus station or behind a bakery. I've been with bakers before."

Holzer nodded with understanding. "Extraordinary people, you Schumanns," he said. "It's not easy being a Jew these days. Turn off the light when you're ready. If you need anything, I'll be in the bedroom, reading. Sleep well."

Horst went to the couch and crawled under the blankets. Through the window he could see that it was snowing again in large, soft flakes. He thought about his father. Perhaps Oskar had joined Dov in The Den or maybe he had gone to Hershl, another shoemaker with a good heart. Were all shoemakers nice people? He pondered on that, but not for long. In the microscopic moment before sleep comes he pictured himself in a strange, beautiful park with cowboys and Indians and branches full of birds. Walter was there, coloring the birds' feathers with long, fragile brushes. It was an enormous park in the middle of a country he had never seen. Ali liked it too, walked right next to him, his paws as silent as the falling snow.

◆   ◆   ◆

By the time Horst woke, the shoemaker, an early riser, had already shopped for fresh rolls. Butter and marmalade crowded the kitchen table, a pot of coffee bubbled on the stove. Horst dressed quickly. He watched with awe as the tiny man easily managed domestic chores. A homemade stepladder allowed him to reach every nook of the cupboard. Rods were attached to the corners of its top step, a hook fastened to its left side, a small leather basket on the right. Deftly, perhaps to show off, Holzer snagged a can of condensed milk from a top shelf, caught it neatly in the basket. "You drink coffee, Schumann? I could make cocoa."

"Thanks very much. I like coffee, especially with milk."

"Help yourself."

Horst wolfed down a roll almost in one bite, anxious to be on the road.

"So. What's today's plan, young man?"

"I'd like to get to Cologne."

"Ah, Cologne. Trains leave from Hagen several times a day."

"No trains. Not this close to Dortmund."

Holzer agreed. "Yes, I see. That's how it is. Very sad. Well then, could you risk the bus?"

"Buses are probably safer. They can't watch every one, can they?"

"No, I think not. Finish breakfast. I'll drive you."

"You don't have to, Herr Holzer. I'll find the bus stop."

"No problem. Your father has done me many favors."

Horst wondered if he should telephone Oskar. No, he decided, better to wait until later. Dortmund was still too near and that made him nervous. Strange, he had left only yesterday, but he already experienced remoteness, a sense of being apart from the city and the people he knew. The feeling began right after he said good-bye to Papa, when he started on his way to Stuttgart, to America, to a brand new set of parents called Malkin. The thought amazed him. He didn't even know what they looked like, but he was sure they were nice. Anyone wiling to adopt a stranger had to be nice. Something else occurred to him that made him giggle. He was only twelve years old and soon he would have another father and mother. It felt weird to think of having two fathers and three mothers in less than twelve years. He tried to imagine what Chicago was like.

Holzer interrupted his daydreams. "You have money?"

"Yes, I have enough."

"Show me."

Horst pulled up his shirt and zipped open his kit. The shoemaker leaned over, inspected the worn case, secured with linoleum strips.

"Not safe, that thing. We can do better. Let's go down to the shop right now."

He measured Horst's waist, cut a wide strip from a square of fine leather, attached a brass buckle, punched holes in one end then stitched a leather patch to Dov's toilet kit and inserted the belt.

"Try it on."

Horst pulled the new belt through his trouser loops, the kit firmly attached.

"Better, no?"

"It's beautiful, Herr Holzer, what a difference. I like it very much!"

"Least I can do. You're a nice boy. You deserve it. Your father will miss you. Now we go."

Horst was astonished by Holzer's car, equipped with padded brake and clutch pedals, the fuel controlled by a lever at the steering wheel. Holzer shot him a side-long glance. "Good German engineering," he smiled, "more convenient than hiring a chauffeur. Also much cheaper."

It took less than ten minutes to get to the bus stop near the Brünninghausen railway depot. "Catch the one that says Hagen. I think it's number ten. I could drive you, you know. Only twenty kilometers."

"Thank you, I appreciate it, but I'd better get used to being on my own."

"Should I call your father? Tell him you were here?"

Horst had made up his mind. "No, my father and I said good bye for now."

They shook hands. "Take care of yourself. Good luck in America." The generous little man climbed into his car and drove off.

Horst's bus came quickly. He paid thirty pfennigs and found a seat at the rear, admired his new belt, tightened its buckle and opened his rucksack. A paper bag lay propped on his clothes. Pinned to it were ten Marks and a note: "You have courage. Your father must be proud of you. I'll subtract the money from what I owe him. God Bless." Inside the bag was food wrapped in wax paper.

He felt secure and cared for. Carefully, he unfolded his map. Where should he stop next? Dov cautioned him against big cities, main bus and train stations. On the other hand, local buses were different; they seemed quite safe and comfortable. As he studied his map the word "Solingen" caught his eye. It reminded him of the knife he bought when he lived with Czerny. That knife was manufactured in Solingen. He dug in his rucksack, found it wedged between socks and opened the blade. There it was, "Solingen," stamped into the steel. He smiled. Thinking of Czerny always made him smile. Yes, Solingen it would be, a fine place to stay for the night.

When the bus reached Hagen, the driver offered Horst directions. "Take Number Twelve to Wuppertal, then transfer."

Number Twelve arrived within minutes, to the relief of people huddled in storefronts, out of the wind, grumbling because of the cold. Just as the bus closed its doors, ready to go, a troop of scouts stepped on, noisy and playful, their leader in Storm Trooper uniform. Horst immediately felt nervous, made himself as small as possible and seriously considered going to Solingen later. Then he reconsidered. If he left now he would only draw attention; instead, he pretended to be deeply involved in his Karl May book. The boys prowled the aisle, visited each other in different seats, yelled and fooled around. One youngster saw Horst reading, burst out excitedly.

"Hey Rudi," he yelled, "here's the Karl May I told you about." He turned to Horst. "Good story, isn't it?" Horst nodded, fidgeted, stared at the page. Luckily the boy soon lost interest and scampered away. Horst breathed easier, but remained tense until they reached the next depot. "Solingen is on a different line," the driver told him. He quickly found where he had to go, paid for his ticket and shared a seat at the back with an elderly lady.

A light snow fell and slowed traffic, but the bus arrived in Solingen punctually. Horst immediately began his search for a bakery. He found one in a cheerful, brightly painted storefront and went to its back entrance where the baker stood, preparing for the next day.

A big, fleshy man, a white apron tied over a bulky, black sweater, he was measuring flour for the morning mix. A floppy cap hung over his eyes, a cigarette dangled from his lower lip.

"What do you want? I'm busy."

To Horst this was a well-known statement leading to an old, familiar scene, one he had played many times and could now perform from memory.

"I need a place to sleep for one night and something to eat. I've worked in bakeries. I'll earn my keep."

As expected, the baker never turned his head. "What can you do?"

"Sweep without raising dust. Measure flour. Prepare icing for pastry. Scour long and short pans. Clean and prepare customer baskets. Monitor oven temperature. Polish display cases." He knew Czerny would be proud of him.

The baker stopped, gave him a hard stare, then grinned. "You've also figured out where to sleep?"

"Yes, in the flour storage. It's warm and dry."

The big man nodded. This was a new one, an adolescent gypsy with bakery experience. Well, what the hell, nothing to lose, so why not? "Okay, boy, we close in half an hour. Go help Rosalie clean cases and change windows. You know how to do windows?"

"Yes, I do."

"Funny, I believe you. Okay, sweep from front to back. No dust, mind you. Sleep in the flour closet until four, then measure rye flour for fifty loaves. You get paid one loaf and three sweet rolls. No money. You're out by five. Understood?"

"Yes."

The proprietor checked his ovens, mumbled to himself. "Really a new one." He turned to inspect Horst. "I should call the police, but you don't seem like a criminal. You're not, are you?"

"No, I'm not."

"Hmmm."

Horst did his work. At seven his host took off his apron.

"I'm locking up," he said. "Sleep where you want. I'll see you in the morning. Don't disturb things or I *will* call the police. I have a feeling you wouldn't like that." He banged the door shut and locked it. Horst finished sweeping. The situation held no anxiety; it was familiar and comfortable. He read until his eyes grew heavy, turned out the overhead bulb and slept without dreaming.

The baker arrived promptly at four. "You did a good job. Measure out the rye and get going," he snapped, "wherever that may be."

Horst portioned out the flour on the prep table, collected a loaf of bread and three pieces of pastry and started to leave. As he opened the door the baker stopped him.

"Listen boy, if you really need money…"

"Thanks. That wasn't our bargain. I'm grateful you let me stay. Really appreciate it." He walked out while the man stared after him.

Horst returned to the same bus station, Cologne his next goal. A reluctant sun rose through a snow-laden sky, added scant warmth to the morning's frost. He shivered. When the bus rolled in an hour later he huddled in a corner near the warmth of the motor. The sweet roll he ate was chewy, but tasted stale. His joints ached and he felt hot and cold at the same time. He sneezed. His throat tickled. For god's sake, he couldn't afford to get sick. Not now! He sank deep into his seat and pulled his coat tight to his body. The sweet roll rose in his throat. Then, without warning, a piercing chill jarred him from head to foot.

27

Roland and Erika Pflug felt like traitors. Burdened by conscience, they packed without enthusiasm. They were fleeing their native country, their children's birthplace and the wellspring of their dreams, yearnings and aspirations. Theirs was not a journey of emigrants seeking fame and fortune, nor an escape from religious or civil persecution. Their flight was entirely a repudiation of their nation's governance. When Rollo first became a Party administrator, mainly at his father's urging, he was idealistic about National Socialism and its promise to bring order out of chaos. He was ill prepared for the inner workings of the Nazi machinery. He tried hard to adapt, but the reality of his position became intolerable. Both he and Rika believed their country's behavior had turned barbarous and immoral. An intelligent couple, they were acutely aware that by fleeing the country they were also leaving to others the merciless task of scourging the fascist menace. This realization made them indecisive and quarrelsome, even with each other. Large boxes, nearly full, stood scattered around the apartment.

"Don't take everything, Rika. It looks suspicious. We're supposed to be going on a ski vacation."

"At least it's packed. That should save you time when you come back."

"Yes. Yes, of course it will."

The children, unaware of events, spent the day with friends. None of the relatives were informed of their plans. Too dangerous. The enterprise felt underhanded and out of character. Rollo had voiced his disgust with Nazi behavior openly. Now, in the process of changing their lives, they were acting in secrecy. It tormented them both.

Rika took the dollhouse apart, wrapped its tiny furniture in newspaper. "Seems strange, doesn't it, Rollo," she said, consonant with his mood. "It's been such a struggle, now we're tearing it down. Are we cowards? Are you sure we're doing the right thing?"

He led her to the couch, became his old gentle self, sat beside her and slowly collected his thoughts, as was his custom. She knew her questions had assaulted his dignity.

"The right thing?" he mused. "Look, my love. I'm a mathematician. I'm stuck with the notion that two and two makes four, that the shortest distance between two points…well, you know what I mean."

He left her side, paced, flopped on the floor, leaned against a box and hugged his knees as if to harness vitality. "The right thing? I'm not sure what that is anymore. You make commitments, to a job, a political party, and a country. You honor those commitments as best you can. Simple. The right thing. Two plus two. By the way, our train leaves at four. What time will the children be home?"

"Soon." She waited. There was obviously more. With Rollo there usually was.

He chewed on his lower lip. "The trouble with our country is that two plus two now adds up to whatever some Party official finds useful. Right and wrong no longer matter." He left the box, crouched before her. "Let's face it. Weapons, uniforms, all kinds of war materials are being produced on a mass scale. I'm a Party official. I know things. There's going to be war, Rika, not too far in the future."

"Why a war, Rollo? The country is just getting back on its feet from the last one."

"I couldn't answer that anymore than I could tell you what nations we'll be fighting. All I know is that while the country is being armed, butchers like Böhm are promoted to power, books are burned, torture camps spring up all over, human beings disappear overnight. Sometimes, as we know, they're bombed in their stores. There's no sense to any of it. We don't belong here."

"I know this isn't a good time, Rollo, and we already talked about it last week, but I'm still not at ease. We're the educated ones, supposedly the country's leaders. Is it right for us to run away? I feel like we're quitting."

He kneeled before her, put his arms around her waist. "Is it right? I wish I had an irrefutable answer, Rika, but I don't. Maybe there isn't any. Moral dilemmas are not solved like mathematical equations. I think what's going on in this country is terribly wrong. I'm also convinced that right now there's nothing I can do to change it. I realize I bear some responsibility for the way things are, not a lot, but some. Knowing that makes me feel less human and morally unclean." He looked up, held her eyes with his. "I know if we stay, we will have to chose. Support them or fight them."

"Truly either or?"

"I remember what you said not long ago. You said they must never think that I don't respect them or the way they function, or they would make me pay for it. You were right, Rika, absolutely right. Terhoven, Böhm, probably others we don't even know about, are starting to regard me as unreliable, maybe even as an adversary. The only way I could manage to stay would be to shape up, to conform, to do things their way. But if I did that, I would soon hate myself; not only myself, but everyone around me."

She took his face in her hands, kissed him lightly on the nose. "Good enough for me, Pflug. Come on; let's get at it, plenty of packing to do."

The children came home. Rollo stashed suitcases in the Buick along with skis, boots, and poles, carefully checked papers, passports, tickets and the like. He would park the car near the station. In Switzerland he would settle the family, keep his appointment with Fischer and pursue job possibilities. After his return to Dortmund the Buick could be loaded with personal belongings, everything else had to be sacrificed, including their furniture, a small price to pay. Then he would drive back to Switzerland as quickly as possible.

Their train crossed the border on New Year's Eve. In 1936 they would be living in freedom.

◆   ◆   ◆

Horst's joints ached terribly. He knew the symptoms. Without medicine his temperature would rise. He had no idea what to do if he became really sick. He had to keep well, stay on the road. He hunched into his seat, feeling dizzy and weak. In Cologne he would find a drugstore, eat something warm. The diesel motor's fumes smelled terrible. He put his forehead to the window, grateful for its icy touch. The bus stopped in Langenfeld, then in Leverkusen. A troop of uniformed SA men took seats near the front. A dull pain squeezed his temples. He knew he was becoming increasingly vulnerable, less capable of dealing with trouble. Waves of nausea rose from his stomach whenever the bus screeched to a halt. The possibility of vomiting sent him into a panic. "I must not," he mumbled, "please god, oh please, don't let me vomit, not now, not on the bus."

Cologne's immense cathedral loomed in the distance as the bus crossed a bridge over the Rhine. Twenty minutes later it entered the main railroad station, a busy depot with many train connections, a teeming locale the Security Police would be sure to check out. Caution was critical. What could he do about his fever? Feeling disconnected, unable to make useful decisions, Horst sat on a bench, vaguely heard announcements about arrivals and departures, saw people stroll by arm in arm, envied them. What was Oskar doing on New Year's, he wondered. Strange, he couldn't picture his father, no matter how hard he tried.

It was urgent to concentrate. He couldn't sit here all night. He found a washroom, splashed his face with cold water, which was refreshing and cleared his head, if only for a moment. He bought aspirin, a roll and hot tea, paid three Marks, but then, just smelling the bread, he almost threw up. The tea tasted good, made it easier to swallow the aspirin. Taking the pills he felt he was helping himself, not merely waiting around for something to happen. Crouched in a corner of the waiting room, desperate to plan the next step, he pulled out his map. Its lines were blurred, but by squinting his eyes he could figure out the names of cities. Walter is probably a much better map-reader, he thought, maybe because his father is a printer. Then he remembered that Walter was dead, something he caught from that nail in his hand, and so it didn't matter if Walter was a good map-reader. It didn't matter at all.

Horst felt very sleepy. That was bad. People would surely notice an unconscious boy in the middle of a station, ask questions and discover he was Horst Schumann, son of Oskar Schumann, a Bolshevist writer the Nazis were looking for. On the map the name Koblenz stuck out in big letters, not as big as Cologne and smaller than Stuttgart, but big enough to read clearly. Should he take a chance and ride the train to Stuttgart? Dov told him not to but the thought of looking for a place to sleep, or even riding a bus, terrified him. He remembered when Milfs paid for his trip to Kastellaun. It was very easy. You put down your money and received a ticket. Just like that. Maybe he could travel that way to Stuttgart. Wouldn't that be great! His head was spinning, but he walked to the ticket window, first looked in every direction for signs of suspicious-looking officials.

"How much is it to Stuttgart?"

The man behind the glass was impatient. "First class or second class?"

Horst wasn't sure what that meant, but second class sounded cheaper. "Second class."

"Thirty Marks."

"Oh." He turned away, disappointed, and sat on the bench. Fifty-two Marks were left in his kit, more than he ever had before, but he needed money for food and other things. He went back to the clerk.

"How much to Koblenz?"

"First class or second class?"

"Second class."

"Twelve Marks."

"One ticket to Koblenz, please."

He paid, carefully counted his money. "Excuse me. What time does the train leave? Where do I go?"

"Eighteen thirty two. Track four."

Still two hours before departure. Track four was empty. He felt nauseated again, bought cough drops for twenty pfennigs. They tasted like eucalyptus and made him so sick he ran to the washroom, stuck his face into cold water and swallowed more aspirin. He didn't know if so much aspirin was good, but what else could he do?

The train finally rolled into the station. Signs on its side said "Köln—Koblenz—Frankfurt a/Main." The cars were empty, their doors open. He put his rucksack in the basket over the seats, crouched in a corner next to the window. This was much better than the cold bench outside.

He relaxed, but the fever got worse. Everything felt spooky, like being in a city called Chicago and also on a train to Koblenz. Thoughts about America cropped up. What would it be like? Of course he would have to learn English. "This is a window," Gitte taught everybody on that scary night in the coalmine. "I open the window. I close the window." She had pronounced it carefully, like a teacher. "This is a door. I open the door. I close the door. Good morning, mother and father." Well, Gitte was also dead, burned in a store with her Papa. He wouldn't think about Gitte now, it just made him feel worse. He would think only about America. In Chicago he would say, "I open the door. Good morning mother and father Malkin."

He dozed and then woke when the train moved. Two older women and a bearded man had joined him in his compartment. He felt bewildered for a moment, but their smiles were friendly. He made an effort to smile too, but it was difficult. He almost panicked when the conductor checked tickets. He touched his kit. It was zipped. Good. Images swam before his eyes, Ali, his fangs showing, visions of Papa, a fine café, hot chocolate. His teeth chattered. He tried hard to think about America, but his fever rose and his mind drifted as the train sped toward Koblenz.

28

On January 2, 1936, Willie Jodel stared at his reflection in a window of his office in Berlin's American embassy and saw mainly the red of his bloodshot eyes. The embassy's annual New Year's open house had been exhilarating, plenty of booze, good food, scads of secretaries and staff assistants from various foreign offices milling about, scouting the talent. A few Germans from their Foreign Ministry showed up, a bit sinister in black uniforms, but resolutely courteous. They claimed to have heard about incredible refreshments, wished to sample Yankee hospitality. Jodel thought they were spying. In the afternoon he had locked eyes with a brunette beauty from Brazil's consulate who took him to places he didn't even know existed, dark, smoky clubs where one danced the rumba and the new La Conga. "Maybe next week," she had whispered softly after she kissed him good night on her doorstep, letting him stagger unhappily into the cold dawn.

"Now the pickled piper must be paid. Welcome to the real world, Willie Jodel," he moaned aloud, holding his head, unfinished work stacked on his desk like implacable sentinels. On top of a basket marked "Do It Or Die" lay a short, pointed query from Rep. Luckman, delivered by diplomatic pouch only two days ago. "My constituents, Mr. And Mrs. Richard Malkin, of Chicago, Illinois, are anxious to know the situation with respect to Horst Schumann, of Dortmund, Germany, whose emigration, for purposes of adoption, is eagerly awaited. At your earliest opportunity please inform my office of said Horst Schumann's current status."

He buzzed his secretary, flinched at the sound. "Sharon, please find Lippert. I need somebody to talk to somebody in Stuttgart."

William Lippert, born and raised in Berlin, spoke several languages including State Department jargon.

"Bill, a touchy one. Representative Luckman's desk. Call Stuttgart for me, would you? Find out about a kid named Horst Schumann? Our file says we sent entry papers and voucher approvals to their Special Exit Visa office."

"When?"

"October. Luckman wants to know what's happening. Luckman, pal. House Ways and Means. Know what I mean?"

From the German Foreign Office, Lippert learned that a Dietrich Hartung ran Special Exit Visas in Stuttgart. He placed the call through the embassy switchboard.

"Special Exit Visas. Zeidler speaking."

Lippert identified himself, stated his request.

"I'll have to look it up. I need to know your title and embassy switchboard number. I will call you back."

"Cautious lady," said Jodel.

After ten minutes his phone rang. "Yes, Herr Lippert. Horst Schumann submitted all necessary documents. He is due for his interview in our offices on January twenty first. Barring unforeseen circumstances he is scheduled to depart from Hamburg on January twenty eight, aboard the *Hamburg*. At the moment this is all the information I can give you. *Auf Wiedersehen*."

"Bless you, Bill," said Jodel. "Sharon, wire Luckman's office, copy to Baggott. 'Horst Schumann due for final Stuttgart interview January 21. Scheduled to sail on Hapag's "Hamburg" January 28, barring unforeseen circumstances. In case of problems will immediately notify you by wire.' Sign my name. Thanks."

Well, that worked out. Things were running more smoothly. German military activity along the Rhine was causing considerable furor amongst old Versailles Treaty partners, but even that had quieted down. In Berlin, however, excitement pervaded the atmosphere, large-scale expansion of facilities for the upcoming Olympic Games visible everywhere. "All this war talk will probably turn out to be nothing but propaganda," he muttered in the direction of his crowded desk. But not for an instant, not even for a tiny moment, did Willie Jodel truly believe this prediction.

◆　　　◆　　　◆

Had he felt better, Horst would have loved the train ride to Koblenz. His life had been spent in Westphalia flatlands, along rivers whose sounds were gentle murmurs compared with the Rhine's majestic symphony. Oskar had often lauded Zeltingen's serene hillsides, the intoxicating smell of grapes in season. Had Horst been less feverish, he might have been delighted by undulating slopes of vineyards above the Rhine's riverbanks, covered in pines and willows. Instead, his body shivering, his brain refused to focus beyond his terror at being arrested. He slipped in and out of agitated dreams. His joints hurt terribly. Thirst made him lurch to a lavatory to cup tepid water into his mouth, then return to his seat with great effort, desperate not to disturb fellow passengers. Barely conscious, he sensed a blanket being pulled to his chin. In the dim light he made out an elderly, pink-cheeked lady as she leaned over and tucked him in. "Rest, young man," she whispered, "you will feel better soon." Lulled by her words and the train's motion, he drifted into a leaden sleep.

"Koblenz. Five minutes to Koblenz," the conductor shouted, marching down the aisle. The rest had not refreshed Horst nor had his fever abated. His head throbbed; his joints ached worse than before. He recognized the woman who had covered him and thanked her.

"You must see a doctor, boy," she said. "You are not well at all. Your mother must take care of you."

The words jolted him. "Yes, I'm sure she will," he whispered hoarsely, "she'll be there when we get to Koblenz." He pulled down his rucksack. "Maybe she'll take me to the hospital," he heard himself say. "Is there a hospital in Koblenz?"

The woman looked startled, not believing the question. "Yes, naturally. Several. In fact a good Catholic one, Das Alte Hospital, near the station. Are you not from Koblenz?"

"Excuse me," he said, I must go to the bathroom."

He stayed behind the locked door until the train came to a halt, waited until everyone had gone, then left the lavatory.

Walking brought more nausea, but he made it through the station, asked a taxi driver for directions to the Catholic Hospital.

"It's not far," the driver said, "looks like you might stay there a while."

The hospital, a square structure of dark-red stones, resembled a medieval fortress. Horst paid the driver, climbed hesitantly up the worn steps, too frightened to go in, too sick not to.

A glass door opened to a vaulted reception area. It was dark and cool inside, a marble floor echoed footsteps, and nuns in blue habits approached and disappeared along hallways. A woman in a flowered dress, seated behind a counter, addressed him.

"Young man, you wish to see someone?"

"No, I'm sick. I need help."

"I'm sorry. You can't just walk in and..." She stopped, suddenly aware of the terror in the boy's eyes. "Sit there. I'll call a nurse." Horst sank on a bench, feeling faint. Only moments later a nun leaned over him. She put her wrist to his forehead and he heard her habit rustle softly. Her face swam before his eyes, but her hand felt cool and soothing.

"This child must be in bed," she said. "Immediately. He's ill. Call Emergency, whoever's on duty."

"But Sister Auguste, he just walked in, right off the street. How do we know if…"

"Later, Frau Blomberg. Now he needs a doctor. Call Sister Angela. She's on duty in Pediatrics. Please ask her to help me."

She took off Horst's rucksack, cradled him in her arms and gently stroked his forehead. "Don't look so frightened, child, nobody is going to hurt you. You are a sick young man, but we will make you well."

Her hands smelled of soap. His cheek rubbed against the starched fabric of her habit. He liked her calm voice and looked up. Her smile, from a serene face framed by a gray wimple, seemed far away, but as reassuring as her strong hands, guiding him to an elevator.

"You have a name? What are we to call you?"

"Horst. I'm Horst," he whispered. "Horst Schumann. I have an appointment in Stuttgart. I must not be late."

"Of course you won't be late. We'll see to it, Horst Schumann."

A room with many beds, boys staring without curiosity. For a moment Horst thought he was back in Paderborn and whimpered with anxiety. When they removed his clothes he clutched his kit, would not let go.

"It's all right, Horst. I'll hide it under your pillow," said the nun called Angela. "You can sleep with it."

He was put to bed in a hospital gown, covered with blankets that smelled like the soap on Sister's hands. A doctor in a white gown pulled a curtain around the bed, felt his forehead and listened to his chest with a flat piece of metal. Horst heard him mutter to the Sisters, winced as a needle stung his arm. I can't be late to Stuttgart, was his last conscious thought.

◆   ◆   ◆

On a Friday afternoon Willie Jodel's wire, verifying Horst Schumann's current status, was delivered by congressional page to the cluttered desk of Nathan Nasatir, Rep. Luckman's administrative secretary. Nasatir was out. Like most mid-level gardeners in Washington's orchards, Nasatir deemed Friday noon as part of the weekend, especially when the boss was back home, pressing flesh. On Monday, of course, things piled up. Rep. Luckman was a popular speaker, a good fundraiser and a pro at dealing with the Hadassah and B'nai B'rith crowd. Appointments had to be made, telephone messages answered, speeches researched, formulated, and drafted. He finally got to to Jodel's wire. Schumann?

Who was Horst Schumann? Some composer his boss was getting out? He showed it to the secretary.

"Who's Schumann, Carol?"

"A kid we're rescuing from the Nazis, Nate. Farber's deal. Better call Chicago. Luckman knows the Malkin family. Hard workers in the primary; better call now before you forget."

Nasatir phoned Chicago, but Farber was downstate, canvassing Champaign-Urbana and wouldn't be in the office before Monday.

When Farber returned the call on Monday, Nasatir had left for the Hill to check polls with Washington's press corps, but his secretary was available.

"Any idea what this is about, Carol? Something from Berlin?"

"A wire, Bert. The Schumann kid is having an interview."

Nasatir and Farber connected the next day. "Where the hell you been, Nat?"

"Busy, Bert, dousing fires. Damn gun lobby bitching about our statement to the Trib. I thought the Trib was on our side."

"I'll handle it. Listen, what's in the wire from Berlin?"

Nathan read it to him twice. Farber carefully wrote everything down.

"Thanks, Nat. Keep up the pressure. The boss will be back Friday."

Farber called the Malkins that evening.

"The twenty-eighth?" Rae yelled into the phone. "Bert, that's in less than two weeks!"

"Add five days, Rae. He's coming on a ship, not an airplane."

"Oh god, Bert, what's this interview about? It's the day after tomorrow. Nothing's going wrong, is it?"

"I don't know about interviews, Rae, but nothing's going wrong. "Luck" wouldn't allow it. I'll let you know if I hear something. In the meantime, if you're making arrangements to have the boy met in New York, you should call Hapag and find out when the ship arrives. They're at 57 Broadway. I'll get the phone number and call you. Relax Rae, we have a winner."

Dick took over the phone. "Can't thank you enough, Bert. You've been a friend. We won't forget."

"Anything for a good Democrat, Malkin. I'll be in touch."

Dick hugged Rae, relieved and excited. "Hey, little mother," he laughed, "let's go to Song Hee's and celebrate. Whatever you want on the menu, even pork foo yong."

"Don't tease, Dick. I can't wait for the boy to be here with us."

"That's what all new mothers say."

◆   ◆   ◆

For the next four days Horst was barely conscious of his surroundings, or of Sister Auguste and Sister Angela, both of whom looked in time and again, mumbled words of encouragement and wiped sweat from his forehead. When doctors came by, accompanied by nurses in habits and interns in green gowns, he didn't notice. He took his medicine, but couldn't remember who brought it, or when. At odd moments he reached under his pillow. Thank God! As long as the kit was there he was safe. Nightmares disrupted his sleep, dreadful apparitions of Papa with a bloody face, of Walter drawing pictures with nails sticking out of his hands. In one dream Günter discovered him in the sewer, stared down with cold eyes, put locks on the lids, leaped gleefully on top yelling, "Dirty Jew, you can't get out. You'll never get out!" A nurse heard Horst scream, changed his sweat-drenched gown, made him swallow a pill and rustled out again.

Finally the fever broke. Horst lay awake, stiff and exhausted. Jittery, he brooded about Oskar. Try as he might he still couldn't remember what Papa looked like, not clearly. Dortmund, too, seemed a far away dream, a place nearly forgotten. He felt like jumping out of his skin. Horst hated being sick and weak and vulnerable. He was thankful to the Sisters for taking him in, but now he was ready to get up and go, first to Stuttgart, then to his ship, then to America. He wanted to do it right now, at this very minute. He was thirsty, poured water from the pitcher, felt shaky from the effort.

The door to his ward flew open and was immediately closed by an invisible hand, but not quite. A small gap between door and frame was sufficient for Horst to hear Sister Auguste in heated discussion with a doctor. He heard his name spoken and listened.

"The patient list, Sister, it gives his name as Schumann. Schumann! Don't you understand? Schumann could be Jewish! Is he circumcised?"

"Yes, doctor, he is."

"Why didn't you tell me? So he is Jewish! We have strict orders. Get him out of here."

"He may be a Jew, doctor, but he's also sick. He has a paper that says he must go to Stuttgart. He's emigrating. Have some Christian charity."

"Don't talk to me of charity, Sister. Don't you dare! Your charity will kill us all. We are forbidden to treat Jews."

"Christ also asked us to show mercy."

"Mercy won't help us in a concentration camp, Sister. Maybe you don't mind going, but I do. Have him out today, now, before they discover we treat Jews in this hospital and arrest us." Horst heard the doctor storm away.

Sister Auguste looked distraught when she came in and stood by his bed. "Sleep, Horst. Rest. Gather your strength. We'll find a way."

He dozed fretfully for maybe an hour. His mind was clearing, shreds of possibilities banding into useful action. He ate what he could of his lunch, napped, and waited for Sister Auguste.

Within the hour, she returned with a paper bag. After she comforted and administered medicine to other children, she pulled Horst's rucksack from the closet, put the bag inside and spoke with quiet urgency.

"Here's food for you. I'm sorry I have no money. You must leave right now. The office is contacting local authorities. Perhaps they have done so already. You have no time to waste. Here are your clothes. Dress immediately. Take the elevator to the basement. I will meet you there with your rucksack and coat. We will go through the kitchen and out the service entrance. I will give you directions to the highway. The train station is not safe, just in case they are looking for you. Be quick."

Horst still felt physically weak, but his mind was definitely clearing. Within a few short minutes he met Sister Auguste at the service entrance. She took his face in her hands.

"Go little boy, go fast. May Christ be with you." She squeezed his hands, pointed him toward the highway and silently disappeared.

Slowly, but without hesitation, he began to walk. How long was he in the hospital? Three days? A whole week? The air was chilly. He tried to move faster, to keep warm and gain distance. After an hour he reached the bank of the Rhine. There he saw the most beautiful bridge he had ever seen, with arches and pillars that spanned the wide river. This had to be the place Papa had told him about, where the Mosel ran into the Rhine. He sat on the ground to catch his breath and admired the sight.

He was very proud of himself. Yes, Stuttgart was still a long way off, he felt very shaky, but he would make it to Stuttgart; soon, very soon. He checked his kit, as he had done countless times since leaving Dortmund, tightened his belt and ate one of Sister Auguste's rolls. Better get going, he thought, before they came looking for him. Feeling rested and a bit stronger, he hitched up his rucksack and walked south.

29

Heiko Böhm fumed with rage. Nothing was going right. One week as Dortmund's *Ortsgruppenleiter* convinced him that office work was not meant for real men. The League of German Girls wanted to hold a rally to raise money for summer camp. Would Herr Böhm approve? The *Völkische Beobachter* and the *Dortmunder Zeitung* politely requested interviews. What time would be convenient for Herr Böhm? The *Nazi Volk-Welfare Society*, the NSV, needed an urgent meeting to assess the coming year's quota. Herr Pflug had been provided with detailed information. What was Herr Böhm's position in the matter? Herr Böhm wanted nothing to do with any of it, dumped responsibility on a cadre of underlings and on Frau Schuster, who resented it. Well, too bad. Those were niggling matters; others were worse. Terhoven called yesterday, the conversation short, but pointed.

"Good day, Heiko. Things going well?"

"I'm learning."

"Excellent. I won't keep you. Berlin sent word that the Propaganda Ministry approved a tour for American journalists. From the Hearst papers, I understand."

"A tour?"

"So the memo says. In February. Westfalen is on the agenda."

"Dortmund too?"

"Who knows? Maybe they wish to ride the Wuppertal suspension railway. Never can tell with Americans, especially when they're newspaper writers, eh Heiko?"

Böhm felt uneasy with Terhoven's familiarity. The man was not known for pleasantries.

"Speaking of visiting Americans," the *Gauleiter* continued, "How's our little campaign going? I don't have to remind you, especially with journalists snooping around."

"I'm working on it," responded Heiko. It sounded inane, even to him.

"Funny, your former boss used those words whenever he tried to avoid an issue," growled Terhoven. "I didn't hire you to give me the same crap! Do I have to come there and personally take charge?"

"No sir. I'll clean it up this week. You'll have a full report on your desk."

"Look forward to it. Heil Hitler."

"Heil…" Terhoven had already hung up.

Böhm recognized priorities. If he hoped to ever leave this pencil-pushing assignment, the *Gauleiter* was not the man to displease. Besides, a little head knocking would be a respite from sitting on one's ass all day and listen to harangues about winter relief, office furniture and a need for new instruments for the HJ Marching Band. Terhoven should have punished Pflug by making him stay on this lousy job.

He picked up the intercom. "Gajewski? Heiko. Come to the office. Yes, right now. Bring Kemmer and Hoffmann."

"What's up?" asked Gajewski, as he entered. His smile revealed brown teeth.

"Action, Egon, action. Here are the files on Lifschitz, his wife Hannah and the kid, David, the Schumanns, father and son, ahh…the Herz file…won't need that anymore, eh?" They chuckled with the bond of conspirators. "Pfarrer Thalmann, although I hear he wasn't in his church the last two Sundays. Check him out. Here's the Grünberg file, with addresses for both house and office. Let's see…Rabinowitz we've taken care of. The Koerners, the famous mechanic and his daughter Lisa. Addresses and phone numbers are on the front covers. Also five or six suspects in the ghetto. Time we put fear into that pack of kosher rats. Find them. Invite them to a party we're giving, right here, beginning tomorrow."

"Dead or alive, Heiko?"

"Alive, Egon. Don't spoil our fun."

"Oh Heiko," said Hoffman, the ex-boxer. "Is Pflug still around? Some guys are wondering."

"On vacation, skiing with his family." Böhm consulted his calendar. "In fact, he should have been back today. You want something from him?"

"Yeah, well, he talked about promotions. We gave him stuff for our personnel files. We wondered what became of that."

"I'll check it out."

The men left. Heiko twirled in his chair. He appeared absent minded, but in fact his thoughts were sharply focused on Rollo. He knew he could call Pflug on the telephone, but something about their last conversation still nagged at him. He knew where the Pflugs lived. He would go there and check things out personally.

Rollo gave a reception when he made Böhm his adjutant. Everyone from headquarters was invited for heaps of food, plenty of beer and lots of fun. Frau Pflug was polite, but Heiko clearly understood her dislike for him. Well, he wasn't interested in winning a popularity prize from Rika Pflug. Her disapproval wouldn't keep him from dropping in today, or on any other day.

He crossed Südwall to Gutenbergstrasse, found the building as he remembered. He stepped into the hallway and instantly felt a foreboding, a sense of disjointedness. Advertisements and envelopes addressed to the Pflugs lay carelessly strewn on the floor. The mailbox was overflowing. Truly suspicious now, Heiko rang the manager's doorbell. A woman's voice called down from the second floor. Böhm identified himself with *Sicherheitsdienst* credentials which, as always, elicited instant response.

"I'm concerned about my comrade, Herr Pflug. Any idea where he is?"

"The Pflugs told me they were going skiing with the children. In Switzerland, I believe."

"Did they mention when they were coming back?"

"No, but looks like not for a while."

"What makes you say that?"

"Well, they took a lot of stuff, quite a few boxes. I told my husband Ulrich, I said 'Ulrich, look how many boxes the Pflugs are taking on holiday.' And Ulrich said, 'Well, you know how women are when they go on vacation, enough for a whole year.' That's what Ulrich said. Then when Herr Pflug came back the other night and packed…"

"Pflug came back? Here?"

"Yes, I'm sure it was him. I heard things being moved, but it was late, so I paid no attention."

"Give me the key to Pflug's apartment."

"But, I couldn't possibly…"

"Give me the key right now or I'll break down the door."

She knew resistance was useless, in fact dangerous. She did as he asked, started back up the stairs.

"Wait. I'll return the key in a minute."

Even before he opened the apartment, Böhm knew the answer. The furniture stood in place, but everything else was gone. The Pflug house was deserted. Totally furious, he slammed the door shut.

Grabowski returned to Heiko's office late in the afternoon, squirmed uncomfortably in the visitor's chair.

"What is it, Egon?"

"They're gone, Heiko."

"What do you mean, they're gone? Who's gone?"

"Grünberg, Lifschitz, the Schumanns, the rest of them. Gone. We hauled in a couple of yids from the ghetto, but the others have disappeared. We asked neighbors, looked all over the city, every place they could hide. Nothing."

"Shit!"

Böhm's face frightened Grabowski.

"Are you telling me they turned into thin air? Hunt for them in the ghetto. Move, man. Get the hell out of here. Find them!"

Damn it," yelled Böhm, when alone. "Goddamn it to hell," and slammed the desk with his fist. "Goddamn Bolshevists! I'll catch you rats if I have to crawl into your godforsaken nests." He banged the desk again. "Frau Schuster!"

She edged through the door, prepared for the worst.

"I want Pflug's files. Everything he's touched and signed. I want all of his records! I want to know what agencies he's done business with, his personal correspondence, a list of those he's approved for emigration, whatever you can find."

"Everything?"

"Do I have to repeat myself? Yes, everything."

He worked until midnight, discovered many disturbing facts about his former boss. He learned that Pflug carried on an active correspondence with mathematicians all over the world, many with Jewish names. He read that Pflug had often protested to Berlin about unequal treatment for women teachers. Nearly blind with fatigue, he came across the list of emigrant applications Pflug had countersigned for the *Kreiswirtschaftsrat*. He scanned the list. Near the bottom was the name Schumann. Horst Schumann.

"Pflug, you goddamn traitor," fumed Böhm, "You let the little bastard escape. Shit! Maybe it's not too late." He tore a sheet from Schuster's steno pad and, convulsed by anger, wrote her a note. "Frau Schuster! The moment you come in send a wire to Stuttgart immigration, to this man Hartung listed on the attached directive. Say 'Horst Schumann is wanted by this office for subversive activities, further details to follow. If emigration procedure has started, stop it. Please keep me informed. Heiko Böhm, *Ortsgruppenleiter*, Kreis Dortmund.'

It was the best he could do at the moment. They would catch every last one of those lousy Bolshevists. Where the hell had they all run? Tomorrow he would have to report the bad news about Pflug to Terhoven. The *Gauleiter* was sure to hate it, although it came as no surprise to Heiko. He had long ago detected something soft in the high and mighty professor. Good riddance! It was he, Heiko, who would show Terhoven who could, and could not be trusted, what a real comrade would do for his Führer. "I'll catch those red bastards if I have to walk into hell to find them," he raved, "and no soap and water this time around." He grabbed his coat and hat, kicked the wastepaper basket clear across the office and slammed the door behind him.

30

Horst walked all day, thankful for sturdy shoes and a tough constitution. The map became his partner, the Rhine a constant and welcomed companion, dormant vineyards on its sloping hillsides harboring villages and towns wrapped in a wintry landscape. He crossed a bridge where the Lahn feeds into the Rhine. A sign pointed to Limburg, only thirty kilometers to the east. Milfs might still live there, drinking beer, his sweaty muscles hammering horseshoes. Horst was tempted to visit his friend, but immediately rejected the notion. Stuttgart was too far away; he had no time for detours.

Near Lahnstein, a truck driver hauling firewood gave him a lift to Saint Goar. "That's the rock of the Lorelei," the driver informed him, pointed to a stone shelf jutting pugnaciously into the narrowing stream.

Horst remembered the drawings Norma Klingen showed him and the legend she told him of a mythical siren, rumored to have dwelled here, singing to ships drifting by and tempting boatmen into blissful damnation and death with her beauty. Norma also taught him the song and Heinrich Heine's bleak lyrics. For some time after he left the truck driver he hummed the Lorelei melody as he made his way up the Rhine valley. Eager with excitement and high on adventure, he grew stronger each day. He hoarded his money, scrounged food at village farmhouses where women, usually kinder than men, insisted that he sit down to eat. "Where are you going?" they asked. "Why are you not in school?" He learned long ago that people didn't believe him when he lied, so he said that he had to go to Stuttgart, that it was urgent. They rarely pursued the matter, too busy with their own lives. Toward night, when he asked if he could rest in their barns for a few hours, they were usually agreeable, but he made himself as unobtrusive as possible and was always on the road before daylight.

When he was too exhausted to walk, he thumbed rides and took buses for short stretches. The longest, costing fifty pfennigs, extended from Wiesbaden to Mainz. Even at its outskirts, he realized Mainz must be bypassed. At many places along the river, close to the city, he watched soldiers in green uniforms and steel helmets restlessly smoking, rifles slung over shoulders or cradled under their arms, apparently waiting for trains or trucks to take them elsewhere. Clusters of children, cheering and laughing, and older people as well, often surrounded them. Horst steered away as soon as he spotted helmets in the distance.

The temperature was milder than it was up north, but to sleep outdoors was out of the question. He was determined not to get sick again. Once, near Nierstein, he found himself without shelter as it grew dark, noticed a "Guest Room" sign in the window of a farmhouse. The woman who opened the door was surprised to see a young boy all alone, but she showed him a room with two narrow beds covered with heavy, warm-looking quilts. It would cost three Marks, she said, including breakfast. That seemed a lot of money to sleep in a bed for one night, but he was worn out and accepted the price. He undressed, happily hugged the warm blanket and instantly fell asleep.

Early breakfast was served at the kitchen table, fresh warm rolls with butter and marmalade and a glass of milk. Anxious to move on, he paid the bill, thanked the woman and walked refreshed into a crisp, clear morning. A dairy farmer, tin cans stacked tight in his truck, picked him up at noon, dropped him off where the Rhine skirts the city of Worms.

At the mouth of a small river harbor he sat on an ornate iron bench to study his map, to decide where to seek shelter that night. The river lapped against the edge of a grove of spruce, flowed calmly between brown meadows. Thick pussy willow bushes jutted against a bright blue sky. He heard footsteps and straightened up in alarm. A stout, red-bearded, middle-aged man approached, wearing a black coat and fur-trimmed hat, peering intently into a book while humming softly. The man looked briefly at Horst, then eased himself onto the bench. For a few moments the two sat silently, quite aware of each other. Once or twice the man turned his head in Horst's direction, as if to establish contact.

"You're going somewhere?" the man finally asked and closed his book. He pointed to the map. "Maybe I can help?" He appeared friendly enough, somehow familiar, with long tapered fingers like those of Lev Grünberg.

"I'm going to Stuttgart."

"Today? From Worms?"

"As soon as I can get there."

"Ahhh," came the reply, with a nod, as if that were perfectly clear. Again they sat wordlessly, stared out over the water. "Important business in Stuttgart?"

Horst chose not to answer.

"I understand," the man said, wistfully. "Can't be too careful these days, especially if you're Jewish."

Horst flinched, put down his map. "How do you know I'm Jewish?"

The stranger chuckled. "Practice. Also by your eyes, the way you're already looking for someplace to run to, just in case. Come on, take a chance and tell me your name."

Horst hesitated before he gave in. "Schumann. Horst Schumann."

"A pleasure to meet you, Horst Schumann. I'm Menahim Hirsch. They call me Red." He lifted his hat, revealed a mop of red curls. "I do a little singing in Worms, in the synagogue. Actually I'm the cantor. Nice here, isn't it?"

"Uh huh. It's beautiful."

"I often come here to enjoy the river and practice my music. It's quiet. Not many people visit during the winter."

Horst felt easier, waited for the man to go on. Hirsch continued. "Stuttgart, eh? Do me a favor, Horst Schumann, and tell me your story. I love a good story, especially from people I've never met. I don't wish to intrude, but it's possible I can help. These days Jews have to stick together, you know."

Menahim Hirsch had a kind face, an endearing smile. Horst decided to trust him and delivered a brief account of his experiences. When he finished, Hirsch moved closer, laid a hand on his shoulder and nodded with genuine sympathy.

"What a world we live in. You know, maybe you're doing the right thing. Jews are leaving Germany, from this city also. Not many, but some. In your case, I can understand. What choice is there? Still, it's a question. My people have lived in this place for generations."

"So did my Papa's."

"Ahhh. Where? In Worms?"

"No. Papa was born in Zeltingen, at the Mosel, my grandfather, too. He was a Rabbi."

"Schumann?" Hirsch was now truly startled. "Your name is Schumann, you say? What was your grandfather's name?"

"Jakob."

"I can't believe it," Hirsch exclaimed. "Reb Jakob Schumann, the Socialist?"

He took Horst's arm, pulled him to his feet. "Tonight you will stay at my house, Horst Schumann. Tonight you will eat at my table with my wife Leora, my daughter Jana and my son, Zvi, also a redhead. You will tell me of your father and I will tell you tales of your grandfather, Jakob Schumann, the Socialist Rebbe of Zeltingen. Your grandfather and my father, I should inform you right now, knew each other well, but there was no love lost between them. Also, they caused a lot of mischief. Come, it's getting dark. My car is over there. Later we will have time to talk."

They walked quickly to Red Hirsch's car. The sun licked at the river's western banks with golden fingers. A cathedral bell rang sonorously in the background. Horst Schumann was sure he had met a friend and it felt wonderful.

◆   ◆   ◆

Frau Schuster complied with Böhm's orders, scoured her files for available data pertaining to the Schumanns, father and son. Oskar's dossier included articles under his byline, Communist propaganda supposedly authored by him, descriptive accounts of his arrests, beatings and, alas, releases; also documents detailing his assets, friends, wives and assorted rumors, innuendoes and pure fictions ascribed to this middle-aged leather merchant, ordained by Nazi fiat to be an intractable menace. About his progeny they knew almost nothing, merely a few undocumented notations suggesting his skill at posting political flyers. With absolute certainty they knew only that he was twelve years old and one of many Jews who wanted to flee the country. However, in Heiko Böhm's proscriptive frame of reference, Bolshevism was an inherited disease to be expunged before it grew sufficiently virulent to infect others, preferably in infancy. For this reason alone Böhm was eager to have both father and son decontaminated at Dachau as soon as possible.

"Have photo copies made of Horst Schumann's file, Frau Schuster. Keep the original and send duplicates to Stuttgart. By the way, if you should hear anything about Pflug, anything at all, office gossip, information from friends, intelligence of one kind or another, you'll tell me, won't you?"

"Of course, Herr Böhm."

She smiled inwardly as she returned to her desk. She had no intention of telling Böhm anything, least of all matters concerning Pflug, whom she admired. She hated Böhm's condescension toward women, his barbaric relish of cruelty, sometimes fantasized about watching him sink in a bog of quicksand as she danced around him. She was also afraid of his wrath and treated their association with caution.

She routed a request for copies of the Schumann boy's file through inter-office mail. The purchasing department issued an order in two days. The copies arrived on her desk a week later. She wrote a cover letter to a Dietrich Hartung in Stuttgart, the name and address on the directive attached to Böhm's note. Late on Friday afternoon she placed it on Böhm's desk, in a pile of other notes and memoranda that required his signature. Böhm, who detested what he considered administrative hogwash, merely glanced at the documents, relied on her experience and good sense. She mailed the photocopies on Monday, the thirteenth of January. They were received and processed in Stuttgart on Friday, the seventeenth, and delivered to Frau Zeidler's desk shortly before she left for the weekend. She had tickets to the theatre, an unquestioned priority. Jewish subversives could wait until Monday. Besides, she wouldn't touch this one; strictly Hartung's responsibility. Before he left the office, Dietrich announced his intention to visit friends in Frankfurt, a familiar metaphor. It meant he would close every tavern in Stuttgart between now and Sunday, lucky to make it to the office on Monday. He surprised her and arrived at noon, but much too hung over for productive work. By Wednesday he felt better and haphazardly attacked that interminable paper mountain marked "To Do *Immediately*." The Horst Schumann material from Dortmund, containing Böhm's earlier wire, lay near the top of the pile. Hartung, in no condition to deal with vexing problems, scanned it briefly and decided this was a matter for "Security." Inter-office mail picked up the folder and delivered it to Deppmüller's desk on Wednesday, January 22.

◆   ◆   ◆

"Your appointment isn't until the twenty-first?" Red Hirsch asked, seated comfortably in an overstuffed chair, sipping wine, analyzing Horst's appearance notice. "Today is only the sixteenth. It's less than two hundred kilometers to Stuttgart, so stop worrying. Spend the Sabbath with us. What's more, you're too skinny. You could use some homemade food. On Sunday I sing at a wedding in Karlsruhe. I'll put you on the train there. This far from Dortmund it should be safe enough. From Karlsruhe it's only an hour and a half to Stuttgart, so relax already, don't be so restless."

It was Horst's first religious service in more than a year. Oskar scoffed at religion, but Horst went occasionally to Walter's house on Friday nights, mostly to please his friend. Unfortunately, George Pariser always turned the Sabbath service into a full-blown marathon, chanted endless, dry-as-bones prayers in Hebrew while succulent smells of chicken soup and matzoh balls, of challah and potato kugel, of Brussels sprouts and sponge cake, and heaven knows what, wafted from the Pariser kitchen. Walter and Yetta, accustomed to the ordeal, endured in stoic silence, but Horst couldn't bear it, squirmed in his chair and drew many baleful stares from a Talmudist antagonized by a mere hint of sensory intrusion.

Without neglecting basics, Red Hirsch's approach to Sabbath rituals was infinitely more humane. His wife, as per custom, blessed the candles, after which appropriate praise was rendered to God for providing great wine and bread. Then, before he loosened his belt, the cantor shared a few reflections,

"I'm thankful we can share this meal with Horst Schumann who is on his way to America. I'm sure the Sabbath is observed there also, mostly in New York, I hear. Maybe in Chicago, too, but who knows? Our guest has had a hard time of it. He's told me quite a bit of his life, but I know there are things he doesn't want to talk about, so let's not intrude. Listening to his story should be enough to remind us how lucky we are that the *goyim* have left us in peace, at least so far. How long will it last? Who can tell? Believe me, we have no right to be complacent. Maybe the worst is over, but let's not count on it. Apparently it's worse in some places, mostly in the big cities. We've read the stories. To keep our eyes and ears open is a good idea. In the meantime I thank God for a wonderful wife, two loving children and a guest whose grandfather was a Rabbi and also stirred up a lot of trouble with grape pickers at the Mosel." He raised his glass. "Here's to his blessed memory. What could be more suitable than a toast with wine to a Socialist toiler in the vineyards of God? *L'chaim.*" He drank to the bottom. "Now, Leora, you glorious pearl among women, let's eat."

The next two days with the Hirsch family were wonderful. Leora, a calm, caring woman, made Horst feel at ease. She washed his clothes and while they dried she shortened for him a pair of Zvi's pants and the sleeves of a cotton shirt. Horst wore both for the service on Saturday. Before they left for the synagogue, Zvi related its history, about the group of Jews who came to Worms almost a thousand years ago with earth from Jerusalem to put in their temple, or so the legend went. In the evening they sang Hebrew melodies, accompanied on the piano by fifteen-year-old Jana. Zvi, two years Horst's senior, suggested a game of chess. The boys played until Horst grew weary and retired to the guest room behind the kitchen, where Leora tucked him in and kissed him good night.

"Sleep well, young man. Everything is going to be just fine. God bless you."

"Thanks," he said, felt emotions like those he last experienced with Norma. "You've been wonderful. I appreciate it very much."

"I know you do. Now sleep."

He woke late Sunday morning, dozed a while, felt truly healthy for the first time since he fled the hospital. The family gathered at the kitchen table for a breakfast that featured chunks of smoked fish and rolls with a hole in the middle. Horst ate his fill of what Zvi called bagels.

"We don't leave until noon," said Red, "so take your time. Tell us about your father."

"He's a Communist," Horst declared. "He writes pamphlets and posters. He's not much of a Jew, but the Nazis don't care. They hate him because he is good with propaganda. They keep beating him up, but he doesn't stop doing it. I don't know where he is now. He said he would try to escape, but he's said that before and he never does it."

Hirsch sighed. "My father's family came from Russia over a hundred years ago. They were knocked around too, by the Tzar, also by peasants. Maybe by everybody. Everything to do with Russians, my father despised. I guess he acquired that from his father."

"Opa Jakob liked Russia, Papa told me. I'm not sure why he was a Communist, but he was. Then he taught Oskar."

"Your Opa Jakob tried to convince a lot of people. He and my father stood on opposite sides, mostly about politics, but especially about religion. My father was a Hebrew scholar, a regular *yeshiva bocher*, a frommer yid who bound *tefillen*, sacred writings, to his arm and forehead every morning. His business was importing hand-written, sacred scripture from Palestine to put in mezzuzahs, which he carved from wood. Together with remnants of wool and silk, he peddled them to Jewish communities along the Rhine and Mosel. Not much of a living, but we ate. That's how he met your Opa Jakob, Reb Schumann. Maybe they didn't truly hate each other, but apparently they had terrible arguments. Samuel Hirsch believed the Talmud was inspired by heaven and designed to enlighten humanity. Reb Schumann? The gospel according to Marx. Religion? Opium of the people. They both loved Germany. I'm not positive why, but it was surely for different reasons."

Horst nodded. "Papa always says he loves Germany, or at least he used to. But now Papa says they're trying to tell us we're not even Germans anymore. The Nazis say we're Jews; that's what we are, and that's all everybody cares about. Either you're a Jew or you're not. I'm glad I'm going to America. I had a teacher in Dortmund who said in America it doesn't matter if you're a Jew."

"We've never had any problems in Worms," said Leora. "Only lately some troublemakers paint swastikas on the synagogue, that kind of thing. The Nazis have been in for a couple of years now. They seem to feel very secure, so maybe they'll leave us alone. A lot of our Jews are staying. They think it will all blow over."

"I don't believe it, Leora, but I hope they're right." Horst's voice sounded empty, his face suddenly drawn looking and much too old for a boy of twelve.

There wasn't the time, or the mood, to say more. Red dressed for the wedding, Leora packed Horst's rucksack, Zvi did school work and Jana practiced piano. With many hugs they said good-bye and wished each other well. Horst and Red talked little on the way to Karlsruhe's train station.

"You still have two days before your appointment. Go to the synagogue on Hospitalstrasse. It's not far from the depot. Look up Rabbi Bamburger, Simon Bamberger, a friend of mine. He's also a friend of the Westheimers who run a small pension nearby. If they have a room, they'll take you in. I stay with them when I'm in Stuttgart. Won't cost you much. Use my name."

"Thanks a lot, Red. I'm so glad you invited me. I had a great time. I almost forgot what it was like to be with a big family."

"Won't be long and you'll have a family of your own in America." Red gave him a card with his address. Horst put it into his kit. They shook hands at the curb. "Take it easy, Horst Schumann. Be careful, don't let them push you around." He climbed into the car. "Good luck and write a letter." He would like to have stayed, but then drove off with a last wave of his hand.

As always around public places, Horst remained watchful, alert to signs of hostile activity. He quickly paid three marks and fifty pfennigs for a ticket and boarded his train a half hour later. He found a seat and tried to be calm, but was far too excited to sit down. He felt like wandering from one end of the train to the other, but thought that would be a dumb thing to do. Only when the train began to move did it enter his mind: After so many weeks of worry and fear, he had truly reached the last leg on his way to Stuttgart! He had made it from Dortmund in less than three weeks, even with a stay at the hospital to slow him down. In only ninety minutes he would finally be there. It seemed like a dream.

After a while he relaxed, mused about those three weeks. Yes, he had seen new places and that was great. He recalled the people along his way and instantly felt grateful to them. He envisioned Herr Holzer and his wondrous car; Sister Auguste, her peaceful face and cool hands; the farmers who picked him up on the road and, of course, Sabbath dinner at the Hirsches. The click-clack of wheels reminded him of that pink-cheeked old lady on the train to Koblenz. He kept seeing her face. They had hardly spoken and would remain total strangers, yet somewhere between Cologne and Koblenz she recognized his need, covered him and spoke comforting words that sustained him in his helplessness. He would never be able to repay the debt, nor would he forget her for the rest of his life.

The train wound through the Black Forest's northern boundaries, passed pretty villages with picturesque names, Maulbronn, Mühlacker and Vaihingen/ Enz. Church spires and steeples rose in the distance, a green and tidy city lay tucked into a verdant valley. Horst's feelings were jumbled. He felt exhilarated, a big step closer to America, but he was also horribly frightened by the prospect of his dreaded appointment. Slowly the train chugged into the station. His journey to Stuttgart had ended.

31

"The Gray City." Hamburg lived up to its reputation as a dense fog swept from the North Sea over the Hanseatic port. As she left her office after a trying day, Hildegard Kube wished for the bright days of summer, but alas, this was only January. The "Hamburg" was scheduled to depart in ten days and preparations were extensive. Hundreds of details had to be negotiated, passenger lists and cabin assignments completed, travel agency vouchers checked against reservations and berth assignments finalized as soon as Eberhardt sent her the "Approved Passenger Manifest." The new exit procedures had only been used once and functioned without a hitch. A messenger had delivered the manifest from Eberhardt on the afternoon before departure. She thought it was peculiar that all the names sounded Jewish. When she ventured to ask him, Eberhardt, making the rounds among all agents, explained it in his usual, disagreeable manner.

"Just do what it says in the booklet, Frau Kube. Nothing else should really concern you. However, since you're so curious, these are Jews cleared in Stuttgart and a few other cities. We conduct one last security check before we issue them exit visas. Surprising what turns up."

"Like on the last trip."

"Exactly. Those three that I stamped 'Not In Order'? Every one an enemy of the Reich. Good thing we found out in time."

"What happened to them?"

"Also no concern of yours," he growled so harshly it made her flinch. "Just do your job, pull out 'Not in Order' tickets and give them and the manifest to our security officer on 'Sail Day'. That's all you have to remember. We'll take care of the rest. Heil Hitler." He had walked out, but not until he ran a finger along the counter, testing for dust.

She had watched the guards shove those three enemies of the Reich into a black wagon parked in the alley behind the office, was only able to guess what their fate might be. Today, as she stepped from her office into Hamburg's thick fog, she considered asking Otto. Maybe he knew. No, don't be stupid, Hildegard, she reminded herself. Mind your own business or you'll end up like those three. She tied a woolen muffler around her neck for extra warmth and walked briskly to Jungfernstieg to catch the streetcar. She hoped Otto and Gottfried, her son, would be out, at a meeting or a skat game at the *Drei Ecke*. After a hard day, she required time alone in her sanctuary. Communion with the Madonna always renewed her spirits; then she would take a leisurely bath and relax.

◆   ◆   ◆

In Stuttgart, Horst asked directions from a kind-looking lady.

"Hospitalstrasse? No problem. Straight ahead on Königstrasse to Lange Strasse, turn right and you come to Hospitalstrasse."

It was the first time he walked in a large city since leaving Dortmund. Shops were closed on Sunday, only a few people were in the streets. Men in black and brown uniforms, often with their families, leisurely strolled on sidewalks. In cafes, people laughed, smoked, and drank beer and coffee, paid attention only to each other. Horst was dressed in Zvi's woolen pants and the good cotton shirt. Leora had also polished his shoes and brushed out his winter coat. He saw his reflection in the depot's washroom and decided he looked nice.

He found the synagogue. Near the sanctuary doors a woman typed at her desk. Horst asked to see Rabbi Bamberger.

"The Rabbi's out this afternoon. Perhaps I can help you. I'm Miriam Lefkol, his secretary. What is your name?"

"Horst Schumann."

"May I know what you want to see the Rabbi about?"

"Herr Hirsch in Worms told me to look him up."

"Ah. How is Herr Hirsch? A wonderful cantor. You are from Worms?"

"No, I'm not." He shifted uneasily on his feet. "Herr Hirsch said the Rabbi might help me find some place to stay, a pension called Westheimer."

"For you and your parents?"

"I'm alone."

"You're alone?"

"Yes."

Miriam Lefkol pushed away from her desk. A story, she said to herself. These days it's always a story. Why should a little Jewish boy be alone, looking for some place to stay? A *Schande*, a real shame. She sighed. "I'm going home in ten minutes. I'll take you to Westheimers; it's on my way. They're friends of mine. Rote Strasse is close to here. In the meantime have a look at the temple. You'll like it."

He walked up and down the main aisle of the temple, was reminded of prints he had seen in one of Papa's books, the one with buildings from Africa and Spain. He wasn't sure, but this synagogue looked just like those pictures, with walls made of little colored stones and an iron lamp hanging from the ceiling. Sure prettier than the temple in Dortmund where he attended only once, for Albert's *bar mitzvah*. Karl and Albert would love these colorful designs. Suddenly he wished desperately for his friends to be with him. Would he ever see them again?

"You like it?" asked Miriam Lefkol.

"Yes, I do. It's much nicer than the one we have in Dortmund."

On Rote Strasse 2, a four-story building, a brass plate announced the Westheimer pension, located on the second and third floors. Miriam rang the bell and a buzzer let them in.

"This is Horst Schumann," Miriam introduced him to a harried-looking lady in a kitchen smelling of cabbage. "He's from Dortmund."

"So where are his parents?"

"He's alone, Luba. Cantor Hirsch from Worms sent him."

'Ah. And how's the Cantor? Sit child, you're making me nervous."

"I have to leave," said Miriam. "He can stay?"

"Today, yes. Tomorrow, who knows? You know what those *momsers* in the Rathaus are like on Mondays. By tomorrow maybe we'll all be…" she popped her eyes, stuck out her tongue, ran a finger across her throat.

"Don't pay attention to her, she's a kvetch," Miriam advised. "Good luck, Horst. Come see the Rabbi. He'll be in tomorrow."

Luba Westheimer put salt in some pots, stirred around in others, dumped potatoes on the table from a bowl. "You know how to peel potatoes?" she asked, handed Horst a paring knife. He nodded.

"Don't leave the eyes in. You're hungry?" He nodded again.

"Finish peeling, I'll fix something. You have money?"

"A little."

"For you, because you're from Hirsch and also because you look like a nice boy, it's two marks a night. For that you get two meals. A great cook I'm not, but die from it you won't. You can afford two marks?"

"Yes."

"When's your interview?" He looked up, surprised. "Nu? Why else would a Jewish kid come to Stuttgart? To see the Palace? I have twelve rooms, eleven of them for people with interviews. You'll meet them at supper, the ones they let go."

He had never seen such confusion, heard such wailing and yelling, such bitter denunciations. One couple had been here for over a week and was now schedule for further investigation. Their laments mingled with shouts of relief from the lucky ones, those who were cleared and were packed, ready to leave for various ports of exit, where passports and visas waited.

"Too bad about Benesch," said a gaunt, awkward man with a wispy beard, stabbing a potato and meatball. "If I told him once, I told him ten times. I said Benesch, don't screw around with drafts to Paris banks. Maybe a year ago, okay, but not now, not anymore. They're organized."

"What happened?"

"How do I know? He's not here, is he?"

In the momentary silence that followed, everyone present contemplated his or her own vulnerability, but after dinner the babble continued in the sitting room, died down only near midnight when Albert, Luba's husband, insisted on turning out the lights. A group of well-dressed women asked Horst about his papers.

"I don't have any."

"Nothing? No documents?" The lady from Frankfurt couldn't believe it.

"I'm here alone," he explained, I don't have anything."

Two families from Berlin kept to themselves; the children played with toys, the women chatted. The men, dressed in expensive-looking suits, smoked cigars, conferred quietly, exchanged documents and retired early. Horst soon became bored with talk about blocked Reichsmarks, Reich Flight Tax and something called Aryanization that everyone agreed was a total *Schande*, the very sound of the word infuriating.

On Monday morning Luba Westheimer handed him a city map. He was anxious to find out how long he would have to walk to arrive at the Rathaus. Tomorrow was Tuesday! Tomorrow he could not afford to be late; his life depended on being punctual. It was as simple as that. He wanted to take no chances and decided to make a practice run. He crossed Königs Strasse to Neue Brücke, turned left on Hirsch Strasse and saw the feared building, which dominated an entire side of the Marktplatz. It took him only ten minutes to get here, but much longer to revive his heart, which nearly stopped beating by what he saw.

From the steps of a fountain, where other Jews milled about to support each other and to gather courage, the Rathaus loomed imposingly. A handsome dome, flanked by ornate cupolas, reached for the sky, its gracefully curved windows reflecting fine old townhouses, their stores already crowded with shoppers. Had the Rathaus been stripped of Nazi trappings, the view would have delighted Horst's eye, but such was not the case. A huge swastika billowed above the central doorway, smaller ones dangled from eaves of the sloping roof. Guards in black uniforms and steel helmets, rifles at parade rest, guarded an entrance where limousines disgorged an array of military personnel. In and out went Party officials in black uniforms, officers in green longcoats, men dressed in leather, others in SA regalia, thongs cinched under chins, hands raised in the Nazi salute, shouting endless "Heil Hitlers."

The thought of entering this building made Horst tremble. He could still see his father as he lurched out of Böhm's basement like a torn rag doll, disfigured, stripped of human identity by men just like those who strutted and swaggered into their fortress. Sheer terror numbed his mind. He dug his fingernails into his palms as he clenched his fists.

Fear and anxiety nearly overwhelmed him. He knew he hated these people, hated them so fiercely his tears were like blood squeezed from his eyes. Abandoned, bereft of protection, he wept for his losses. He once had a Mutti and sister, had loved them, but now they were dead. He loved Papa, but would he ever see him again? He had loved Walter and Gitte and they were also dead. "Did you have to do that to Walter?" he mourned, kicking the fountain with frustration. "He only wanted to paint birds and flowers. Why did you want to kill him?" He pressed fingers against his swollen eyelids. "Why do you want to kill me?" he screamed at the building with a soundless voice. An old question and always the same silent, mournful reply: "Because you are a Jew."

The swastika snapped in the wind. Close by, men with furtive eyes, in long woolen coats, flailed arms for warmth, whispered to each other, searched for deliverance in shreds of paper, in assertions honed during endless hours of sleepless nights. "Because I am a Jew?" Horst Schumann cried out to an unhearing god.

Why had the hatred grown so fast? How had it become so vicious? What did that fierce little man in the Limburg hardware store believe that could make Milfs, that powerful giant, tremble with fury? Papa's customers, Gretchen's parents, even the Communists who came to the house, all of them thought it would go away, the banners and the marching and the man screaming his lungs out on the radio, the one they called Führer. It didn't go away. Instead, he and his friends had to hide in sewers and mines. Günter broke both of his arms, but nobody punished him. Eckert killed Walter and nobody cared. Gitte and her father were bombed to pieces, but the men who did it laughed as they drove away. They smashed Papa's body, but no one protested. Maybe the Hirsches in Worms believed it couldn't happen to them, but he knew they were wrong. Those men in the Rathaus would make sure no Jew was spared. Schmuel and Papa and Gitte and Isador and Walter too, they already knew. Why? Why were they tortured or dead? Because they were Jews.

Now he knew what confronted him and felt better prepared for tomorrow. With time to spare, he ambled toward the *Schlossplatz*, to the castle, the theater and the gardens, just looking. On Dorotheenstrasse he splurged on a hot chocolate, wanted Oskar to share it with him. Where was his father now? Was he well? Was he even alive?

The morning had drained him, but when he returned to the pension in the late afternoon Horst felt more confident. Luba Westheimer served him a special treat, a piece of cake and a glass of milk. Later he rested, tried to read, but he couldn't concentrate. He daydreamed his favorite dream, the one about America, and dozed off. A supper gong woke him in time to join a renewed babble, Jews who shouted and whispered, waved documents, complained about foreign currency allocations, breaches of contract, the iniquities of the latest racial laws, the hated *Rassengesetze*. After dinner he played chess with a man from Mannheim who chain-smoked cigarettes and whose hands shook so bad he knocked over pieces. Horst finished one game and politely excused himself. He much preferred to go back to visions of his promised land.

At eight the next morning Luba gave him a roll and hot coffee, yelled at him at nine-thirty, wished him *mazel* when he put on his rucksack and walked down the stairs.

He did not permit himself the slightest hesitation, looked neither right nor left, walked through the Rathaus doors and presented his appearance notice to a man in a green uniform seated at a desk at the foot of a stairway.

"Go to the fourth floor, turn left to Suite 422."

A woman behind a counter took his notice. "Sit in the waiting room until we call you."

Wooden chairs lined the walls, a second door exited to the rear. An older man nervously shuffled documents. A girl in a brown uniform, a sheet of paper in hand, burst through the rear door.

"Schumann. Horst Schumann."

His heart skipped a beat, his legs felt like lead. He struggled to his feet and followed her down a hallway. She opened a door, told him to enter and closed it firmly as soon as he walked through.

At a long wooden table at the far end of the room sat a slim, dark-haired man in an SS uniform and a blond, older woman in a black suit and white blouse, a swastika in her lapel. Files and ledgers were spread in front of them.

"Step forward." Through steel-rimmed glasses the man scrutinized his appearance notice, confirmed his identity.

"Your full name?"

"Horst Schumann."

"Who is with you?"

He didn't understand, looked at them questioningly.

"In Stuttgart. Who is with you in Stuttgart?"

"Nobody. I'm here alone."

"Your father, it says you have a father. Where is he?"

"In Dortmund."

"Why is he not with you?"

"We have no money. I had to come alone."

They turned their backs to him, conferred in low tones and thumbed through contents of a brown folder. The woman pulled out several documents, placed them neatly on the table and made notations.

"Your papers state that you're emigrating to America" said the man. "What are you taking with you?"

He didn't understand that question either, again looked at both of them.

"Listen, you dumb little Jew. Answer me or I'll make you talk. What are you taking with you?"

"Everything I've got is in my rucksack."

"What's in there?"

He took it off and started to pull out the contents. "I've got a Karl May book, a shirt, a pair of socks…"

"That's enough." The man removed his glasses, rubbed his eyes as if wearied by the process. He and the woman conferred briefly. "Give this lump of dirt his papers, Frau Senger. Get him out of here," the man mumbled, selected another folder from the pile and began to study it.

The woman told Horst to step forward to the edge of the table. Her voice was hard and flat: "This is your security clearance for departure on the *Hamburg* on January twenty-eight, a week from today. Your photo is sealed into your identification. Don't lose it. It would take months to replace. Without this identification you don't exist. Present yourself at Hapag's Hamburg office. The address is printed on this paper. Here is your health certificate which you will also present. Do you understand?" He nodded. "Sign the receipt for these documents."

He signed a ledger sheet marked 'Schumann, Horst.'

"In Hamburg you will be issued a ticket, passport, exit visa and boarding pass by our Security Office on the day of departure," she continued. "Do you follow me?"

He nodded, his heart beating fast.

"Your American sponsor…" she looked in the folder…"a Richard Malkin of Chicago, Illinois, deposited with the United States Embassy an amount of American currency equivalent to sixty-five Deutsche Reichsmarks. I have a voucher in that amount made out in your name. If you need funds you may redeem it now, or you may do so in Hamburg." She waited impatiently for an answer." Do you wish to redeem it now or later?" she repeated.

He had no idea what "redeem" meant, so he nodded. She took sixty-five marks from a steel box and pushed them towards him with a receipt.

"Sign here." He signed, clutched the money in his fist.

"Listen carefully. I will not repeat myself. We have informed you of procedures leading to your departure from Germany. We have issued you a security identification with your sealed photograph. We have given you a Certificate of Health signed by a licensed physician. We have redeemed a voucher issued in your name by the Embassy of the United States in the amount of sixty-five Deutsche Reichsmarks. Furthermore, you swear that you have withheld no assets aside from those previously identified, or intend to acquire such assets prior to departure. The penalty for perjury is severe, I assure you. Do you understand what I have said?" He nodded. "Do you agree with that statement?" He nodded. "Sign here to verify." He signed.

"Any questions?"

He had none.

"Put your money and papers away and get out," said the man.

Horst stuffed everything in his kit, his fingers shaking. The woman walked him to the door. The girl in the brown uniform was waiting on a chair in the hall.

"Katz is next, Karin. That way out" she said to Horst, pointed to a stairway.

He stumbled down to the lobby, past soldiers guarding the entrance and continued to the center of the market place, trembling with relief. He had walked into the cave of the beast and come out alive. "Oh god, Papa," he said out loud, "I've done it. They're letting me go. They're letting me go in a week."

Floating on air, he hurried to the train station. He knew the way by now. He had seen Hamburg on his map. Hamburg was far to the North, the train the only way to get there in time. He had enough for a ticket.

The clerk at the information counter consulted his schedule.

"A train to Frankfurt leaves Stuttgart at 4:00, arrives at 6:45. You can make a connection to Hamburg at 9:21 and arrive tomorrow afternoon at 2:07." Tomorrow afternoon! Horst could hardly believe it.

He ran back to the pension, breathlessly told the Westheimers the good news. With genuine happiness and many *mazel tovs* they packed for him salami and cheese, fruit and two large pieces of cake.

"Go with God's blessing, young man," Luba beamed. He paid his bill and hugged Luba. He walked to the depot, bought his ticket and boarded the train. He loved the ride, felt totally light-hearted. America, here I come! In the distance he looked out on the Neckar, saw the castle at Heidelberg shortly before it grew dark. He devoured the salami and cheese, wolfed down the cake before changing trains in Frankfurt. In the morning, at the edge of Westfalen, he had a slight, but momentary, sentimental twinge. As the train crossed the Elbe he stared with amazement at the harbor and the ships, large and small, some steaming up and down the river, others clear out of the water with men working on them. The train pulled into Hamburg's main station at 2:04. He went through his accustomed routine, checked his kit, tightened the belt, made sure it was secure and on January 22, 1936, Horst Schumann put on his rucksack and walked into Hamburg's cold, sea-born air.

◆   ◆   ◆

Franz Wilhelm Deppmüller, Chief of Security on Dr. Becker's administrative staff, telephoned Frau Zeidler in Dietrich Hartung's office. When was a young Jew named Horst Schumann scheduled for his interview? She looked it up, informed him the interview took place yesterday, that Schumann was cleared and most likely on his way to Hamburg, if not there already. "So, Hamburg," said Deppmüller. "And his departure date?"

She shuffled through reports received from the Rathaus only that morning, found the Schumann folder and the date. "He's scheduled to leave on the twenty-eighth, aboard the *Hamburg*."

"The twenty-eighth? Good, that gives us five days. Plenty of time. Thank you, Frau Zeidler." He started to hang up. "Oh, one more question. When was Hartung informed of Böhm's wire from Dortmund? It was sent on the thirteenth."

She felt the question coming, frantically searched for a sensible answer, anything to keep her sad, alcoholic boss from falling into the pit he was digging.

"Totally my fault, Herr Deppmüller. So many applications to process the last two weeks, I neglected to give this one to Herr Hartung until Wednesday. I apologize. I promise it won't happen again."

He paused, too long for comfort. "See that it doesn't. And Frau Zeidler…"

"Yes, Herr Deppmüller."

"I sincerely hope anyone who works for me in the future is as loyal to me as you are to Hartung."

He hung up, scowled and made a notation to talk to Becker. Hartung was becoming impossible. These kinds of slip-ups had to stop. What to do with the Schumann file? Obvious, send it to its logical destination. He checked with the mailroom.

"Deppmüller here. I need to get papers to Hamburg Security by the twenty-seventh. Any problem?"

"Airmail is leaving right now, sir. Can we pick it up?"

"It's ready. Will it be in Hamburg in five days?"

"Guaranteed, Herr Deppmüller."

He wrote a brief note, apologized for the lateness of delivery; things piled up, never enough hands to do the work, the sort of nonsense he, like everyone else, laughed at. It didn't matter as long as the information arrived in Hamburg on time.

Hamburg's Security office delivered Böhm's wire and Deppmüller's note to Eberhardt's desk on the 26th. He placed them in his "Approved Passenger Manifest" folder. The deadline for final corrections, to close the trap on parasites trying to slip through, was not until tomorrow. He scanned the list, three from Stuttgart, one from Frankfurt and two from Berlin. With the new Schumann file that made seven, twice as many as the last time. More rats trying to escape or was security improving? Eberhardt preferred to think it was better security; not yet perfect, but improving.

32

For twenty-five pfennigs Horst bought a map of Hamburg. He felt safer finding his way around without asking questions, easily located Alsterdamm, the address given to him in Stuttgart. Only a short walk from the station, at the edge of a lake, which looked frozen, "Hamburg-Amerika Linie" was stenciled on office windows that ranged an entire block. Just to see the name reassured him; it was almost like being on the ship already. He found Number 25. Behind the windows a heavy-set, gray-haired, middle-aged woman talked with several well-dressed people. He didn't want to interrupt so he strolled along the lake, the first one he had ever seen in the middle of a city. When he returned, the woman was alone. She looked up when he entered, smiled pleasantly and came to the counter.

"Good day. How may I help you?"

Horst took out his security identification.

She examined it on both sides. "You're here from Stuttgart?"

"Yes. I'm going to America next week."

"You're a little early, Herr…Schumann. Please come back with your parents, any time later this week. A few days early are best." She returned his card.

"I don't have any parents. I'm alone."

"You're alone?" Hildegard Kube frowned, consulted her passenger list and found his name, the ticker paid through the U.S. Embassy. "Were things explained to you in Stuttgart?"

"They told me to check in here for my ticket and passport."

"That's right, but not until Tuesday morning."

"Oh."

She saw his disappointment. What a nice boy, she thought, but why was nobody accompanying him? "Where are you staying in Hamburg?"

As always, to be alone in situations like this embarrassed Horst. He stood with his eyes large, forlorn and full of sadness. Frau Kube wanted to put her arms around him, to give him comfort and reassurance.

"Surely you must be staying with somebody?"

"I don't know anybody. I don't have any place to stay."

She sat down at her desk, puzzled and moved. Sweet Jesus, she said to herself, what am I to do? She walked back to the counter. "Maybe I can find you a place to sleep."

"I don't have much money left. Just enough for food."

She needed time to think. To offer him money seemed wrong somehow. It also seemed wrong to let him walk away without help.

"I close at five-thirty. Why don't you look around until then? By the way, my name is Hildegard Kube."

"I'm glad to meet you, Frau Kube. I'm sure I can find things to do."

"Good. Come back at five-thirty. We'll figure out something. Try not to worry about it."

He waved to her from the sidewalk.

She watched him disappear down the street. In the middle of winter and no place to sleep? Dear God, please help me find a solution. Hildegard Kube never doubted that God listened to her, especially when He was needed.

Horst ambled along Alsterdamm, crossed Lombardsbrücke and strolled down the Alster shore. Trees were bare, the ground frozen, but the sun was out and some boys in uniforms played soccer on the brown grass, using rucksacks for goal posts. He watched for a while and wished, as always, that he could join. The sun began to set, a church bell rang five times. He walked back quickly. Frau Kube shouldn't have to wait for him.

"I might get into trouble," she said, "but I can't let you sleep outdoors in the middle of winter." She looked closely at him, saw a child of God just like herself and sorely in need of help. The expression in the boy's eyes made her shiver. In the art museum she had come across eyes like his once before, a long time ago. A lady artist named Kohlwitz or Kollwitz, she wasn't sure, had painted eyes she never forgot, like the black holes she had seen in pictures of Jesus on the cross. The eyes looking at her now were like that and she couldn't bear it.

"We have a supply room. It's warm. There's a toilet and a sink with water. The water isn't hot, but you can drink it if you get thirsty." She wished he wouldn't stare at her with so much hope. It almost made her cry.

"You can sleep there if you don't disturb anything. I have to lock the front door, but I'm here in the morning. I'll bring you something to eat. I'm sorry, it's all I can think of right now."

"I've slept in many different places. Some of them weren't nearly as nice."

She had no problem believing him. "You must promise to stay in the supply room. If anyone sees you, we're both in trouble. Really bad trouble."

"I promise, honest I do. I don't want to make trouble."

She showed him where to turn the lights on and off. "Keep the door closed," she said, "or they'll see the light from outside." A towel hung on a hook in the bathroom. "I'll bring a fresh one tomorrow. I have to leave now."

She quickly shook his hand, turned off the office lights, closed and locked the front door, and felt faint. Nothing like this had ever happened to her, but deep inside she also felt warm and very alive. She needed to calm down, traversed Adolf Hitler Platz, crossed Mönckebergstrasse and entered St. Petri Cathedral. The sacredness in the church always soothed her heart. A few women and a man were quietly praying. "Oh Lord," she whispered in the direction of the Christ over the altar, "I am terribly frightened. I broke the law. Forgive me, but the boy had to have help. I put myself in your mercy. Amen." Relieved, but still nervous, she went home. Thank God, Otto and Gottfried were out. A warm bath and a light dinner refreshed her. Afterward, in her sanctuary, her mind lingered on those strange eyes that told such sad stories.

◆   ◆   ◆

Horst made himself comfortable. The room was carpeted and that was nice. A bit of food remained in the rucksack, not a great meal, but better than nothing. Supplies on the shelves consisted of stationery and envelopes, file cards, ledgers with thick green covers, boxes of pencils and pens, rubber stamps, office materials. Careful not to disturb a single thing, he went to the bathroom, washed with a piece of soap and dried off with the towel. He read his Karl May. Would he ever finish this book? Right now fierce Comanches attacked a Fort full of soldiers, hoping to get scalps. He had goose bumps as he read about fiery arrows zinging through the air, about savages who climbed the Fort's barricades, swinging their frightening tomahawks. He wondered if there were Indians on the streets of Chicago, what he would do if he met one. He forgot all about uniforms and sewers, about fear and loneliness and the death of friends as he vanished, if only for a short, blissful time, into a universe of masterful scouts, swift horses, brave soldiers and feathered warriors, contentedly losing himself in a child's world of fantasy.

◆   ◆   ◆

The following morning Frau Kube unlocked the office before eight thirty. Everything appeared to be in order. In the supply room she found Horst fully dressed, dozing on the floor. She woke him gently, then watched with pleasure as he wolfed down the onion bread and cheese she had brought.

"I can't spend time with you, I have too many things to do," she said, "but you can explore the city. Go to the harbor. It's very exciting. Walk along the Elbe and watch the ships sail in and out. I can show you on the map where the *Hamburg* docks. You'd like that, wouldn't you?"

"Oh I would! I would like that very much."

His enthusiasm was contagious. He was just a young boy after all, his eyes not nearly as sad as yesterday. "Come back at five thirty, before I lock up. You have money for food?"

"Yes, enough. I don't eat a lot."

He was being brave. She saw how he tore into food, how skinny he was. Tomorrow she would bring something more substantial. At his age, her Gottfried could eat a whole cow. Horst put on his coat, tied his muffler around his neck and lifted his rucksack. Hildegard had no idea what possessed her, but she just couldn't help it. She hugged him and kissed him on the top of his head. He walked out the door, waved to her and was gone. She sighed and began the day's work. So much left to do; it was the twenty-third already.

◆   ◆   ◆

In the next four days Horst explored Hamburg's harbor, wandered around its innumerable canals, watched welders and painters hang from platforms as they repaired ships in dry-dock, found St. Pauli's fish market where objects were sold the likes of which he had never seen; exotic flowers, tools and knives and fish as flat as pancakes. The smells were overpowering, at once terrible and wonderful. He walked the Grosse Elb Strasse, far out to where ships steered around sandbars, saw vessels beyond his wildest imagination with smoke stacks as tall as houses, blasting deep-throated fog horns as they moved up the channel. When he found the *Hamburg*, docked at a busy anchorage, being loaded by cranes and swarms of dock workers coming and going aboard, he was so excited he couldn't tear himself away, nearly forgot to go back to the office. Frau Kube had brought a blanket and a fresh towel. She had been very good to him and he thanked her with all his heart.

"Na ja," she said, as she prepared to close up, "almost your last night, Horst. Then you can sleep on a good bed, fresh sheets every morning, more food than you've seen in your whole life."

"You've been on the *Hamburg*, Frau Kube?"

"Oh yes, several times. We had a Christmas party on her last year. We're often invited to company celebrations. She's a beautiful ship."

"I'm so excited! I can't wait!"

She would miss him when he left. He was appreciative, a lovely boy, the first Jewish child she had ever talked to for more than a moment. Why did people despise the Jews? Why did Otto and her own Gottfried hate them so much? She simply couldn't understand it. After all, Jesus was a Jew. That was a fact, although it always confused her. Well, in a couple of days the boy would be on his way to America. She didn't know how it was for Jews in America, but it surely had to be better than here. She boarded the streetcar at Jungfernstieg and thought about Horst on the way home.

◆   ◆   ◆

Gottfried Eberhardt considered himself a meticulous worker, a valued company employee and a respected cog in his Party's machine. He took pride in orderly process, expected it from everyone in his sphere of operation. Tomorrow was departure day. He always supervised a myriad details in connection with that event. Now his contribution to the voyage's success was nearly completed. Only one other task to perform and he could leave for the weekend with a clear mind. He looked forward to the weekend. Perhaps he would go to Berlin, visit old comrades, take in a soccer game at the stadium and maybe a concert, but first things first. He unfolded the passenger manifest, carefully checked the inkpad and stamp, made sure they were clean. He opened the manila folder that contained the list of undesirables, the ones to be kept off the ship and turned over to Security. In the manifest's 'Not in Order' column he put tiny dots next to their names, verified them, verified them again, and then checked once more. No margin for error at this stage. It would not do to send inappropriate persons to…well, wherever enemies were sent these days. He'd heard about a new camp close to Berlin. Not his concern and not part of his job. With utmost precision he filled each appropriate rectangle with the red stamp and initialed it at its border. Auerbach, Avrom; Jäger, Joseph; Levy, Arthur; Nofziger, Julian; Perl, Solomon; Schumann, Horst; Zelig, Mordecai. He blotted the sheets, careful to avoid smudges, assembled them in proper order and rang for his secretary.

"The manifest, Fräulein Briese. Please deliver it to Frau Kube. She's waiting for it."

"Right away, Herr Eberhardt."

He watched her leave, cleared his desk, put on his well-tailored overcoat, cheerfully waived at office personnel already busy closing up, and went home, satisfied with a job perfectly executed once again.

◆   ◆   ◆

The envelope was delivered to Hildegard Kube at 4:00 p.m., well before Horst was due to return. Everything in connection with the voyage was complete except for this last detail. Following Eberhardt's explicit instructions, she had already removed tickets of those interviewed in Stuttgart and other cities and put them in a special, marked folder, to be turned over to Security in the morning. Now she needed only to remove the tickets of those that Eberhardt had stamped 'Not in Order' and put them in a separate envelope. She hated this final task; it felt like preparing obituaries.

She wondered who had landed on the list this time. The men and women who came from interviews were a fearful crowd. Nearly all had been in the office today. They checked in, looked worried and asked a million questions. Some dragged in suitcases, argued with her and made themselves obnoxious. Totally exasperated, she had posted a sign in the window: "All passengers with security identification cards must come here tomorrow at 8:00 a.m. <u>PUNCTUALLY</u>. You will be taken to the passenger hall next door where exit documents will be distributed. <u>DON'T BE LATE!!!</u>" That had helped and they had dispersed.

She removed the manifest from the envelope and picked out the names marked with red stamps: Auerbach Jäger, Levy. She turned to the next page. Nofziger, Perl, Schumann. Schumann, Horst! Her heart went cold, her breath stopped; she nearly collapsed at her desk. There it was, no mistake. Horst Schumann, stamped 'Not in Order.' The death sentence! Hildegard Kube was not a brave person. Until a week ago she had performed few acts that demanded courage or inner strength. She had lived a placid life, married to a placid man. Her pride lay in her son and in her devotion to Jesus. As far as she could remember she had never broken a law, found disobedience to rules and regulations abhorrent. Nor was she a particularly compassionate person. The warmth of her reactions to Horst had taken her by surprise. She felt decent and virtuous by helping the boy. To allow him to sleep at the office frightened her, but nothing like the turmoil she experienced now. She tried to think of some way to rescue the boy. Even to contemplate such an action shook her to the core of her being. Was the devil tempting her? Was the archfiend asking her to defy the law? No, that could not be. This was not, it simply could not be, the devil's work!

In the depth of Hildegard Kube's soul an awful rage burst into flames and blazed like wildfire. This was not fair! This boy was no monster, but a sweet, peaceful, decent human being. Her inner, secret Jesus filled her consciousness, suffused her with a clear and unmistakable message: *This boy must be saved, no matter what the risk!*

She was acutely aware of the peril, the punishment she would most likely suffer if she were caught interfering. She pictured herself on a trip in a black wagon, like the one she had seen in the alley. Was saving the boy even possible? How could it be accomplished? Her mind raced, rejected one idea after another until she finally hit on one remote possibility. She felt weak in the knees, desperately reached for a decision. Then she left off the struggle. Her belief in Jesus, her trust in His message, prevailed.

When Horst arrived she sent him away. "Don't ask questions. Sleep at the station or wherever you can find a place. Tomorrow morning, be here promptly at eight. You must not, you absolutely must not let on that you know me. If you do, it could mean the end for us both. Do you understand?" Horst nodded, very confused and deeply frightened. Something terrible happened to upset her like this. Already in Stuttgart he had overheard rumors, at the pension and at the fountain in the square, ugly rumors about final security checks, about Jews not allowed to go on the ship, about men and women who then disappeared. He had paid no attention. In Stuttgart rumors flew everywhere. Now he understood, once again reminded of life's endless potential for disaster. "I'm so sorry, Frau Kube, I hope I haven't done…" "Go," she snapped, shoving him out the door. "Don't waste time. Just be here tomorrow."

She telephoned home, told Gottfried to make supper for himself and his father, that she had to stay late, that unexpected paper work had to be finished. She locked the office door, let down the rolling window shades and went to work. She knew that what she was about to do was insane, it would never work. She was signing her own death warrant. Then she had to smile, realized that although her heart was pounding, she had not felt so inspired, so absolutely and so totally in touch with her Christ since the day of her first Communion.

Only a few months ago her office had received from her company's supply division a new product developed for the Reichspost by I.G. Farben. An enclosed instruction booklet stated that the contents were bleach-based chemicals intended to remove ink and stamped impressions from paper. The booklet acknowledged that the process was experimental at this time; that test results were deemed somewhat unreliable. Trial before use was advised. If swallowed, vomiting was to be induced and a physician consulted. The bottle came with a brush attached to its top. She had tried it briefly, relegated it to a desk drawer as too difficult to control; the typed copy and stamp she used for the experiment came out smudged. However, there was nothing else. It was this or nothing at all.

She prepared a clean blotter and put a stronger bulb into her desk lamp. Then she searched for a gadget recently sent by an office supply company, a small magnifying glass set into the tip of a ruler, and found it in her desk. That would help a great deal. "Thy will be done, on Earth as it is in Heaven" she said, and bent to the task with the devotion of the true believer.

She held the magnifying glass over small sections of the stamp, attacked it in fractions of millimeters and cautiously blotted each erasure. After the first hour she worked in a trance, thought of each dot of ink as a bead in her rosary. Her eyes burned like hot coals, but she ignored the discomfort. She continued without pause until midnight and then stopped to examine her work by holding the form against the light. Yes, one could see a difference; the erased square was slightly transparent. She shrugged that off. Why would the Security people hold the paper against a light? There was no reason for them to do so and she felt certain they would not; they had not done so the last time. The red stamp and inked initial had ceased to exist; not a trace remained. She prepared for the final entry, Eberhardt's check mark. She experimented with several pens, found one whose color precisely matched Eberhardt's. She studied his mark under the magnifying glass; it was short on the down stroke, carelessly longer on the upstroke. She practiced several times, and then resolutely executed the mark. It looked totally indistinguishable from the others. She inspected the page the way she thought Security might examine it tomorrow. It looked flawless to her. As ordered, she put the tickets of those who were surely doomed into a separate envelope and marked it "Not in Order," just as she had done before. She put all other tickets and the manifest in the safe and locked it. She gathered up the papers on which she had practiced, ripped them in pieces and deposited them in the trash container located at the street corner. She called a taxi and, while waiting, cleaned her desk, checked carefully once again for unsafe evidence and found none. The taxi came a few minutes later and drove her home. Totally exhausted and still shaking with anxiety, she undressed quietly and slid into bed. Otto was snoring and never moved.

Horst stayed awake all night. He knew that whatever happened, directly concerned his fate. He had seen it in Frau Kube's stricken face. He was tired and terribly weary of the battle. He tried to sleep on the depot floor but sleep wouldn't come. He trudged to the harbor long before sunrise, saw the *Hamburg* in its berth, its gangplank guarded, a beehive of activity surrounding the ship, supplies being loaded, bilge water being pumped. He looked at the vessel with unbearable yearning, then walked to the Alsterdamm and arrived promptly at eight.

The clamor was deafening. There were well dressed Jews with fancy luggage who kept to themselves and Jews from the ghetto, their belongings in pillowcases. A leather-coated Security officer and his assistant picked up the ticket envelopes and the marked manifest from Frau Kube and herded the milling crowd into the hall adjacent to the ticket office. At the loading ramp two buses were parked, attended by uniformed guards. Inside, everyone was ordered to sit on rows of wooden benches. A technician tested a loudspeaker. Two SS guards flanked a rear door.

"Ladies and gentlemen," the man holding a clipboard said into the microphone, as he scanned their tense faces. "I am Eugen Schulte. I bring you greetings from our Führer. He bids you farewell. The entrance doors are now closed. I congratulate you on your punctuality." His tight face never moved a muscle. "Anyone not here has now lost his exit visa. *Schade.* Before we can proceed, a few of you need to clarify some…well, let's call them misunderstandings, that have surfaced since your interviews. Nothing to be concerned about, I assure you. We are certain you will be able to explain everything." He pulled the tickets of those rejected from the marked envelope and very carefully checked each name against the manifest. "The names I now call will move to that door at once." He pointed to the rear exit. "You will be taken to a comfortable room at the harbor where you will enlighten security officials about certain allegations that have been made; all a mistake, of course. Now then: Avrom Auerbach. Josef Jäger." Schulte allowed himself a small smile at the sight of the crumpled man. "Jäger indeed," he mumbled. "Arthur Levy. Julian Nofziger."

In her office, Hildegard Kube held her breath as the names rang through the wall. She had experienced only one such roll call before. At that time she had shut her mind to the process, but now she listened with an anxiety that made her dizzy. "Solomon Perl. Mordecai Zelig." After that she heard nothing. She had done it. "Oh thank you, dear Jesus! Oh thank you!!"

Those whose names had been called were herded into the alley. No one dared to watch them leave or enter the waiting black vehicle. The look in their eyes told their story. Everyone in the hall knew that these unfortunates were unlikely to be heard from again.

"Now then: The rest of you will present your security cards at that table. You will receive your passport, stamped with an exit visa, your ticket and a boarding pass. For all of that you will sign a receipt. As quickly as possible you will then leave this hall and seat yourself in one of the buses parked outside at the loading ramp. You will be driven to the harbor. On the way there you will remain silent and exchange nothing, absolutely nothing at all. When you arrive at the dock, you will immediately go aboard. You will then sail to America, which richly deserves you." He lowered the arm that held the clipboard.

The excitement in the room was tremendous, but suppressed. Nobody dared to offend, not now. Horst received his documents and took a seat on the bus. Moments before it pulled out he turned to look back. In her doorway stood Hildegard Kube, hands folded as if in prayer. Their eyes met. Horst nodded and smiled. She returned the smile, then quickly closed the door behind her.

As if in a dream, Horst showed his boarding pass to the guards and walked up the gangplank. Most passengers had boarded long before, crowded the railings and waved to friends and relatives on the dock. A marching band played, but Horst didn't hear it. He felt disconnected from the real world, didn't trust his senses and couldn't believe this was really happening. Unaware that he was doing so, he followed the crowd to the ship's fantail as the bilges pumped water. A tow tug came alongside, gangplanks and hawser lines were pulled up, the foghorn gave a departing blast and the *Hamburg* pulled slowly out of its berth and moved up the Elbe toward the North Sea. They passed under bridges and past boats in their docks, but Horst remained oblivious. People waved from shore, but he didn't really see them. They neared the landmark where a ship's colors are hoisted and its history told on an amplified loudspeaker, but he didn't listen. At dusk, as the liner moved into deep water, Horst Schumann remained standing at the fantail and gazed far beyond the ship's wake. He watched the land slowly disappear, not yet convinced it was happening. A fierce hunger growled in his belly.

Then, he resolutely traversed the length of the *Hamburg*, a long, exhilarating walk past happy people toasting the trip with champagne, past contented couples who sat in deck chairs, wrapped in warm blankets. Finally he came to the heaving bow; his fixed stare scanning the unbroken horizon. Wind and saltwater stung his eyes; a few seagulls, hunting food, wheeled over the ship. At last the truth dawned on Horst Schumann, all at once and with great power. "I am free," he shouted to the birds, as tears spilled down his face. "I am free. Oh god, I am free." He thought of Oskar, was saddened for a moment by the image, but also elated. Wherever Papa was now, he would be so proud and happy for him. "I made it, Papa, I am free. Oh Papa, I did it. I did it!" He yelled it again and again to the heavens, delirious with the exaltation of a newborn soul. Nearby passengers were amused by the outburst and brushed it aside, but those few who knew where he came from, those who had been there, they nodded and smiled and they understood.

Afterword

It hasn't been all "beer and skittles," but ever since that fateful "Sail Day" in 1936, life has treated me well—most often very, very well. I arrived in Chicago as a scared, skinny and solemn youngster. My new parents welcomed me with open arms, were patient with my wounded spirit, gave me a superb education and encouraged me to play all the baseball I could squeeze into the busy life of someone learning to become a bonafide American. In World War II, I served my country for four years as a sailor, much of it overseas. I graduated from a fine university, married a beautiful artist, sired five glorious children, divorced, re-married (a splendid, totally *simpatico* German woman) and began the first of more than five decades—and still going strong at the present time—teaching literature, theatre, film, and writing workshops at American universities and abroad. I hosted my own television show, L.A.'s popular "Theatre Beat," for nearly fifteen years and have lived in glorious parts of the country, California, Santa Fe, Denver, New York, and now in gorgeous Asheville, North Carolina, surely the Paris of the South.

I have often returned to Germany and other European cities, sometimes as visitor, often as teacher, always on the lookout for evidence relating to my father. In the bookshop at Buchenwald, that most loathsome of horror camps, I found a photograph of Oskar entering Auschwitz in the midst of a petrified herd of ill-fated Jews. It was the first time I knew the awful truth and it was a deep stab in the heart.

I've dragged my reluctant soul into the *Steinwache*, that bestial Dortmund police station, now a museum dedicated to documenting the odious years of this novel. I have tried, unsuccessfully, to locate Dov and other brave companions of my childhood. Grete moved to Sweden, where she remarried.

On a sojourn to Lippstadt, I was told that Pavel Czerny and his wife Elsa had closed the bakery and fled the country, presumably to Czechoslovakia.

With deep regret I learned that Cantor Hirsch remained in Worms even after his synagogue was destroyed on *Kristallnacht*. A former neighbor of theirs told me that the Hirsch family, with all other Jews in Worms, was rounded up in 1939, not to be heard from again.

After the war, I visited with Frau Kube in Hamburg and came to know the details of her extraordinary act of bravery and kindness, which surely saved my life. She lost her husband to emphysema and her son to a Russian winter. We met at the splendid "Four Seasons" restaurant, cried together as we hugged, bawled quite a bit during soup and salad, then joyously toasted our reunion over the dessert.

About the Author

Hal Marienthal holds a doctorate in Communications from the University of Southern California, has taught at leading U.S. universities and has been a writer, producer and performer in the film industry. Dr. Marienthal is currently on the faculty of the University of North Carolina-Asheville, where he teaches screenwriting workshops.

978-0-595-36859-4
0-595-36859-X

Breinigsville, PA USA
19 May 2010
238367BV00002B/43/A